SUPERVAN
&I

SuperVan & I

The memoir of SA's greatest driver & his alter ego

SAREL VAN DER MERWE with **Steve Smith**

Published by Zebra Press
an imprint of Random House Struik (Pty) Ltd
Reg. No. 1966/003153/07
Wembley Square, First Floor, Solan Road, Gardens, Cape Town, 8001
PO Box 1144, Cape Town, 8000, South Africa

www.zebrapress.co.za

First published 2012

3 5 7 9 10 8 6 4 2

Publication © Zebra Press 2012
Text © Sarel van der Merwe and Steve Smith 2012

Cover photograph © Morne van Zyl

PUBLISHER: MARLENE FRYER
MANAGING EDITOR: RONEL RICHTER-HERBERT
EDITOR: THEA GROBBELAAR
PROOFREADER: RONEL RICHTER-HERBERT
COVER AND TEXT DESIGNER: MONIQUE OBERHOLZER
TYPESETTER: MONIQUE VAN DEN BERG
INDEXER: MARY LENNOX

Set in 11.5 pt on 15 pt Adobe Garamond

Printed and bound by Interpak Books, Pietermaritzburg

ISBN 978 1 77022 170 3 (print)
ISBN 978 1 77022 268 7 (ePub)
ISBN 978 1 77022 269 4 (PDF)

Over 50 000 unique African images available to purchase
from our image bank at www.imagesofafrica.co.za

To the memory of my father, Sarel van der Merwe Snr, who introduced me to fast cars, which resulted in many major adrenaline rushes

CONTENTS

ACKNOWLEDGEMENTS

This book was written under duress. Over the past few years, a pressure group (led by my wife and supported by quite a few of my friends) was formed, their only objective a campaign of nagging, threatening, bugging and general irritation to get me to write my autobiography.

However, because of a strong resolve and some very good reasons not to write such a book, I managed to withstand this pressure for years and only succumbed when Steve Smith joined the chorus.

My reasons for withstanding public opinion were well thought out and valid, namely:

1. Who was going to buy the bloody thing? Having spent the past 65 years in my own company, I have come to the conclusion that I am not a very interesting person; not even I would therefore necessarily buy a book about my exploits. It would be very embarrassing if the book came out and only the pressure group bought copies.

2. Writing an autobiography seems so *final*. I would still like to race every now and again, but what if car owners see this book and think that, because it has been published, I have finally retired for good? What if the grim reaper thinks I am ready for the final race? What a bummer.

3. Laziness. Laziness is often referred to in a very derogatory fashion. Very few people are aware of the thought, time and effort that go into perfecting this art form. After years of devoting myself to its cause, I feel that I have perfected it, and it is probably the main reason for delaying this book for so

long. Now that I have finally surrendered, I suppose I should apologise to all the people who might be insulted, threatened, hurt, defamed or just generally pissed off by this book. Not that I give a shit, but it just seems like the right thing to do.

Nobody survives for 65 years without a strong support base. In this respect, I was blessed with a circle of friends that I would not change for anything in the world. My sincere thanks to the following people:

From my early childhood, I want to thank Dries Lategan, Meent Borcherds and Gerrie du Plessis – playing with toys ... to playing with girls ... to paying for weddings.

From my early motor-sport encounters and still with me today: Johan Evertse and Schalk Burger (Bitterbal).

From the team management side: Geoff Mortimer, André van der Watt and Michael Barnard.

Motor-sport pals: Michael Briggs, Keith Coleman, Enzo Kuun, George Fouché, Maxie Jonker, Fanie Theron and my lunatic friend Llewellyn Anthony.

The departed ones: Tony Viana, Nico Bianco, Abel de Oliveira, Bernie Marriner, Mike Fourie and my parents.

My kids: Sarel, Nicolene and Nohlene for trying to make sense of their lives out of the chaos I at times caused.

To Danielle, who for the past 22 years has unconditionally supported me and put up with my shit.

To all the girls – it was fun.

Omitted from the above are the half-witted idiots who are campaigning for the national speed limit to be reduced to 100 km/h. To them I wish an infestation of killer lice where they least want it.

For those youngsters interested in following a career in motor sport, the following advice: Motor sport is a lot like sex – you start with what is available at the time. As you get more adept at it, you upgrade to better models. Finally, you have access to the latest models (some of us are even lucky to get paid for it). As you get older, you will find that you are no longer offered the latest equipment. When you get to my age, you are limited to the vintage and veteran models and the only way of getting the latest stuff is to buy it.

A word of advice to the general public: Do not take sportsmen and women too seriously. At the end of the day, we are all only entertainers.

SAREL VAN DER MERWE

PAARL

AUTHOR'S NOTE

Fear. It sharpens the mind.

I knew I was going to be scared. Which, of course, only made it worse. Being unexpectedly scared– now that's not so bad. It's when you know something scary is on the cards and have time to mull over the prospect that the fear ratchets up a notch or three.

It was 7 a.m. and, as had been my ritual for the past few months, I was heading up the N1 to Sarel van der Merwe's house in Paarl. At precisely 7.30 a.m. (Sarel appreciates punctuality) I'd pull up to his beautiful farmhouse-style home and he'd be at the door to welcome me. He'd fix us both a good, strong cup of sweet morning coffee and for two hours or so we'd sit and talk about whatever aspect of his hugely entertaining life was on the agenda for that morning.

It was a bucket-list experience for me. The fact that our chats were going to culminate in a book was a happy bonus – the real pleasure was sitting in Sarel's lounge listening, laughing and gaping in astonishment as stories from his life unfolded.

This particular morning, however, I knew things would be different, all because of the car I was driving. Part of what I do is to review and write about cars. I do it partly to pay some of the bills, but mostly I do it because of the cars. I love reading about them, I love looking at them, and mostly I love driving them. And if you're a motoring journo, you get a new car to drive every week.

Sarel always appraised the cars I rocked up in. If it was a sports car (or any Alfa), he would run a hand over its flank and give an approving nod. If, however, it was a lesser life form, you'd inevitably hear his deep laugh, followed by: 'What piece of shit have you arrived in this morning!?'

This low-slung white coupé would suffer no such indignities. In fact, it was highly doubtful that Sarel and I would do any talking once he clapped eyes on the Audi RS5. If there's one brand that South African motorsport fans associate with our greatest ever driver, it's the four interlocking rings of this German manufacturer. Thanks to Sarel's rallying exploits in the legendary Quattro rally car, his Wesbank- series dominance in the high-tech Quattro saloon, and his SA land-speed record in a 500 turbo, Sarel and Audi are an iconic partnership.

Their R8 supercar aside, the RS5 is the quickest road-going car Audi has ever made. With its 450bhp, 4.2-litre, V8 engine and all-wheel-drive Quattro drive-train, this car accelerates like a missile and corners like a Scalectrix. So nope, there was no good, strong cup of sweet morning coffee waiting for me that day. Instead I was instructed to hand over the keys, move to the passenger seat and buckle up.

It was when Sarel said, 'I wonder if Audi have restricted its top speed to 250 km/h?' that I realised just how scared I was about to become.

I won't tell you how fast we went along those quiet back roads of Agter-Paarl – suffice to say that the platteland became blurry in the way stars do in sci-fi movies. Never once did Sarel or the RS5 put a foot wrong, and we stayed on the road despite our warp-speed velocities. But that didn't really matter. Fear gripped me nonetheless. It gripped me everywhere except, for one split second, when it let go of my bladder. Cresting one particular blind rise with very little in the way of rubber touching the asphalt, I involuntarily released a small dribble. Not much, just a little 'ppssst'.

And in that moment, I think I understood Sarel just a little better.

Thanks to all the interviews, I knew the details of his life, but until that moment I never quite understood the world he inhabited. It's a foreign realm where the scenery can rush past you at 385 km/h … where you live on a knife's edge … where one very small mistake can end your life. Intellectually I knew all of this, but for 15 minutes I spent some actual time in it. Or in *part* of it. It wasn't even in the part where one also has to fend off the challenges of other, equally skilled drivers on a racing track.

What I realised on that the beautifully cambered road near Sarel's house was that this world is inhabited by a special type of person. Not only is it the kind of person with a stronger bladder than the one I possess, but it's the kind of person who is invariably going to take less notice of life's conventions. After piloting a 1200bhp endurance sportscar around Daytona's famous racetrack for the best part of 24 hours (and winning the event), the pace and the customs of normal life must seem, at best, a little drab …

And thank you

I know about magazines, but I'm still learning about books. And it's thanks to the team at Zebra Press that I'm making head-way with this newly acquired skill. Firstly to Marlene Fryer, my publisher: my suggestion of Sarel van der Merwe as the subject of an autobiography was something of a left-field choice. In a country that's nuts about rugby, cricket and soccer, a book on a retired racing driver wasn't a natural choice. I'm very grateful that Marlene chose to go ahead with the project and gave me the opportunity to tell the story of one of South Africa's great sporting characters. Hers was a brave decision given the pressure the print industry is currently experiencing, and for that I'm particularly thankful.

Without the rest of her team, of course, what you're holding in your hand would've been a vastly inferior product … in fact, you might not have been holding the book at all. It's thanks then to Ronel Richter-Herbert for helping me craft the story, Thea Grobbelaar for her editing skills, and publicist Kim Taylor for her immense expertise in marketing and promoting *SuperVan & I*.

Thanks also to my good friend and photographer Morne van Zyl. Morne also took the cover portrait of Herschelle Gibbs for my first book, *To the Point*, and once again, more than pushing the shutter button and getting the lighting right, he was instrumental in conceptualising how we should portray Sarel. Have a look at www.mornevanzyl.com to see just how good this guy is.

Finally, to my family – Medina and Holly – for all their love, support and encouragement. 'I can't talk now, sweetie, Dad's working …' was a phrase Holly heard more often than I would've liked. And Dee, the fact that I ever had a magazine feature published, let alone a book, is largely due to spending the last 26 years with you.

Steve Smith

GLOSSARY

Aerodynamic – how effectively the car slices through air

Aerodynamic drag – the car is slowed down by air flowing over its body

Aero-package – the various wings and bodywork additions that manage airflow over and under the car

Bhp – brake horsepower: measure of an engine's power

Black-flagged – track marshals wave a black flag to indicate a serious infringement by a driver, who's then obliged to retire from the race

Chevron – a reflective warning sign on a track usually indicating a sharp corner

Chicane – a tight double-corner on a race track (left followed by right or vice versa) designed to slow cars down

Class A – The most powerful class in a particular motor-sport formula

Class B – The second-most powerful class in a particular motor-sport formula

Differential lock – also called a diff lock, when engaged it means both wheels on a common axle rotate at the same speed. When traction under each of the wheels differs – i.e. as is often the case off-road – this offers much better traction

Downforce – the downward thrust created by air flowing over a car's body; makes it stick to the road for improved handling

Drive-through penalty – a driver infringement means he must come into the pits, stop for a predetermined amount of time – often 10 seconds – before rejoining the race

Drivetrain – the components of a car that generate power and deliver it to the road surface: engine, gearbox, drive shaft, wheels

Ex-works – can refer to a car or driver. It's a driver who used to drive for an official manufacturer team, or it's a car used by an official manufacturer team

Fettling – refers to tweaking or working on an engine or chassis until it's performing optimally

Full-works – an official manufacturer-backed race or rally team, like Ferrari or Porsche

Gear linkage – the set of mechanical linkages that connects the gearbox to the gear stick

Ground-effects – the manipulation of air under the car's body that effectively sucks it to the track for better handling around corners

Group B – a set of regulations introduced in 1982 for GT racing cars and rally cars. It resulted in some of the quickest, most powerful and sophisticated rally cars ever built

Group C – also introduced in 1982, it was a racing formula for Le Mans–type endurance sports prototypes

Group N – a racing formula for close-to-standard spec road-going cars

GTP class – Grand Touring Prototype: essentially the American version of Group C (see above)

Haal uit en wys – show me what you've got

Hardegat – arrogant

Homologation cars – refers to (an often limited) production run of a road-going car that a manufacturer has made solely in order to legitimately race the car in a particular formula

Inboard disc brakes – as opposed to the disc brakes on the inside of the wheel, these brakes are on the axle

Jaaging – racing

Kak/kakkest – shit/shittest

Kapenaars – Capetonians

Klap – slap

Laaities – youngsters (slang)

Left rear wishbone – a wishbone is a type of racing suspension-strut that attaches the car's wheel to the body

Marque – a brand of car

Modified car – a race car based on a standard road-going car, but has several modifications to improve its performance

Moer – hit (v) or huge (adj.)

Moer of a – helluva

Off-camber – refers to corners where the road slopes down towards the outside or the corner. A car wants to drift off the road on such corners

Oom – uncle

Oversteer – this occurs when a car turns into a corner more than the amount commanded by the driver, i.e. the car's steering characteristics are causing it to turn in too sharply

Pace notes – the information at the navigator or co-driver's disposal that not only map out a rally's route, but also provides road-surface info

Paraat – alert/ready

Poes – cunt

Porting – A tuning process that modifies and reshapes the intake and exhaust ports of a car's engine to increase air flow and therefore improve performance

Privateer teams – a race or rally team that's not an official manufacturer team. They might buy a car from the manufacturer but they run it on their own

Production Class – refers to a racing or rallying formula of cars close to normal road-going spec

Qualifying trim – Some formulas allow race cars to have softer tyres or more powerful engine settings specifically for qualifying sessions. This would make the car fast but fragile

Race-spec – following on from above, this refers to the harder tyres and engine settings that would mean slightly slower lap times, but allow the car to last the whole race distance

Racing pads – brake pads designed for racing and rallying. They operate at higher temperatures and will last longer than standard brake pads

Regs – the regulations that will define a particular formula: engine capacity, suspension set-up, aerodynamic aids, etc.

Re-map – retuning the engine to produce more power

Rev range – the high and low limits an engine will rev at. Over-rev and you risk terminal engine damage

Roll cage – made from tubes welded together and attached inside the car's interior, it forms a lightweight, but very strong, protective shell around the driver

Rooi onderbroek – red underpants: colloquial term for an Englishman

Rooinek – redneck: colloquial term for an Englishman

Run-off areas – parts of a race track designed for safety. If a car spins off the track or approaches a corner too fast to be able to make the turn, this extra space allows the driver to slow down before hitting any track barrier

Seun – son

Single-cam – refers to the camshaft, a part of the engine that operates the valves. Single camshaft engines are generally older models. Most modern engines have double camshafts or 'double overhead cams'

Skelm – mistress/bit on the side (coll.)

Snot en trane – snot and tears

Sports prototype – a car built specifically for racing. It has no basis in any road-going car. The term usually describes Le Mans–type endurance race cars

Spotter – part of the race crew who, from some elevated position, keeps an eye on the race and informs his team's driver via radio of any developments – like a crash up ahead. Used mostly in NASCAR

Suiwer – pure

Telemetry system – the sophisticated car-to-pits communication system that not only lets the pit crew talk to the driver while racing, but also transmits back info on the car's performance

Torque - Part of the basic specification of an engine, the power output of an engine is expressed as its torque multiplied by its rotational speed of the axis

Torsion bar suspension – old-school car suspension system, it uses a torsion bar as its main weight-bearing spring. It's still used today in some SUVs and trucks. Porsche used torsion bars in their 911 up until 1989

Touring cars – a racing formula of heavily modified road-going cars that started in Europe. The formula ran in South Africa during the 1990s but ultimately proved too expensive

Turbo lag – a characteristic of turbo-charged cars. It refers to the slight pause between pushing down the accelerator pedal and the actual delivery of the power to the wheels

Twin-cam – see 'Single-cam' above

Two-stroke motor – a small, lightweight engine used in motorcycles, outboard boat motors and, during the 1970s and earlier, in some small cars. They're easy to build and maintain, but have high emissions

Understeer – this occurs when, despite the driver's input, a car does not turn in sharply enough and drifts towards the outside of a corner

Up-rated brakes – when a car has been fitted with brakes better suited to the rigours of competitive motorsport, i.e. they will stop a car quicker and last longer

Windgat – arrogant

Works driver – a race or rally driver who is racing for an official manufacturer team

Xtrac – a UK company that manufactures high-performance automotive gearboxes

1

THE EARLY YEARS

A tale of two Porsches, and the roots of my desire

It was 10.30 p.m., 15 June 1984 ... and I was doing 385 km/h.

Not only had I never gone that fast before, but I was hurtling around an unfamiliar track, in an unfamiliar car. And it was dark too. This wasn't just any racetrack either. This was Le Mans.

I was shit-scared. Easily the second most scared I'd ever been. And there were three reasons for this.

One: 385 km/h is very, very fast. If you think 200 km/h is quick, let me tell you that 300 km/h feels a whole lot quicker. And approaching 400 km/h is like another realm altogether.

Two: not only was I doing 385 km/h at night, but I was doing it down the testicle-shrinking Mulsanne Straight.

And three: I had been far more scared 23 years earlier, but we'll get to that a bit later.

Before those French idiots went and put a chicane in the middle of it, the Mulsanne Straight at Le Mans was the longest piece of straight track in motor sport. At seven kilometres long, cars like the mighty Porsche 956, which I was currently strapped into, could reach, and sometimes pass, the 400 km/h mark.

Now usually going down a straight in a racing car isn't that difficult. Often it's an opportunity for a seasoned driver to relax a little and take stock of the race he's currently involved in. The Mulsanne Straight at night, though, is another story altogether. I don't care how seasoned you are.

The thing about the Mulsanne is that it has this little right-hand kink about three-quarters of the way down. You have to take it flat out. Your instincts might tell you to brake, but you have to trust the Porsche's ground-hugging aerodynamics that will stick the car to the track and help you make it through.

The other thing about the Mulsanne is that it ends in a blind 90-degree right-hander. Naturally, you do have to brake for this one. Heavily. After such a long straight – it probably takes about 90 seconds from start to finish – the car's brakes are cold, so you have to touch them early just to heat them up a bit, then stand on them as hard as you can. The car's speed has to come down from 385 km/h to round about 60 km/h in 200 metres. Needless to say, the deceleration is dramatic.

Here's the tricky part: it's not that easy to know where exactly you are. Are you approaching The Kink ... or the 90 degree-er? When you're flying down this piece of asphalt in the dark at that speed, there's very little in the way of visual clues to tell which part of the Mulsanne you're bulleting down. And to do this for the first time only exacerbates the situation.

Out of the blackness I could vaguely make out a set of chevrons ahead of me. I say 'vaguely' because we hadn't yet had a chance to set up the car's headlights properly and they were all over the show. Were these chevrons the chevrons for The Kink? Or were they the chevrons for the 90-degree corner at the end of the straight?

This was a crucial piece of information.

If I had somehow already gone through The Kink and this was the end of the straight, I needed to brake very quickly or it would all be over. And I don't mean 'over' as in it would be the end of my race. I mean 'over' in more of a 'dead' kind of way.

There was another reason I couldn't afford to get it wrong. My career was basically riding on this lap. Earlier that year, out of nowhere, Tony Martin, Graham Duxbury and I had won the prestigious 24 Hours of Daytona at Daytona Beach in the USA. Our Kreepy Krauly–liveried March had surprised the more fancied Porsches to win one of the world's greatest endurance races. Based on that result, I had been invited by the Fitzpatrick team to race a Porsche 956 at Le Mans a few months later. I needed to prove that Daytona was no fluke.

This is what I had been wanting all along. I might've started my career as a rally driver and made my name as a multiple rally champ back in South Africa, but my real passion was the racetrack. Here, at Le Mans, I was finally in Europe with the big boys, in a serious racing car.

Going out for the first time at night in order to qualify had not been part of the plan, but as the new boy in a three-man team, I was last in the pecking order. My teammates were Briton David Hobbs and Frenchman Philippe Streiff. Hobbs was the most experienced driver in the team; Streiff was the up-and-coming hotshot who had designs on a seat in Formula 1... and I was the unknown entity from South Africa. I was already 37 then – quite old to be making a bid for a career in the top echelons of motor sport.

Le Mans rules dictated that all three drivers had to qualify the car. The problem was that when Hobbs went out to set up the car, the engine broke and it took the whole day to sort it out. Once that had been fixed, Streiff had to run his qualifying laps, which meant that when I finally got into the car, it was already about 10.20 p.m. Qualifying ended at 11 p.m.

By the time I was out on the track, I only had two laps – a sighter and then a full quali lap, where I really had to go for it. So I did. And fortunately for me, those chevrons were only for The Kink. By the time I hit the braking markers for the 90-degree corner at the end of the Mulsanne, I was able to slow down the car sufficiently to make the turn.

We didn't have in-car radio contact with the pits in those days, but when I came around again, my crew hung out a pit board with 'OK' in big letters. I knew I'd qualified. It was a helluva relief. I'll never forget that night down the Mulsanne... very, very scary.

MY FIRST WHIFF OF RACING FUEL

But not the scariest moment I ever had in a Porsche. That occasion occurred in 1961 … the day I stole, and then pranged, my father's new 1959 Porsche 356 Speedster. The reason he owned such an exotic car was that my father – also named Sarel, like my grandfather and great-grandfather before him – was very involved in motor sport. (Ja, I named my son Sarel as well.)

I remember exactly when it all started, too. It was 1956 and I was 10 years old. We were at Palmietfontein, a now defunct racetrack that was located just outside Johannesburg, where a big race was taking place that day, and I remember British driver Peter 'Pat' Whitehead was there in his Ferrari. Whitehead was famous for being the first person to whom Enzo Ferrari ever sold a Formula 1 car – a Ferrari 125.

As we watched the race, not only did I think it was the greatest thing ever, but, it turns out, so did my father. So much so that it inspired him to go out and buy a Triumph TR3, which he started rallying. He later swapped that for an MG Magnette, and by 1959 he'd bought the unfortunate Porsche Speedster I'd mentioned earlier.

My father had more than a little racing talent and was, in fact, the first South African rally champion, in 1959. It wasn't an officially recognised title yet – the Pretoria Motor Club started the championship, which the following year was taken over by the Automobile Association and declared an official SA championship. Although my dad competed in a few nine-hour endurance races on the track with his friends, he concentrated mostly on rallying. My father was a privateer who had his own quantity-surveying business, so he never really competed as seriously as I ended up doing. He was also very involved in the organisational side of motor sport back then.

He was, for example, involved in the building of Kyalami. We lived in Pretoria and my father was a member of the South African Motor Racing Club – they were the builders and first owners of the famous circuit when it opened in 1960. He was also involved in the Zwartkops racetrack. So ja, as a young boy growing up, I was always exposed to motor sport.

I guess I should, at this point, tell you a little bit more about my childhood. It's as good a time as any – we'll get back to the cars in a minute.

I was born in Joburg, but we moved to Pretoria when I was about three or four. It was a pretty carefree time for me. We lived in a big home in Waterkloof – the quintessential white Afrikaans upper-middle-class family. I went to Laerskool Anton Van Wouw and Afrikaanse Hoër Seunskool. I had a lot of friends who lived nearby, so it was easy to carry on, have fun and cause shit.

The shit-causing part sometimes got a little out of hand. In my final year at Affies, I got 106 cuts, which was apparently something of a school record – probably still is now that they've stopped corporal punishment. I'm actually quite proud of it.

Academics were never really my thing. In primary school I was always one of the top three or four students, but in high school other pursuits attracted my interest. Plus, there were many more pupils in the classes at Affies, so I could get away with a lot more. Unlike at primary school, the teachers didn't know my parents, so I could do the absolute bare minimum without being caught. As I could pass without too much effort, I spent most of my time playing and causing kak. I could never understand why you had to swot stuff that you were never going to use again anyway.

On one occasion I went to fairly great lengths to avoid studying …

My parents had gone on an overseas holiday, and my grandparents had the unenviable task of trying to control me. I had a big exam coming up – one which I hadn't studied for and knew I would fail. Knowing what my father would do to me, I decided to disable my writing hand. I gave my finger an almighty crack with a bulky encyclopaedia and managed to convince my grandparents that the swollen digit was too badly hurt – possibly even broken

– to write the exam. My ploy worked. With my hand in plaster I was off the hook and I passed on my year mark.

Like all young boys, I played most sports, including cricket, rugby and tennis – basically whatever was going. I was better at some sports than others, and I would continue to play other sports throughout my racing career. Of those, I enjoyed golf the most, and I eventually played off a 7 handicap when I was racing in the US in the 80s. The one pastime I disliked intensely was swimming – mostly because they made us take to the water in the early morning when it was bloody freezing. They wanted me to swim in galas on a Saturday morning, which I thought was a silly idea and flatly refused to do. To this day, I refuse point-blank to swim in cold water.

Back to the cars, though ... As I was saying about motor sport, I loved it right from the start. I even attached a stopwatch to my bicycle and would race around the garden timing myself. The bike was a Raleigh and I'd completely wear out the tyres' sidewalls with all the hard cornering. I'd then swap those tyres with the ones on my younger brother's bike. As he knew nothing about racing, he was never able to figure out why the hell his tyres kept wearing down so often. Even then I knew motor racing was something I was going to do one day.

It was the golden age of South African motor sport, where we had events like the Springbok Series for sports cars and our own Formula 1 series. Towing a caravan, my family and I would follow the Springbok Series around the country, with my father occasionally taking part in some of the races. The living arrangements were a little cramped, but the experience was well worth it for me. The series normally started at Kyalami, then went on to Natal. They built a new track there in the 60s – Westmead – but it didn't last too long. From there the series moved to East London and it finished in Cape Town, so it was four races in those days, though we never made the Cape Town leg. We'd always stop at Nature's Valley, where my parents had a holiday house.

All the big international names of the day would come to South Africa to race – guys like Jack Brabham, Jim Clark, Jo Bonnier, Stirling Moss and Trevor Taylor. I still have a book with all their autographs, which I managed to collect myself, except for the one of Stirling Moss. My dad had to get it for me. Not that I didn't try myself, mind you. I had seen Moss leaning against the pit wall at the 1960 South African Grand Prix in East London and walked up to him to ask for his signature. Formula 1 wasn't anywhere near as controlled as it is these days, and, during practices, the public could wander around the pit area. Anyway, Moss basically told me to bugger off, as he was busy. It was quite a shock to me and I never forgot it. Maybe he was thinking about something important; I don't know, but I held a grudge for 25 years.

I got my revenge, though.

Many years later, in 1986, when I was an international racing driver and competing in the American IMSA series, Sir Stirling Moss, as he was now called, was the series commentator. At the first race, in West Palm Beach, the organisers arranged for Moss to meet all the drivers. He came down to the pits and was asking everyone to sign the race programme. When he got to me, I told him to bugger off, as I was busy. My response came as a bit of a shock to him. But I couldn't help myself – I burst out laughing and then explained why I'd reacted that way. He apologised profusely and said that his mind must've been elsewhere at the time. We enjoyed a bit of a chuckle together.

These times in the early 60s actually taught me the fundamentals of driving, and specifically driving a racing car. Not only was I watching my father race and learning from him, but I was also around the best drivers in the world. They were accessible and I would just stand there and listen to them talk. I remember meeting and speaking to Jim Clark at the East London caravan park. It had been raining heavily and the drivers couldn't practise. For a bit of a laugh, they erected a gymkhana course in the car park and had some fun. It turned into a mud pit very quickly, but it was a real education to see Clark and South African drivers like Ernest Pieterse handle cars in those conditions. Pieterse was a good friend of my father's and a talented single-seater driver in the early 60s – I remember him winning the 1962 SA National Formula 1 title in an ex-works Lotus 21.

So ja, I was never actually *taught* to drive – it was just something I seemed to know how to do. When I was in Standard 5 – I must have been 12 – my mother, Nicolene, had an Auto Union DKW car. She came to fetch us at school one afternoon and, as it was easy to do if you weren't careful, managed to flood the car's carburettor. She couldn't get the car started again, and the parents of one of my friends had to give us a lift home. Later that day I walked back to school where the car was still parked, started it, put it in gear and drove it back home.

Naturally, my parents weren't particularly happy about this – I could hear them having a muffled discussion about how they had to put a stop to my driving – but I knew my father was secretly proud. Later that week my parents had some friends over for dinner and I heard my dad tell his buddy that a woman floods the car, yet a 12-year-old boy gets into the car, starts it and drives it home. And that just shows you how inept women are. He was teasing my mother a bit, obviously, but I think he was quite chuffed with me as well. What he didn't realise was that this talent of mine was going to cost him a lot of money a few years down the line.

By the time I was 15, I was regularly driving my mother's car, though neither my parents knew about my little excursions. We lived on the old Klapper Fort road right at the top of the hill at the back of the city. I was writing my Standard 8 exams at the time, and in those days they were a big deal. Although it wasn't an option for me, one could leave school after Standard 8 and learn a trade, so there was some pressure associated with these exams. Once my parents had both gone off to work, my buddy would come over and we would steal one of my parents' cars to drive to the exam locale and back home afterwards. My parents had three cars at the time: my mom's, my dad's everyday car, and then the car my dad raced.

One morning before one of the exams, my buddy and I were faffing around only to realise that we were late and would miss the exam unless we made up some time. Luckily for us, my father just happened to have the perfect car for making up time: the Porsche 356 Speedster. The roofless Speedster was no ordinary Porsche 356 convertible. This was an ultra-rare piece of machinery.

Unlike the normal 356, the Speedster had a low-cut windscreen and no side windows. With the rudimentary cloth roof up, it also had a lower profile than the standard 356 Roadster. Performance-wise, other cars in its class at that time were the six-cylinder Austin Healeys, the twin-cam MGAs and the special-bodied Alfa Zagato Sprints. Compared to today, of course, they weren't that fast – you'd probably beat one in a diesel bakkie – but they were impressive for the time.

In the late 50s, a car that could do over 100 mph was a bloody fast motor car, and the Speedster could do around 112 mph. I don't think there were ever more than three or four Speedsters in the country, they were that rare. Today a Speedster in mint condition can go for a couple of million rand, but I have no idea what it cost my father back then. In 1966 my father imported a Mercedes 230SL convertible and I know he paid R6 000 for it.

Not that I cared about any of that …

'We'd better take the Porsche,' I said to my buddy, and off we charged at a hell of a lick. *Too* much of a lick, unfortunately, as at Brooklyn Circle a woman suddenly pulled out of a parking space in front of me. I had to swerve quickly to avoid her, but being an inexperienced driver, I lost control of the Speedster and side-swiped a parked Mercedes-Benz. I mean, we went straight into the Mercedes's side.

The Porsche's fenders were bent back right onto the wheels, and I never really knew how badly the Merc was damaged, because I didn't stop to look. But I do know that they were made of considerably thicker steel than the little lightweight Porsche. The Speedster was not looking well. I panicked, sped off home and left my buddy to hike to school. My only means of defence was to barricade myself inside my room – a fairly pointless attempt at trying to avoid the inevitable wrath of my dad.

Obviously a lot of people had witnessed the accident and seen the Porsche's number plate. Not that this detail mattered much … there weren't many Porsche Speedsters in Pretoria at the time. Nonetheless, my father got the inevitable phone call at work.

'Sir, do you own a Porsche, registration TP10150?'

He said yes.

'Well,' said the police officer on the other end of the line, 'then you just drove away from the scene of an accident.'

My father obviously made it clear that he'd been at work all the time.

'Then somebody in your Porsche just hit a car at Brooklyn Circle.'

My father very quickly put two and two together and informed the policeman that he'd better get to our house before my father did, or he'd have a murder to investigate as well.

Having foreseen what was likely coming my way, I had also armed myself with my father's revolver – another factor that didn't exactly endear me to him at the time. It took the cops quite a while to talk me out of the siege I'd laid, but even after a lengthy negotiation, my father made sure their work still wasn't done. To my utter shock, he made the cops cart me away to the police cells. I remember sitting at the police station with the cops phoning him to come and fetch me … and my father refusing.

'If I fetch him, I am going to kill him.'

My imprisonment lasted for days. My mother had to bring me food and the cops took me to school. That, of course, made me a playground hero, because everybody thought that staying at the police station was very cool.

Ja, I think my father was pretty close to murder. I was allowed back home after a while, but he completely ignored me for six months – didn't say a word to me – though eventually things thawed out.

And my father wasn't exactly a saint behind the wheel, either. He even managed to roll a car twice in one weekend. The first time was kind of legit – it was during a rally, so that's part of the game – but later that same night, he and his buddy Ewold van Bergen rolled another car on the way back from the after-rally party. I've no doubt they'd had one drink too many. My father also once rolled the Speedster – at a race my mother, my brother and I were watching. He got chucked out of the car, but apart from some bruising, he was okay.

My Speedster crash, by the way, wasn't my first either. And perhaps that might've had something to do with my father's anger.

My first crash occurred when I was 12, in my mother's Ford Fairlane. Sometimes, when my parents went out at night, my buddies and I would 'borrow' her car and drive it around the neighbourhood. Once I came around a corner too fast, just missed a telephone pole and, while looking around to see by how far I had missed it … drove over a culvert. The impact took out the radiator, propshaft and so forth.

Another of my activities my father fortunately knew nothing about was when my mates and I would 'steal' cars in Waterkloof. At weekends we'd walk around the neighbourhood at night, looking to see if there were any parties taking place. We'd then try the doors of the cars parked outside the party venue and, if any were open, we'd get in and go for a free-wheel joyride down the hill, all the way to Magnoliadale, which must've been about five kilometres away. No doubt there was plenty of head-scratching when people eventually traced their cars a few kilometres down the road from where they had originally parked.

Anyway, to conclude the Porsche Speedster story, the car was repaired, but my father never raced it again and he eventually sold it. I'm not sure if it was because of the accident or because he was starting to get more involved in rallies and driving DKWs.

MORE DICING THAN RACING ... OR FLYING

A few years later, in 1965, I eventually got my licence. Given my escapades in cars up until that point, my driving test was surprisingly uneventful. I'd been driving for six years by then, so my ability behind the wheel was never an issue – the only thing that could have cocked it up would have been if I'd tried to show off. Becoming a legal member of the South African driving public, however, was very important to me, and I was the epitome of the calm, attentive and well-mannered motorist. I went through the entire exam doing everything required perfectly, and the nice bloke in the grey uniform gave me my licence.

It was wonderful. Now I could legally cause kak. Okay, 'legally' still isn't entirely accurate. It was legal in the sense that I was allowed to drive; it's just that the kind of driving I was doing wasn't exactly legal. Me being me, day-to-day driving was never going to be an attractive proposition. So, to satisfy my ever-growing desire to race a motor car, the next best thing was street racing, which was pretty big in Pretoria in those days. Street racing was a regular event on Sunday nights and pretty well organised. I'd take my mom's DKW and pitch up at a place called Ray's Roadhouse. Some of the guys took it very seriously and would arrive with a full pit ensemble consisting of their buddies, jacks, racing tyres and racing fuel. Actually, some of the cars even ran on AV gas ... aviation fuel that they bought at Wonderboom Airport. It burnt like hell, but it wasn't exactly the safest kind of fuel. Some cars even blew up.

Street racing is basically another term for illegal drag racing. It was a straight-line shoot-out, often down Vermeulen Street, and it was so well organised that people would block the traffic lights just so that they could have a proper run. They even had different classes running. It was a major event. With my mother's

DKW F12, I was in the 1 000cc class, along with the Ford Anglias and Minis. The lightweights, like us Deeks, would run first, followed by the main manne, like Richard Sterney in his 1640 Cortina. Later, guys would pitch in in their V6s. There was no prize money or any other rewards; it was all about bragging rights.

The cops, of course, tried their hardest to stop the racing, but we had spotters with hand-held radios who would find out where the cops were. I remember the Pretoria police driving Studebaker Larks back then – not that it helped them at all. Our spotters would simply say, 'Okay, the cops are coming. Close it down.' Everybody would just park their cars and stand around and talk kak. The cops would stay for a while to check us out and then, thinking nothing was going on, eventually duck. And then the dicing would continue.

The cops tried to shut the street racing down quite a few times, but we always had a three- to five-minute warning. This went on for years and years. The newspapers would report that on Sunday night the cops would be clamping down once and for all, and they would duly arrive in force … only to find nobody there. Occasionally they would see some guys dicing and try to catch them, but apart from the few lower classes, the cops and their Larks couldn't even run with the Anglias – those guys would just drill them.

I don't remember there being any major accidents, which is surprising, I guess, given the reputation street racing has these days. But there was the occasional fight when the Joburg guys arrived in their cars – we were quite territorial, I suppose. But I remember it as a really wonderful time.

Funnily enough, I don't think I ever told my father about the street dicing. He knew that I wanted to race motor cars, but back then in South Africa, there wasn't such a thing as a professional racing driver. Overseas, yes, but back here you basically needed a career to finance your racing. Even if you were a works driver – and only the rally scene had real factory-backed teams – it still didn't pay enough.

So I needed a career. And as far as my father was concerned, it wasn't going to be as a racing driver. It was 1965, and my father still had his DKW racing car and equipment, though he wasn't really competing any more. He knew that with all this stuff lying around, I'd want to hit the racetrack. To prevent this from happening – as you've seen by now, I had a history of 'borrowing' his cars without his permission – he sold all his racing paraphernalia and the car to Coenraad Spamer, who'd become well known in local motor-sport circles for his exploits on the track and at hill-climbs in various Deeks. In fact, my father specifically told Spamer that he didn't want the car any more because I had my eye on it.

So I decided to become an air force pilot.

One-year national service was compulsory then – it had to be done either straight after school or after your tertiary studies. I was originally drafted into the army, to be stationed at Bloemfontein, but I decided instead that being an air force pilot might be a good substitute for the racetrack. I duly applied to the air force and was accepted. All trainees attended the Air Force Gymnasium in Valhalla near Pretoria, and I got through the whole rigmarole – the selection phase, the training and the rest of it, which was pretty intense and physically tough.

I passed everything … but then I was caught AWOL one weekend. We had ducked out to visit our chicks, but one of the guys didn't wait for us to pick him up to get back into base. Instead he hiked back but was involved in an accident, then shot his mouth off and the whole thing came out. That was the end of the party for me. I was promptly kicked off the pilot's course.

'If we can't trust you on the ground, Van der Merwe,' said the officer in charge, 'how the fuck can we trust you in the air?'

Good point.

I was arrested and confined to barracks – no belt, no shoelaces, supposedly to stop a person from hanging himself. That was a non-issue for me – I was just annoyed that I had to walk around in boots without laces. Idiotic.

By this time everyone at the Gym had been allocated jobs – some guys were working in stores, others drove bulldozers, some were in the control towers ... basically everyone had something to do. So when I came back, I was like a lost fart in a thunderstorm, and for nine months they put me in an office and gave me a series of mind-numbingly boring, minor admin jobs to do. I am not good at, nor am I particularly interested in, minor admin jobs. Not back then ... and not now.

The air force made one crucial error, though. They left me in an office that had a telex machine. I soon found out that I could send anyone an official telex, including my commanding officer. I promptly sent him one to inform him that I had been 'transferred' to Air Force Headquarters in Pretoria. So every morning for about two months, carrying a little kit bag, I'd jump onto the back of the Gym truck heading for HQ ... and then jump off once we were outside the gate. I had civvies in my kit bag, and I'd go into the public toilets, get changed and saunter off to visit my buddies.

Unfortunately, I didn't count on Air Force Gym checking up on how all the transferred guys were doing in their new jobs. When they phoned HQ to ask about my progress, obviously no one there knew anything about me. That afternoon, when everyone returned to the Gym and we had the usual parade, the sergeant major called me and said, in a suspiciously calm voice, 'Van der Merwe ... you just stand there and think about where you were the last two months.'

In order to keep an eye on me, the sergeant major made me work in his office for the remainder of the year – I think he quite liked me because I was always causing kak, though he would never have admitted it. But confining me to his office wasn't the smartest move the air force could've made. The sergeant major was responsible for signing the weekend passes, and I had access to all the papers, which, of course, allowed me to sell weekend passes. All I had to do was slip in a few of my own among the legit passes and he'd sign them. For this service, I'd charge my clients one rand per pass. Not a helluva lot of money, even then, but it made for a decent drinks kitty.

We also had a sergeant by the name of Nel, who was a real arsehole. He wanted us to do something – I forget what, but no doubt some arbitrary job just to show who was boss. I just stood there and stared at him.

He looked at me: 'You want to fuck me up, don't you?'

I said ja.

'Right, let's go to the boxing ring then.'

So I did. And, boy, did he knock the shit out of me. Gave me a real working over. That said, the fact that I was prepared to take him on actually made him like me. I even got a little preferential treatment from then on. So that's essentially the story of my whole army career. We'd sit and scheme all day long, do stuff, and then get into shit.

With my attempt at a career in the air force (I would get my pilot's licence many years later, when I bought my own aeroplane) having crashed and burnt, the issue of my future career was still no closer to being resolved. Once the year was up and I'd *klaared* out of the air force, my father was on my case.

'What are you going to do now?'

'What can I do?'

'Anything you want.'

'Okay … How much is it going to cost for me to become a doctor?'

Cue rough estimate from my father. As I said, he was a quantity surveyor – he was good at this stuff.

'Right, I don't actually want to become a doctor, but can I have the money to go racing?'

Silence.

'There's no such job – you're going to university.'

Which is how, in 1966, I ended up at Tuks University in Pretoria studying for a B.Comm. I passed the first year without causing too much damage to anything or anyone. The second year, however, was a different story. Two auspicious things happened to me in 1967 – I competed in my first ever actual, legal race. And I discovered the wonders and pleasures of women. Both would dominate my life from that point on...

2

THE RISE OF SUPERVAN

I've been there, done that, bought the T-shirt. Seriously. It's red

Before we continue our little timeline, it's probably a good idea to introduce you to someone. Think of it as a case for the defence.

For some strange reason there are some folk out there who might think I'm a little on the arrogant side and, yes, I may possibly have pissed off a couple of people in the past 40 years. But that's not really me. That's someone else.

Ladies and gentlemen, my star witness ... SuperVan.

Motoring journo John Oxley first came up with the nickname after the 1973 Pretoria News Rally, where, driving my standard Datsun SSS, I managed to beat SA champ Lambert Fekken in his works Ford Escort. It was my first ever rally win and the press made a pretty big deal of it. I quite liked this new name. Superman's overalls might've been slightly tighter than mine and he wore his Y-fronts on the outside, but it nevertheless seemed like a good comparison.

The name stuck. The Afrikaans press tried Super Sarel for a while – maybe Superman was just too *rooinek* and *rooi onderbroek* for them – but they eventually adopted SuperVan as well. And, as I would soon discover, there were certain benefits to the name ...

You see, to my family and immediate circle of friends, I'm actually a fairly reserved and private person. Publicly, though, I'm someone else. You could see this other persona starting to develop during my high school and air force days, but he really only became fully formed once I started racing.

The more I began to compete in motor sport, the more often SuperVan emerged. I needed to adopt another persona, as motor sport demanded someone a lot more outspoken and aggressive than me. *Hardegat* is the word. I felt I needed to back up my exploits on the track with a suitably impressive character off it. SuperVan fitted the mould perfectly. More than merely a nickname, SuperVan became my alter ego.

He was certainly 'large and in charge' after that first rally victory in 1973. The prize giving was held at the Pretoria Motor Club, and I had the DJ play the Mac Davis tune 'Oh Lord It's Hard To Be Humble' as I went up to collect the trophy. My choice of song probably annoyed a few people, which was my intention. I was doing all I could to make my name and, like any new gunslinger in town, I was ready to take on all comers.

Sure, it was arrogant, but it was also an indication of how completely focused I was on not only being the best, but making it crystal clear to my fellow competitors exactly who the top dog was. As the saying goes in motor sport, 'The first person you need to beat is your teammate', and I always made damn sure they knew where they stood. And that, obviously, was a position or two behind me.

I'll give you an example. In 1984 I was racing the IMSA series in the US, driving a Kreepy Krauly–sponsored March with fellow South Africans Tony Martin and Graham Duxbury. As the number-one driver in the team, I was the one setting up the car. In other words, I was the one doing stuff like tweaking the suspension settings until they were exactly to my liking.

I was also faster than my two teammates, but I'd got wind that they'd grumbled to our chief mechanic. According to them, the reason for the gap in our lap times was mainly because the car had been set up for me and not them. Both Martin and Duxbury had come from single-seater formulas back home and they were highly regarded drivers. How could this ... this ... *rally driver* be embarrassing them? *Heh heh.*

'Fine, tell you what,' I said. 'I'll give you guys a day's head start. You take the car and set it up exactly the way you want it. Test those settings until the cows come home … and then I'll come the next day and drive the car with your settings, and we'll compare lap times. How does that sound?'

Mumble, mumble.

So that's what they did. They set the car up the way they wanted it and the next day I strapped myself into a car that would supposedly not be giving me such a big advantage.

I went quicker straight away. But of course SuperVan wouldn't leave it at that. They not only needed to know that I was faster than them; they had to know that I was better at setting up a car as well.

'Right. These settings of yours are shit. Now we're going to set the car up my way, and believe me, the car is going to go quicker. If you don't like driving it like that, take your things and fuck off.'

I changed it back to my preferred settings, and not only did I go even faster, but even they improved their lap times! I'd made my point. Perhaps it wasn't the most subtle way of going about it, but the point had been made.

Was SuperVan being an arsehole? Probably. But all I wanted was the best possible result we could get, and if you step on a few toes in the process, then it's tough shit. In this case I was driven by a need to establish myself in the US, but even when I was later dominating local rallying in the Audi Quattro, SuperVan made sure things went his way. For example, when I was practising prior to one rally, I was unhappy with the way my Quattro was performing. I had a go in my teammate Geoff Mortimer's car and found I liked it better. It didn't matter that Mortimer was also our team manager … without a second thought I instructed him to unbolt his seat and replace it with mine and I took over his car.

I knew I was faster than him – why kill myself trying to beat him just because my car was slower? Because even in the slightly slower car, I knew without a doubt that I'd still beat the guy. It would just make our lives easier if I took the fast car from the word go. SuperVan simply had no qualms about pulling rank in this sort of situation. No doubt it pissed Mortimer off. That, as far as I was concerned, was his problem. SuperVan had mechanics, and even team managers, fired because he thought they were doing a shit job. At the end of the day, SuperVan takes the flak for a bad result, not them.

Not only could SuperVan do all that tough-guy stuff on the track and on dusty rally roads, but he also allowed me to be SuperVan whenever I was in the spotlight. When I wasn't racing, for example, I didn't really socialise that much, other than with close friends. This was particularly the case when I started travelling internationally to race in the US and Europe. When I did manage to get back home, the last thing I wanted to do was go out to various parties and functions.

I was also often battling jet lag, having to negotiate so many time zones. At home I used to wake up at 2 a.m., watch TV or read, and then go back to sleep at noon. I've never been keen on sleeping pills – or any medication, for that matter – so I just had to listen to my body and sleep when it wanted to sleep.

I hate flying too, which doesn't make me a very sociable companion. I hate chatty passengers, especially on international flights. If I'm in a window seat, I go straight to sleep. Or if I'm in an aisle seat, I'll have a brief conversation with the person at the window, which usually goes something like this: 'Are you planning on getting up to use the bathroom or anything like that during the flight?'

'Um … probably, yes.'

'Well, I'll be going to sleep quite soon and, given my size, you won't be able to climb over me. Why don't we make both our lives easier and just swap seats now and get it over with?'

'Um … okay.'

At which point I would then annex the window seat and go to sleep. Unless, of course, there happened to be a beautiful woman next to me and the transatlantic flight promised SuperVan an opportunity to renew his membership to a rather exclusive club.

Whereas I preferred to stay at home in between races or rallies, SuperVan was the life and soul of any after-rally or race party. He was quite happy to be the centre of attention. SuperVan could do things I couldn't and he could get away with all kinds of shit. He could take on the world. And he was also my escape clause.

He was a big womaniser, too. My girlfriends, wives and mistresses knew it all too well.

'Ja ... so you're SuperVan today, I see.'

SuperVan would become such a distinctly different persona from the guy I normally was that even my close friends eventually began to remark on it. They knew that over a race weekend or at a rally, SuperVan would be out and about. My competitors started to know it, too. As I became more successful and began to win more rallies and races, I also became more verbal with my observations on their abilities versus mine. Understandably, this rubbed some drivers up the wrong way and, in their conversations, the word 'SuperVan' would often be accompanied by several expletives.

I didn't mind that at all – it meant I was getting inside their heads – but there was a downside to SuperVan. He was prone to making some ... let's call them 'impetuous decisions'.

Some of these occurred in my personal life, which I suppose is hardly surprising for someone who talks about having 'wives, mistresses and girlfriends'. And some occurred in my career. SuperVan made some ego-driven decisions that, in hindsight, perhaps weren't the smartest. As you'll find out, I left VW/Audi for Ford in 1991, and that was definitely my ego talking. If I'd stayed with the Germans, I would've won four more Wesbank Modified championships and built an unbroken, long-term relationship with them.

VW/Audi is also just a more solid company; they're still in motor sport today. On the other hand, since Ford packed up in

Port Elizabeth and became SAMCOR, it's been a balls-up, to be honest. They are battling to this day, and for years have been in and out of motor sport. VW/Audi did pull out of motor racing for a while, but they've always been on the rally scene and have continued to win, as they've got a good product.

Having said that, I'm still on very good terms with the VW/ Audi group. They even used me in the ad campaign that launched their new VW Amarok bakkie, and I use a fleet of Amaroks in my Spirit of Africa business. But still, it would've been better if I'd stuck with them all the way.

I defected to Ford because winning in the Audi had become too easy. I wanted to prove that I could get into the Ford I'd so roundly thrashed in the Audi the previous season and turn the tables. People were beginning to think my domination in 1989 and 1990 was down to the Audi, which SuperVan could never allow.

SuperVan could also never allow a well-behaved party. Any motor-sport function he attended had to be turned up a notch or 10. Take the 1978 Monsanto Rally, for example ...

Held in Pietersburg, it was the last event of the season, and I had just won the championship. An early night was never on the cards. But neither was running off with the sponsor's wife or scaring the crap out of the Venda 'government'. Those inverted commas are, of course, a nod to the fact that this apartheid-era homeland was recognised by no world nation other than South Africa.

I must admit I don't remember all the details of the evening, though there are moments that stand out. The function was held at that world-class establishment, the Pietersburg Holiday Inn, and the vodka and Cokes – a personal favourite of mine – were flowing freely. For some reason SuperVan took a shine to the young wife of the rally's main sponsor and decided right there and then to pick her up, throw her over his shoulder and rush out of the function venue into a nearby room. I kicked open the double doors ... and was confronted by a rather alarmed Venda government debating important matters of state.

It wouldn't be the last time I interacted with the Venda government that night. The next incident that occurred was even more undiplomatic. Much later, after the sponsor had marched his wife off home, the party moved up to my room. One of the mechanics, with whom I got on particularly well, had snuck off to bed, but I was having none of it. Apparently he was two doors down the passage and I set off to wake the bugger up. Cleverly, though, he'd locked his door.

No problem for SuperVan. I went back to my room, climbed over my balcony to the adjacent one, and from there climbed onto his balcony. The fool had left the sliding doors open. I tiptoed into the room – not an easy feat for someone who had been drinking litres of vodka and Coke, but doable for SuperVan – and in the darkness saw him lying on the bed. I stood back, took a flying leap and jumped onto the bed, screaming something in Afrikaans about this being no time to sleep.

Turns out my intelligence had been inaccurate.

It was not my mechanic's room and it definitely wasn't my mechanic. It was, in fact, a member of the Venda government, and judging by the look of wide-eyed terror on his face, all his white Afrikaner nightmares had become reality. And this at the Pietersburg Holiday Inn, which was something I'm sure he hadn't seen coming.

All hell broke loose.

In between fits of laughter I tried to explain my error and apologise, but this being the second time I'd burst in on him, the ministerial gentleman was taking no chances. The manager was called, as were the police, and all sorts of accusations were bandied about, culminating in the conclusion that a coup had been made on the state of Venda.

At another post-rally function – also in Pietersburg, actually ... not sure what it is about Pietersburg – we ended up having a fire-extinguisher fight in the hotel's hallways. I seem to remember fellow driver and multiple SA rally champ Serge Damseaux being involved in that one, too. If you know Serge, he's normally a very quiet guy, but SuperVan had the knack of helping other people find their own inner SuperVans. The two of us got so out of hand when the manager threatened to close the bar that he eventually just locked us inside and asked us not to try to get out. We caused something like R6 000's damage, which was a lot of money in the 70s.

The next morning, Stuart Pegg, navigator of fellow driver and another multiple SA rally champ, Jan Hettema, rounded up all the guilty parties and we apportioned the costs. We paid up and left. The damages always came out of our own pockets, as obviously our antics never went down well with the teams' managements. Especially with Toyota. They fired me after one particularly big night, more about which in the next chapter.

Besides the associated costs, team management also feared that all the boisterous behaviour would end up in the press. They needn't have worried too much: (1) members of the press were often, if not always, playing leading roles in said parties. And if they weren't actually physically responsible for the collateral damage, they were at least there, applauding it. And (2) they were loyal to us.

The press guys were part of the motor-sport scene. They were not only journalists, but also motor-sport fans who travelled with us from event to event. There were never more than four or five guys covering the events in those days, so they were part of the gang – we were a real close-knit group. In many instances we became firm friends and no one was interested in writing scandal-mongering articles. Besides, as I said, they would have had to include themselves in their stories.

John Oxley and I were good friends – he was writing for *Car* magazine, among others. And I knew old Ben van Rensburg from my earliest days as a driver. He was already doing the motor-sport beat for the Afrikaans papers when my father was racing – he turned 80 last year. André de Kock of the *Citizen* was another.

Throughout my career, I have had a very good relationship with the press. Part of it, obviously, can be attributed to my sparkling personality, but I've also always been prepared to tell them exactly what I think. So I was often saying something controversial that would therefore make it newsworthy. I understand that professional sportsmen and women can't say anything to piss off their sponsors or administrative bodies, but, hell, a lot of boring rubbish comes out their mouths these days. Not me. If the car was kak, SuperVan would say it was kak.

As you can imagine, this did not go down well in America, where I raced extensively during the 80s. Everybody's got this holier-than-thou approach to the press. Put a mike in front of a driver there and suddenly he starts thanking every sponsor, from the smallest to the biggest sticker on his car. And, let me tell you, there are a lot of stickers on those US cars.

We had a lot of problems with the Corvette GTP I was racing and, if asked about the car, I would tell it like it was. The car was shit, and that was the end of the story. General Motors didn't know what the hell to do with this lunatic loose cannon from Africa. But I was just being honest, which the press always appreciated. That was, and still is, SuperVan for you. He's always had the balls to say whatever he is thinking. Diplomacy was never very high on his list of priorities.

No doubt psychologists would have a field day analysing this separate persona of mine – especially when I start referring to myself in the third person. Usually that rings the kind of alarm bells that signal the sound of a straitjacket being firmly buckled up. Maybe they'd diagnose it as a protective cocoon I'd constructed to protect my real self from the harsh realities of life, which must clearly hark back to the time I crashed my father's Porsche and was subjected to his severe wrath and retribution. Who knows – those psychologists are such clever chaps.

No doubt they would point to the fact that both my parents died relatively young, which would surely make this bolshie SuperVan character a carefully constructed barrier against any further emotional pain. Possibly. I was close to my parents. My father raced cars and he hung out with all the famous drivers of the time. He may have been very strict and not have shown much physical affection to his kids, but he was a hero to me.

Shame, I did drive the poor man mad when it came to his cars, though. Besides the Porsche Speedster incident, I also managed to mess up his new Merc. In 1958 he bought a brand-new, black Mercedes-Benz 220S – one of those small, rounded saloons. I must've been about 11 and I was busy painting one of my Dinky Toy cars white. Looking for a place outside in the sun to let it dry, the fender of my father's car seemed the perfect spot. Unfortunately, a few small drops of paint dripped onto the Merc, and instead of just waiting for it to dry and then brushing it off, I went and got a cloth. My attempts to wipe off the paint turned a couple of small, white drops into one big, grey smudge. Needless to say, my father was not impressed, and there was big trouble that day.

He was strict, but I knew he cared about me. That was just his way. He was never particularly encouraging about my motor-sport career and he'd never let on that he was watching me. But I'd often see him in the crowds. Sometimes at a rally, I'd spot him behind a tree, though he'd never tell me he was coming to watch. After he passed away, I found a scrapbook of his with newspaper cuttings of my achievements.

Sarel Snr died of lung cancer in 1979 at the age of 57. By then I had won two SA rally championships, and I was leading the standings that year as well. It's always been a big regret of mine that he never got to see my overseas successes. He would've liked that.

My mother had died two years prior to that, in 1977. She was even younger … just 53 when breast cancer got her. She went through chemo, which prolonged her life for a year, but chemo in those days was particularly unpleasant. Although I was at the Nature's Valley house for a festive-season holiday with my now ex-wife and kids, we came back to Pretoria for Christmas at my mother's request. She clearly wanted us there for the event, knowing that it would almost certainly be her last. Six days later, she was dead. She passed away during the night.

Very soon afterwards, Dad was diagnosed with lung cancer and, having witnessed what my mom had gone through with chemo, refused any treatment. He lived another 18 months. Two of my grandparents would also pass away over that time. Within two-and-a-half years, I lost four members of my immediate family. It was a very rough time, and that would certainly give credence to any SuperVan-as-emotional-barrier theory.

Here's another theory, though. Perhaps SuperVan is just a death wish given a cool name. Maybe with my parents dying so young of cancer, I knew my chances of going the same way were pretty high. Maybe that's why I continued to pursue my dangerous career path, driving faster and faster cars. And also why I was an avid cigarette smoker, flipping a middle finger to the spectre of lung cancer, for many years (I quit in 2011). Or why, during the 80s, I would have as much sex as I possibly could with as many different women as possible at a time when HIV/AIDS was beginning to make just about everyone else zip up.

I remember being at a dinner party with Paul Newman, and the subject of HIV/AIDS came up. Apart from being a Hollywood legend, Newman was a big motor-racing fan – he was both a very good driver and a team owner – and he and I were both competing in the American IMSA series. I'm pretty sure had he not been an actor, Newman would've made it as a pro driver. Anyway, I'm not sure how the topic came up, but it did, and I remember him saying, 'People ask me why I race, and I tell them it's because I'm too scared to fuck.'

SuperVan could, of course, also be just a convenient press construct that I used to my advantage. In this guise I could basically do anything I wanted, safe in the knowledge that I had a SuperVan-shaped get-out-of-jail card at my disposal. Yes. And then it became such entrenched behaviour that it actually formed a part of my mental make-up. Schizo Sarel – forever fused to my psyche. I suspect one or two of my ex-wives/mistresses/girlfriends might be nodding their heads in agreement at this point.

I guess the most disparaging analysis would go so far as to call it an ego-driven exercise in brand-building taken to the extreme. I consciously encouraged the use of the term SuperVan and backed it up with the appropriate *hardegat* behaviour in a deliberate strategy to develop this larger-than-life persona. Well, at least then you couldn't say I was a split personality ... just a rather cynical marketer.

I'm no psychologist, so I couldn't give you the answer except to say that I know myself pretty well. I know my faults, I know my strengths, and I know what I'm capable of. If there's one thing motor sport has taught me, it's that you can bullshit everyone, but you can't bullshit yourself. I could tell you SuperVan was all just a veneer, laugh it off as a convenient persona that I could switch on and off at will. But the reality is that SuperVan is so much a part of who I am that, at best, the switch is subconscious.

To be successful in sport, particularly motor sport, you have to have an ego. It's a basic job requirement. In that environment you have to be forceful, both on and off the track, otherwise you won't get anywhere near the sharp end of the field. You might as well just drive the safety car. SuperVan is basically my ego that was given a cool name. As I said, I'm really a fairly reserved person and, yes, SuperVan did allow a more extroverted personality to develop. But that kak-causing part of me had clearly been there all along – he just needed to be given the green light. And I tend to floor it when the light goes green.

Look, I can be diplomatic when I have to be, but, hell, it's a bit of a struggle. Now there's a state of mind I really have to work on. Not so much with SuperVan, though. He's always present and accounted for at the racetrack – that was expected of him – but he'd often stick around afterwards, causing all sorts of kak in my personal life. Hence the multiple wives, mistresses and girlfriends.

These days, SuperVan isn't required that often, but he does make the odd guest appearance. I still do the occasional race, most often in the Historic Saloons series, mostly driving Peter du Toit's big 7.5-litre 1963 Ford Galaxie. This Galaxie was one of two cars brought out here by Bobby Olthoff to drive in the Springbok Series back then. I remember the car as a youngster – it captured everyone's imagination, and Olthoff used to have these great dices with the little 1.6-litre Lotus Cortinas of Koos Swanepoel and Basil van Rooyen.

On the tighter circuits, like Roy Hesketh and Killarney, the nimble Cortinas would hound the Galaxie for all it was worth and often beat it. But on the faster circuits, like East London and Kyalami, the Galaxie would have the upper hand. It was such a bloody monster of a car that you either loved or hated the thing. I admit I used to root for the Lotus Cortinas in those days because they were the underdogs – the terriers snapping at the Rottweiler.

World F1 champ Jim Clark and Sir John Whitmore even came out for the Springbok Series and they also drove Lotus Cortinas. Together with Swanepoel and Van Rooyen, you had four Lotus Cortinas chasing this one lone Galaxie. It was fantastic racing back then, and I think that's one of the reasons Historic Saloons have become so popular with race fans in this country. Spectators don't care much about lap times – as long as the racing's good, it doesn't really matter what times anybody's doing.

The Galaxie I drive today was Olthoff's spare car – the real heavyweight. The other one, which they raced most of the time, had a lightweight bonnet, fibreglass bumpers and shit like that. I don't know how much less it actually weighed, but it must've been in the region of 150 kilograms to 200 kilograms. Or, to put it another way, that's like having two extra people in the car with you. I don't think Olthoff raced the heavyweight more than twice – only when the other car was broken.

I love this shit. These old big banger V8s have massive power, and the finely tuned aerodynamic downforce of a dustbin. They go like hell and slide around all over the show. SuperVan can express himself pretty well in one of these. As some poor sod in a little Mini Cooper found out recently …

I was having a great dice with a couple of other old Yank V8s at Killarney when this chap in a little Mini Cooper decided to poke his nose in. My 7.5-litre Galaxie obviously had way more power than a 1.0-litre Mini, but because the Galaxie weighs roughly the same as an oil tanker, its brakes tend to go off towards the end of a race. This allowed the nippy little bastard in the Mini to catch up with us. The Mini's famous go-kart-like handling meant he'd closed up around the twisty part of the track, and I could now see him in my rear-view mirror. It was annoying enough, given that my fading brakes had dropped me from first to third behind a Biscayne and a Camaro, but now the fucker in the Mini was actually lining up to pass me. Exactly. What was he thinking?

Sure as hell, exiting the corner that leads onto the back straight, he decided to dive up the inside and nip in front. I know there are these legendary stories from the 60s about how agile little Minis could beat much bigger cars, but *come on*. Seriously. This isn't the 60s. And they weren't driving against SuperVan. Besides, I'd had enough of being passed for one day, and that Mini could probably fit in the Galaxie's boot.

SuperVan shut the door in his face. Very sharply. I could feel a little bump as the Mini bounced off the Galaxie's armour-plating and, in my side mirror, see it teeter on two wheels for a few seconds. Judging by the wide-eyed expression he was wearing, the poor guy clearly needed to change his overalls after the race. It was his own fault, though.

You take on SuperVan at your peril …

3

THE FLAG DROPS

First my rallying, and then my racing career takes off

And back into the timeline we jump ...

As I said at the end of Chapter 1, 1967 was the year that I discovered women, which, interestingly, coincided with a sharp decline in my academic performance. So sharp a decline, in fact, that by October I knew that I was going to fail the year. But I had a plan. I informed my father that I was going to leave Tuks, finish my degree through UNISA and get a job.

Fortunately, my father thought this was a pretty good plan. Even more fortunate was the fact that Datsun were prepared to hire me as a clerk in their accounts department. I suspect this might have had something to do with my father's friendship with Ewold van Bergen. A multiple SA rally champ, Van Bergen was now also heading up Datsun's motor-sport division. I never asked my father if he had had a hand in getting me the job and neither he nor Van Bergen ever said anything to me. Van Bergen, as you'll read, would go on to play a major part in my motor-sport career.

I'd already had my first taste of official motor racing by then, and working for Datsun presented an opportunity for more. In that year I had borrowed my mother's DKW to marshal on the Total Lourenço Marques Rally that started in Pretoria and ended in what was then Lourenço Marques (now Maputo). The Deek was pretty much my car by then – I had used it to get to and from varsity and then just sort of hung on to it.

The Total LM was *the* big rally in those days, and even if I was just marshalling, I was still a part of the scene. At the end of the event, the organisers always hosted a little side race in Lourenço Marques called the Polana Hill Climb. I entered in my mother's car in the 1 000cc class. And, to my surprise, won the bloody thing. My class, I mean, not the whole Hill Climb. Of course, when I came back, I shoved the trophy under my father's nose. He merely said that it wasn't too bad, but I could see that he was chuffed.

Spurred on by this little class victory, I bought a DKW Junior from Coenraad Spamer for R600. Spamer, remember, was the guy to whom my father had sold his Deek car and parts. Considering I was only earning R140 a month, R600 was quite a big investment, but I helped pay it off by assisting Spamer with all the modifications on the Deeks he raced. I guess he was really helping me out more than the other way round.

By 1968 I was racing on the track fairly regularly. I'd realised that if you raced in Natal, they would give you travelling money, plus, if you won, you'd even get a little prize money. I'd race the Deek in the production class – and usually win – then enter the modified class as well and, if I was lucky, sneak a third. On a good Natal weekend I could end up making about R30, which paid for my accommodation and petrol to get back home (it cost R2 to fill the tank in those days).

This was great. 'Hell,' I thought, 'this professional business is really working out well.' I was racing, I was winning, and I was actually making a little bit of cash. Unfortunately it didn't last too long, and by 1969 it was clear that the Deek wasn't competitive any more. Newer cars like the Ford Anglias were starting to kick its arse on the track. By the end of that year, I had made up my mind to try my luck in England – perhaps I could wangle a job as a mechanic in a racing team there and so get my foot in the door to drive …

At the beginning of 1970, I organised a three-month tourist visa and bought the cheapest ticket I could find. It was a return ticket via Rome, which meant catching trains and buses to get to the United Kingdom. If I could get into one of the saloon-car teams in England – the series was pretty big there, with Yank tanks like the Ford Galaxie I'd been driving up against less powerful but more nimble English cars, like the Lotus Ford Cortina – I might eventually end up as a racing driver.

Unfortunately, as I was not a qualified mechanic, no one was interested in my services. The entire exercise turned into a bit of a disaster, and the only place I could find work in London was at the docks, loading goods – not exactly what I'd had in mind. London was supposed to be this hip and happening place. But not for me. I had very little money and the weather was shit – cold, grey, wet and just plain miserable. That wasn't the worst of it, though …

I got married. To a barmaid. And not one of the pretty ones, either.

It was nearing the end of my three-month visa, and one evening I was at a pub where I'd often hang out. I was feeling sorry for myself and telling some friends that I wouldn't be around for much longer unless I found some fair English lass to marry me.

'Give me 50 quid and I'll marry you,' said a voice from the other side of the bar. She wasn't exactly an English rose, but she was English, and that was good enough for me. So I married her for £50 and earned a stay of execution. The marriage was never consummated; it was just a marriage of convenience so that I could remain in the UK.

As these things tend to do, though, the plan backfired. Even though the marriage gave me nine more months in England, by the end of the year it was clear that it was not going to happen for me there, and I made my way back home. Waiting for me in South Africa was a girl I had been seeing before I left for Europe and, for a few reasons I'll tell you more about later, we decided to get married.

The problem, of course, was that I was already married – a small detail I hadn't divulged to anyone, especially not my parents.

Now I had to get divorced, and you can't believe the shit you have to go through to get a divorce under those circumstances. I went to see a lawyer to find out how I could make it all go away.

'Oh my God,' he said, which, frankly, is not something you want to hear from your lawyer. 'This *is* a problem. You've got to advertise in newspapers for three months – two newspapers here and two newspapers in England – and if there are no objections, you'll be granted a divorce.'

Thankfully there were no objections from a certain pub in London, and in the end the divorce came through about three weeks before I got married to my South African girlfriend.

It was 1971, and things were looking bleak. Not only was I almost a bigamist but, worse than that, it looked as if my motorsport career had died. I needed to make a plan. And whatever plan I was going to make, it certainly wouldn't involve my father – that much was clear: 'If you want to go into motor sport, you have to pay for it yourself. No one gave me money to race, and the same applies to you.'

On the plus side, I was able to get my old job back at Datsun, which generated some money for a car. And a car meant that I could go rallying. Track racing was without question my first choice, but it required too many expensive modifications to a standard car. In rallying in those days, however, it was possible to enter and do fairly well in a stock-standard car. The same car that you would, for example, drive to and from work each day – a very necessary requirement for me, given my light-in-the-pocket financial situation.

So I bought an Alfa 1750 – it was a pretty saloon with a big boot. I enrolled a buddy of mine to be my co-driver, and we entered the 1971 Total Rally in August. Never one for messing about, I'd decided that my first rally would be the biggest rally in the country. My first rally, unfortunately, would also herald my first professional crash. And it wasn't a little fender bender either – I managed to write off my brand-new Alfa.

The incident happened at night, when we were following in the dust of the car in front of us. Some idiot in a Renault Gordini had overshot a turn-off and he came reversing back up the road. I was pushing the limits trying to make up time, and suddenly out of the dust the Gordini's reverse lights appeared.

'Oh fuck,' I clearly remember thinking, 'we're going to hit this bastard.'

Which we did. We hit the car so hard, we knocked it right over a fence. And that was the Alfa – and I guess the Gordini – in its *moer*. All I had was a big piece of scrap metal. And it's not as if one takes out car insurance for rallying. What could I do except buy another car? I needed something to get me around every day, but I certainly couldn't afford to crash this one too. In other words, no rallies. My career had stalled again. It took me about eight or nine months to financially recover from the Alfa.

I bought a Toyota, a 1600 Corolla, and by mid-year 1972 I was rallying that car, which didn't go down too well with Ewold van Bergen. He had retired the year before – that Total Rally where I had 'totalled' my Alfa had been his last rally – and was now fully involved in the running of Datsun's official South African motor-sport division. Before then, all Datsun's rally efforts – basically Van Bergen's – had been funded out of Japan.

I suppose one could understand Van Bergen's point of view – working for Datsun but buying a Toyota wasn't going to cut the wasabi. Datsun's management suggested/persuaded/forced me to buy a Datsun SSS. Obviously I was given a good deal, but I still had to buy the car on HP, as it was the only way I could afford it.

I should also mention that by then I had crashed the Corolla as well, so the Datsun was a rather essential purchase. I was quickly discovering that this rally palaver wasn't turning out to be quite as cheap as I had thought.

But the Datsun – the square-shaped P150 SSS – was a decent car, and I started doing quite well in the regional Transvaal rally championship. It seemed I was either winning my class or crashing. Then I wrote off the Datsun as well. By now 1972 had moved into 1973 and I needed another Datsun SSS. This would be the third car I was paying off on HP and the only one on the road. Significantly, though, it would be third time lucky for me. I'd entered the Pretoria News Rally, which was a Transvaal championship. Significantly, Lambert Fekken, the national champion in a BDA Escort, was also competing. Nothing like having a big dog to gun for ...

I remember it being quite a muddy rally, but I managed to beat Fekken with my standard Datsun. My timing was spot on for once, and the high-profile Total Rally was next on the calendar. I was beginning to discover my inner SuperVan at that time and made no bones about the fact that I should be given a works drive in the Datsun team. Eventually Van Bergen called me into his office – I don't think he had a choice, really. I mean, here was a Datsun employee in his own, self-funded car, who'd just beaten the national champ. The fact that this employee was such a cocky young bastard didn't make it easier for him!

Van Bergen was no pushover – he hadn't got to where he was without being hard-arsed.

'Okay, you can come and drive a standard car for us in the Total Rally.'

Standard car? What did he mean, 'standard car'? I was the best driver around! Surely he could see that?

DATSUN PART 1

What I wanted was a drive in one of the modified cars. Datsun ran two factory modifieds, and then a standard car for me. The modified cars were the more powerful, faster and more prestigious drives, but Van Bergen was having none of it. It was the standard car or nothing. And in those days, 'standard' meant 'standard'. You weren't allowed to change anything, not even the shocks. Nothing.

Louis Cloete drove one of the modified cars and, for that year,

Datsun imported a Pom – Tony Fall, the British champion – to drive the other one. Fall won the rally, but my result was the one that grabbed the headlines. I came fourth overall in the standard car, which was basically unheard of. In a national rally, no standard car had ever done anything like it against a field of modifieds. Things were finally starting to go my way, and I had an inkling that a professional driving career might just be on the cards for me. It wasn't on the track, as I'd hoped, but, for the moment at least, what I had was good enough.

For the 1974 season, Van Bergen made me a full-works Datsun driver. But, much to my annoyance and against all my protests, I was still driving the standard car. I was their number-one standard-car driver, but it nevertheless pissed me off. I backed myself and I wasn't shy to voice my opinion on how much better I was than the team's modified drivers, Louis Cloete and Neels Vermaak. But Van Bergen, the canny bastard, still wouldn't budge. It really goaded SuperVan into showing them what he could do.

And what he did was win a national rally outright.

In his standard Datsun.

It was the 1974 Duckhams Rally in Cape Town, and I beat the likes of reigning multiple champ Jan Hettema and all the other modified cars to claim my maiden victory.

I had a new car for this rally – I had replaced my SSS with the new, sloped-back Datsun 160U. It was still bog standard, though. To be fair, it was a wet rally, which negated the modified cars' power to some degree, but it was a huge achievement nonetheless. And I knew it. Feeling more and more comfortable in my SuperVan suit, I wasn't scared of or intimidated by anyone. I thought I was better than all of them, and I would tell them so at any opportunity. I really enjoyed being the upstart. I would say things like, 'I'll beat you.' And then, when I beat them, I'd say, 'You see, I told you so. Now next year I'm going to drive a modified, and then what the hell are you guys going to do?'

True to form, despite the fact that I'd won the rally, Van Bergen kept me in that car for the remainder of the season. 'Great drive, but you're staying put. Next year I'll make you team leader in the modified class, but until then you are first going to drive this car for another year.'

It annoyed me no end, but, as I got older, I realised how smart he really was.

This win was one of the big watershed moments in my career. I'd proved myself as a top driver and a works seat was mine. I ended fifth in the championship that year – I'd had another couple of minor crashes, but still, it was an impressive result in my standard car.

I was also making an impression on the racetrack in my own standard 160U. I was, in fact, leading the Group N championship in my class ... until I got done in by the idiots at motor-sport control. As I would discover again and again, this was somewhat par for the course with MotorSport South Africa's (MSA) organisers.

The Duckhams Rally that I had won clashed with a Group N race at Kyalami. The rally finished on the Saturday morning, so even though I could fly back to Joburg for the afternoon race, I had missed qualifying in the morning. As politely as I could, I asked the organisers if I could just do one lap for a grid position, but they wouldn't allow me. I had to start at the back of the grid. This fired me up, and I came from stone last to finish second. Impressive, but not good enough. It cost me the championship.

It really pissed me off, and after the race I stormed off to have a word with motor-sport control. I might have uttered a few colourful phrases and issued some dark threats. And so started an ongoing feud I would have with the gentlemen, and occasional lady, controlling motor sport in this country. As you'll see in Chapter 10, we still have our differences.

That same year, I also did the legendary off-road race, the Roof of Africa. Held over very rough terrain in Lesotho, it's a notorious car killer. And, true to form, as with every flippin' car that year,

Datsun gave me a stock-standard car to race in. I think we went through 28 shock absorbers during the event. I remember how, at a service point, one of the mechanics tried to remove a shock. He had his head under the wheel arch and, as he took hold of the shock, it was so damn hot from operating way beyond its capabilities that he not only burnt his hand, but also nearly decapitated himself as he jumped up. We were the only standard car to finish the Roof that year.

Despite my successes behind the wheel, I couldn't afford to leave my desk-jockey job yet. I was still working as a clerk for Datsun, but my new status did have some spin-offs. I was put to work as an accountant handling the motor-sport account, which was great; but, even better, my job required me to relocate to the motor-sport facility. Now I could walk down to the workshops and actually watch my modified car as it was being built for the next season.

Everything was starting to come together for me. By 1975 I was driving a modified car and actually getting paid to do it ... R500 a month. Plus, I was earning R500 a month as an accountant. All of a sudden I had a grand a month. That was some serious shit. I could get out of the debt hole I had dug for myself and still have some cash to flash around.

By now I was spending more time rallying and racing than I was in my suit and tie, and eventually the chief accountant called me in.

'You're spending way too much time on the road these days, Van der Merwe. You've got to decide whether you want to be a rally driver or an accountant!'

It took me all of two seconds to make up my mind.

... AND ALFA

And that is how I became a proper professional motor-sport driver. I marked the milestone by winning my first three rallies on the trot. Then, halfway through the season – a season I was dominating in my Datsun – things got a little tricky. Alfa came along and offered me a race drive in a modified Alfetta on the track. Although Datsun were not happy, there wasn't much they could do about it. Telefunken, Alfa's sponsor on the track, were also Datsun's big rally sponsor. So Datsun had to back down, at least temporarily.

But the truce didn't last, and eventually Van Bergen called me into his office. In my experience, being called into someone's office usually meant kak, and this was no different. He told me that the Datsun management were not happy with the fact that I was their works driver, yet here I was getting so much publicity for driving an effing Alfa. In those days, track racing was given more press coverage than rallying, and the publicity I was generating was not acceptable. I would have to choose.

So I said, well, okay, stick your Datsuns. And that was that.

Van Bergen was helluva cross, but, as I've said, racing was what I really wanted to do. I was pretty happy. Not only was I able to race a modified car on the track for the first time – and one with some decent power, no less – but Alfa also gave me a standard Alfetta to race in the standard production class. Plus – and this part must have annoyed Datsun the most – I still went on to win the national rally title, even though the Alfetta was a fairly crap rally car. Thanks to all the points I'd accumulated in the first half of the season in the modified Datsun 160U, I was able to hang on and claim the championship for Alfa. An added bonus was that Alfa gave me a company car too, so I had a nice Alfetta Executive 2.0-litre parked in my garage.

A (SHORT) TIME WITH TOYOTA

By the end of 1975, I was hot property on the local rally scene, and by December Toyota came knocking on my door with a nice fat cheque and an offer to join them for 1976. Scamp Porter – a well-known racing driver in his day – was managing Toyota's competition department, and his brother Phil was the marketing director.

'Okay,' I said, 'but what about a racing car as well?'

The deal was struck. I would drive a Toyota Corolla SR5 twin cam in rallying and a Renault 5 on the track. Toyota were also selling Renaults then, hence the Renault racing car. We tricked up the little French car and ran it in the modified class. Though it wasn't much good, they built the car because it was the only way to get me to sign up.

As it turned out, things weren't that great on the rallying side either ...

It started off okay – I won the season opener, the Castrol 1000 Hills Rally, for Toyota, and was leading another four after that, but then every time the bloody diff would pack up. Naturally, this displeased me somewhat. Then, about a month before the Total Rally, which was always the big rally of the year, we were doing the Total N'thabeni Rally in Natal and once again leading the field. Somehow the battery came loose, made a spark and ignited the fuel tank next to it. The car exploded.

The flames burnt my hair off. Worse, still – also part of my moustache. *No one* messes with my moustache. But that was the rally done for us. We were stuck at the Newcastle Holiday Inn with a burnt-out Toyota Corolla. What could we do but have the mother of all parties ...?

My memory is a little sketchy on the exact details, but I seem to remember the party starting with tropical fruit that evening. There was a big dinner, and hollowed-out pineapples, packed with fruit salad, were displayed on the tables. Some guy with a recently shaved moustache apparently took a pineapple and threw it at somebody else, which of course called for a retaliatory lob, soon followed by the inevitable free-for-all.

The party later adjourned to my room, which then somehow morphed into us pushing fellow competitor Jan Hettema around in a baby's cot. Hettema and the cot got pushed down some stairs – something the cot clearly wasn't designed to do – and Hettema and a pile of white timber landed at the hotel manager's feet. The fact that Hettema was my big rival was just an unfortunate coincidence. Terrible luck.

The hotel manager wasn't at all happy about the situation, and he and I engaged in a debate, which ended with him calling the police – the sore loser. It was a whole drunken drama. The rally crowd gathered outside the entrance to the hotel as the local constabulary arrived to put me in the back of the van and take me away. About a kilometre down the road, the cops pulled over and said, 'Right, so where are we supposed to take you, Mr van der Merwe?' This was about four o'clock in the morning.

Fortunately a friend of mine had a house nearby, so they dropped me there. My car, however, was still at the Holiday Inn, so I waited until the cops had disappeared and then started jogging back to the hotel. It wasn't too far – less than a kilometre. The cops soon found me running slowly along the road and were keen to know what the hell I was doing and where I was going.

'No,' I said, 'I go jogging every morning.'

Anyway, to bring my little adventure with Toyota to a conclusion, the following Monday morning I got a call from Toyota to come and see them. Phil Porter led the jury: 'Sarel … your lifestyle and Toyota's marketing objectives don't quite fit together. You'd better take your things and duck.'

So they fired me.

Getting fired is never easy to take under any circumstances. My parting shot was: 'Okay, you can fire me, but I can guarantee you that by the time I stop rallying one day, I will have won more rallies than Toyota.' Which I did. And I never drove for Toyota again.

The problem was that I was without a drive three weeks before the Total Rally.

BACK TO DATSUN FOR PART 2

Fortunately, my phone rang … it was none other than my former boss and sparring partner, Ewold van Bergen.

'Do you want to do the Total?'

'Ja. Okay.'

Unfortunately, it didn't go so well for me at the rally. I had one helluva crash while leading in a modified 160U, and that put me out. Things had started off well enough, and I'd won all the initial stages. I was still leading going into the first night, but then one of the carburettors came loose and started sucking air. Because of time spent repairing it at the service point, by the time we got going again, I had dropped back to fifth or sixth. It was dusty as hell that year, and in the poor visibility, running down the field – and obviously driving over the limit, trying to catch the other guys – we hit a tree. That was the end of the Datsun.

By now I had no chance of winning the championship and I could only try to help Datsun's team leader, Jochi Kleint, win the title. We'd even swap cars, depending on the event. We were running a 140Y as well as the 160U, and even though both cars had the same 2-litre engine, one was often more suited to the conditions of a particular rally than the other. The 140Y had a solid rear axle, which was better in some rallies than the 160U. It was also lighter.

I was being a very nice guy, don't you think? Not buying it? Ja, I can't say that it gave me a warm, fuzzy feeling to help my teammate, especially when I was leading stages and ahead of Kleint in the rally and then consequently had to stop and take time penalties to let him through. Still, I had to do it. Ewold van Bergen had also built a modified 140Y for me to race – basically a bribe to get me to play the good-team-member game. And in a rather ironic about-turn, Datsun agreed to let me drive an Alfetta again – but only in Group N this time. To top it all, Van Bergen also promised me that I could be team leader again the next year.

As it turned out, my help wasn't enough and Jan Hettema and his Ford Escort BDA won what would be his last SA championship. Still, I knew our car was good enough to compete with the BDA in 1977… if only we could get rid of some unnecessary weight. In my opinion, the car was a good 200 kilograms too heavy.

After much discussion, Van Bergen finally agreed that we could lighten our cars. Even though he was a development engineer, as well as a former driver, all the development he'd done was for Datsun Japan, and they always wanted the cars to look as standard as possible.

With Van Bergen's blessing, in the off season I stripped the hell out of the Datsun. We had fibreglass panels made – we even made lighter sump guards. All in all I shaved off about 250 kilograms, which worked like a charm. In 1977 the car was right on the money. We beat Hettema and his BDA, and the title was mine again. I was pretty dominant that year, and even when I didn't win a rally, I would still be well placed.

I won my first major race championship that year too – the Group 1 title – in my modified Alfetta. SuperVan was both the SA rally champ and the holder of a major saloon-car championship. This was how the world was meant to be.

But 1977 also presented me with one of those fork-in-the-road moments that we all face in life. I had a big decision to make, and whatever option I took would have significant long-term repercussions. In that year, the Total Rally was part of the world championships. The big guns, like Sandro Munari in his famous Alitalia-liveried Lancia Stratos, were competing, as were the late Ove Andersson in a Toyota Celica and Harry Källström in a Datsun 160J.

Datsun brought out two works cars and they wanted me to drive one of them with Källström. But I wasn't keen. Because my car was lighter, I deemed our local car a better bet. Datsun South Africa nonetheless insisted I drive the import, as not only was it a factory effort from Japan, but it would be good for my career … blah, blah, blah. I agreed and did quite well. In fact, I was actually leading the rally until about halfway through. Knowledge of local conditions helped me a bit, I suppose, but back then quite a few of the international guys, like Andersson, were regular visitors here, so they, too, were familiar with the area.

Anyway, halfway through the rally something in the engine let go, and that was it for me. Having had misgivings about this great Japanese factory car, SuperVan was, once again, pretty pissed off. I knew my local car would've done better and that I could've won. I was leading by 1:43 – something I will never forget.

And so we come to the fork ...

Because of that race, the competition manager of Datsun in Japan offered me a drive at a world-championship event overseas, but insisted that, because South Africans weren't exactly welcome in the world then, I had to get another passport first. This was my first brush with politics in sport – something that would figure prominently in my life in later years.

Another passport? Where the hell would I get another passport? So I said, thanks, but no. If you want me, it'll have to be with my South African passport. Take it or leave it. They decided to leave it. The Scandinavian countries were the main problem, as they were leading the boycott of all things South African. I'd therefore almost certainly be prevented from competing in the two high-profile events on the world championship: the Finnish and the Swedish rallies. Because this happened before I'd started travelling widely, I didn't know where the hell I would get another passport. I suppose I could've tried to find out, but I didn't even bother. I would later discover that I could've obtained one from quite a few countries, Lesotho probably being the likeliest.

But, in addition to the passport problem, I also wasn't crazy about the way the Japanese went about doing things. It was their way or the next bullet train out of town and, as you may have worked out by now, I don't respond very well to being told what to do. They had brought some special Dunlop tyres with them that they would only let Källström use. My car had the harder Michelins we used in our local rallies. However, as soon as I started smashing Källström into the trees with faster times – I was six minutes ahead of him eventually – I was suddenly given the tyres.

'Great,' I thought, 'at least these chaps are sensible; they're coming around to my way of thinking. Now we can make some real changes to the car's set-up.'

Ja ... no.

They weren't having any of it. The Japanese think they are the best engineers in the whole world and everything they say is right. They wouldn't change a thing during the course of the rally despite my experience of local conditions and car set-up. Not that it would have mattered, because the engine let go at the end of the day. To make matters worse, when the engine did let go, they said to me, oh yes, they were expecting something like that, because they had tried a new trick on that particular engine that they thought might not work. Why the hell bring the bloody car all the way to Africa if you knew well enough that it was going to blow up? So yes, that sort of put me off too, as I didn't think I could really cope with that kind of kak on an ongoing basis.

When I look back now, it was probably one of the biggest decisions I made in my career. If I had joined Datsun International, I could have established myself in world-championship rallying ... but then I would have had no track-racing career. I often think about that watershed moment. Do I regret the decision I made? I could have gone to Datsun as a works driver and done well enough to get a dream drive with Ford's World Rally Championship team. You could see by the six minutes I was ahead of Källström that the car was not being driven to its true potential. Källström wasn't that good, if you ask me, and I reckon I would've made him look silly. I could've had some promising results on the world stage, which would've made the Ford drive a real possibility, and that might have given me a realistic chance of becoming world rally champion.

So perhaps in some respects I do regret the decision, but then again, I would never have raced at Daytona or Le Mans. And that's why I know I would probably make the same decision again.

So I stayed in South Africa ... but I still wanted to move. Not countries, but teams. The car I really wanted to rally at home was the Ford Escort BDA. From what I could see, not only was the Ford the perfect rally car, but the Ford team also had a very professional set-up. Jan Hettema, Roelof Fekken (Lambert's brother) and Eric Sanders were their current drivers. I started to scheme ...

Turns out I didn't have to scheme too hard. Datsun made the decision fairly easy for me.

About a month after that Total Rally, I was racing in Natal at the Roy Hesketh Circuit. I had two cars, remember – the modified 140Y Datsun and the standard Group N Alfetta – and my two teams were staying at different hotels. The Alfa lot were staying in Pietermaritzburg, and the Datsun lot at the Rob Roy Hotel near Howick. The best mechanic, Koos Roos, who was my own personal mechanic at Datsun, was obviously booked in with the Datsun crew, but I convinced him to come and stay with me in Pietermaritzburg, as it was far nicer.

This didn't go down well with the Datsun team manager – a Pom by the name of Dave Trevett. We used to call him Dosy Dick. By now Van Bergen had moved further up the Datsun hierarchy and he was Dosy Dick's boss.

Trevett was so angry that 'their' mechanic was staying with me and the Alfa crowd that he fired Koos on the Monday morning. The poor guy phoned me with the news. I got into my car, drove to Datsun HQ, and stormed into Trevett's office. He was sitting there having his morning tea. This did not soften my mood.

'What the fuck have you done?'

'What do you mean?'

'You fired the best mechanic!'

'Well, that's my decision.'

'Well then, you had better reverse that decision or I am going to fuck you up.'

He would neither reverse his decision nor would he get out from behind his desk and allow me to *moer* him, the coward. So I lifted the whole desk, including his little tea service, and dumped it on top of him. Was it the right thing to do? Maybe not. But it was fun.

Needless to say, for the second time in my fairly brief career, it was the end of me and Datsun. And again, with me leading the championship and only two or three rallies left to go, I was without a drive.

By the next morning, everybody knew Datsun had fired me for the second time, and it didn't take too long for the phone to ring. Geoff Mortimer – another local motoring legend, who'd later be my teammate in the Audi Quattro rally team – was running a team for Chevrolet that year and offered me a drive in the Chevair. It was a smart PR move on his part – if I went on to win the SA championship, Chev would get all the glory despite the fact that I'd won most of the races in a Datsun. And that's exactly what happened. Again.

The bonus for me was that, unlike the Alfetta I drove after I left Datsun the first time, this Chevair was no dog. Just the opposite, in fact. It was basically a re-badged Opel Ascona, which was the Ford Escort BDA's main competition in Europe. It had loads of power thanks to a 2.4-litre Blidenstein motor and was a wonderful car to drive. I also did the Roof of Africa that year for Chevrolet, driving a souped-up Chev Nomad – a yellow thing with a white roof and a big turbocharger. I came second – I would've won it too if it weren't for six flat tyres in the last stage.

The following season, though, would present me with my much-desired drive. Ford phoned ...

4

HITTING THE BIG TIME

Ford, the Quattros ... and the world's kakkest Golf

FORD. FINALLY

Of course I said yes to Ford. I'd been wanting to get behind the wheel of a BDA for the previous two years. Understandably, Geoff Mortimer was upset. He had saved my arse, allowed me to win the championship and all the rest of it. On the other hand, I'd given Chev a fair amount of publicity by winning it in their car. Truthfully, though, I knew I'd shafted Geoff, but the Ford offer was one of those I just couldn't refuse. Apart from the BDA Escort, they dangled a thick wad of notes in front of me.

I went from the R12 000 a year I was earning in 1977 to R20 000 the following year with Ford, which was a substantial increase. Not only that, but they gave me a full-on BDA rally car as a practice car. I kept it at my house in Pretoria and they just came round and serviced it. There were plenty of dirt roads to practise on then – the canals around Rustenburg and Brits, and there was Mooikloof too before it got built up. There were some wonderful dirt roads in that part of the world.

It's not as if they were blocked, either – these were still public roads and I would just go there and drive. Even in my Datsun days, I would take my rally car down to our Nature's Valley holiday house and then wait for night-time before *jaaging* up and down Prince Alfred's Pass. It was often misty or foggy, which was good because you'd often encounter poor visibility in a rally and you had to know what to do. I did most of my practising at night, actually – which was probably why I was always quickest during the night stages on rallies. Back then, rallies ran through the night. Only later did they start this soft-cock daytime stuff. The Castrol Rally, for example, was a four-day affair, and the first section – apart from a two-hour break – would be 37 hours. That was proper rallying – not this crap that they do nowadays with little point-and-squirt cars.

I really felt as if I had hit the professional scene at Ford. Apart from the competition-rally BDA and a complete works car to practise in, I also finally had some seriously competitive cars I could race in. As happy as I was with the rally set-up, I was like, great, but when are we going *racing*? At first Ford couldn't offer much. We started with a 3.0 S Cortina in Group 1, which allowed only limited mods to the car. Initially the V6 Cortina was too heavy and not competitive. It was a one-make tyre series that gave us no harder tyre options – we'd basically run out of tyres halfway through a race. But things improved when Ford introduced the Cortina XR6, and finally the limited-edition XR6 Interceptor model.

Group 1 in those couple of seasons was probably the best racing we ever had in this country. All the big car-brands were involved – it was a real showpiece. Apart from the Fords, there were Tony Viana and Paolo Cavallieri in their 535 BMWs, the GTV V6 Alfas of Abel D'Oliveira and Nico Bianco, and the rotary-engined Mazda Capella coupés of Dave Charlton, Nols Niemand and Willie Hepburn. This was some of the best racing ever seen in this country – always a bunch of cars fighting for the lead. We were all very well matched and nobody ever got away.

But some of them tried to – often stretching the rules way beyond breaking point. What would happen was that the scrutineers would seal the engine after the race and then, the next morning, you had to be at the track again so that they could check that your car met the legal requirements. I remember that D'Oliveira's crew was caught out that year. It was discovered that the sneaky bastards had snuck into the engine bay overnight (to remove an illegal part they'd run during the race, perhaps?) and had actually removed the Alfa's suspension and worked on the engine from underneath.

Yes. You always got guys who'd use the race regulations as a mere starting point rather than as the definitive rules for the formula. Luckily, being a factory-team driver, there's never any temptation to go down that road. Getting caught was way too damaging for the manufacturer, so cheating was not an option. There was one case, however, when one of our team cars did blur the line somewhat …

Ford gave Tony Viana a spare XR6 to drive in one race … and lo and behold, he went and left the two actual works drivers – Geoff Mortimer and me – in his dust. Apart from this being more than a little rude, it was also very strange. Did Viana simply have the talent to beat the XR6's two regular drivers in a car that he was unfamiliar with? Or had he indulged in some illegal tweaking? SuperVan might have had an opinion, but unfortunately there was no way he could tell for sure. Ford team boss Bernie Marriner, however, was smiling. His team posted a 1-2-3 victory.

Towards the end of my time with Ford, we also ran the Manufacturer's Challenge class – Hepburn and Mortimer in V8 Chevs, Ian Scheckter in the straight six-engined BMW, Charlton in a Fiat with the Ferrari engine, and me in the Ford Escort with a V6 Cologne engine from a Ford Capri. It provided some spectacular racing that fans still talk about today – particularly the dice between Scheckter and me that ended with one *moer* of a crash at Kyalami in 1980.

I'll tell you more about that in Chapter 12, but let's go back to that first year, rallying the BDA Escort in 1978 …

My move represented something of a changing of the guard in South African rallying. Ford got rid of multiple SA champ Jan Hettema to make way for me. He'd won more rallies than anyone else – 35 or 36, I think – but also the most championships – five. I was only just getting into double-figure rally wins and had only won two championships, in 1975 and 1977. Personally, it was therefore a pretty big deal for me. Hettema was like God in local rallying and I'd basically overthrown a deity. I think from his own point of view he knew the writing was probably on the wall. Like I said ... you can bullshit everybody, but you can't bullshit yourself.

As it turned out, Hettema and I did a straight swap. Datsun would hire him for the 1978 season, hoping, no doubt, that he would leave Dosy Dick's office desk alone. Which he did. And from then on, I made sure that he also left the SA championship trophy alone. I was so focused on knocking him off his pedestal that I might occasionally – perhaps, maybe – have pushed it a little.

During one very wet and muddy rally through the forests outside George, I came across Hettema on the side of the road. He had started ahead of me but had got a flat and was busy changing the tyre. As it was a narrow road, I couldn't pass him because his driver's door was open. I hooted, but he ignored me and just carried on changing his wheel.

As we were in the heat of battle, I went from zero to highly annoyed in about a second and, with my car, bent his door back until it was flat against his front fender. I stuffed up my lights a bit – they were shining all over the show – and we lost a little time due to uncontrolled laughter, which is never conducive to pinpoint car control.

Hettema arrived at the service point a few minutes after us, his eyes blazing through his mud-spattered face thanks to the large hole where his front door had once been. He was absolutely enraged. All he could do was shout, 'Jou kont! Jou fokken kont!' The whole rally fraternity saw him emerge from his doorless car, completely covered in mud. It must have been humiliating for him, but I didn't think of that at the time.

As I mentioned, there were a couple of things that really impressed me about Ford – the car and the management.

The car was wonderful – light and very nimble. It didn't weigh much – around 1 000 kilograms, and we even ended up building a 900-kilogram version – and the engine put out a very handy 240–250bhp. You had to learn to drive it on the throttle and, because it was quite a small, narrow car, if you hit something, you actually had to drive your way out of it. If you lifted off the throttle, you rolled.

It was simply the best rally car of its era, and even when manufacturers like Opel came out with 2.3-litre engines, the BDA was still competitive. We managed to stretch the engine capacity to 2.1 litres with around 270bhp, and although it was still slightly underpowered, the whole package was just so good. Apart from the superb handling, you just couldn't break it.

The only time we ever lost a BDA engine was during a rally on the Indian Ocean island of Réunion in 1979. The Communist Party was fairly active in Réunion then, and obviously white South Africans weren't high up on their Christmas-card list. (I wonder if communist parties have Christmas-card lists? Probably not.) Anyway, after the first overnight stop, someone – no doubt wearing a Che Guevara T-shirt – cut my bloody cam belt.

There was no doubt that I had been targeted as a South African driver. Initially I was supposed to start at number one on the road, but the organisers even warned me that 'some people' might leave rocks on the road and it might be a better idea for me to start third. The cam-belt incident had probably occurred in the parking lot prior to that day's stage – they must have cut it half-way through. I drove from the *parc ferme* to the starting line with the engine idling. By then the belt had let go, which scrambled the valves. That was the end of the rally for me.

My first drive in the BDA was a bit of a disappointment, too. No Commies involved this time, though. I was still getting to grips with the car's handling when I managed to roll it. Not a full 360-degree roll – I just put it on its side. Some spectators eventually helped us roll it back onto its wheels, but by then I'd lost too much time. By the second rally I was on it, and that year I claimed my third SA rally championship.

A lot of my success at Ford could be ascribed to my relation-ship with team boss Bernie Marriner. Bernie was one of the biggest operators ever in the business. I don't know how the hell the guy did it, but he always managed to come up with a whole pile of sponsorship money, which even allowed us the occasional overseas adventure. We used to take our cars over to the UK and take part in the Welsh Rally, the Scottish Rally, the RAC (Royal Automobile Club) Rally and the Circuit of Ireland. We even competed in the Reno Rally in the US.

Bernie's modus operandi was to say to a sponsor, look, don't pay us any money – we'll just send you the bills and you settle them directly. Then, at Ford, he'd say okay, we're going rallying in Europe, but don't worry, the sponsors are paying. The money, therefore, was never paid into the Ford account and would be spent on getting us, and the cars, overseas.

This much competing improved my abilities considerably. The competition in the UK was a lot tougher than in South Africa, so I was forced to lift my game. I didn't win any races – remember, these were our own, locally developed Fords – but I would run up front and actually win stages in the RAC Rally.

The other disadvantage we had was that, as I hadn't competed overseas before and no one knew me from a bar of soap, we would get very low starting numbers. Normally I would start around 30th, and then – by the time I got going – the road surface was already pretty buggered up. Only later did I move into the top 15, then the top 10, and finally into single digits.

Conditions were also very different from those back home in South Africa, and it took a while, for example, to get used to the ice. I remember one Scottish Rally where we were doing really well. We were running with the guys who counted, having a hell of a dice. In fact, we were in the top three for the first two days. But on the third day, there was a dip in the road and I went off. But *really* off. We literally flew into the forest and the car ended high up in a tree. We had to get out and climb down. Plus, we'd never do a full season – only selective events here and there – which didn't help our standings either.

As mentioned, driving in these different conditions against higher-calibre opposition helped hone my driving skills and improved my tactics. When I came back home, it was a lot easier for me to be quick right out of the blocks no matter what the conditions were. Clearly, that is what is lacking in local motor sport these days – today's guys don't enjoy international competition any more. You simply can't measure yourself until you have driven against the best. Ford made that happen for me.

Look, I'm not saying I had everything my own way at home. There were some very quick South African drivers around – most notably Eric Sanders in a Datsun Stanza. He'd sometimes post a time on a stage and I'd think, 'How the fuck did he manage *that*?' It would be a tough section and he'd take 10 seconds out of me.

The problem with Eric, though, was that he was a card-carrying member of the lunatic fringe. He was a disciple of the all-out, balls-to-the-wall style of driving. He would manage some great times during certain stages, but the problem with the all-out, balls-to-the-wall approach is that you crash fairly often. Which is something Eric did. Fairly often. He had a decent car, too. The Datsuns were running some fancy engines from Japan with more horses than we had.

Sanders would post a ridiculous time now and then or he might come in second or third, but I never really thought that I would lose the championship to him, as at some point in the rally he would crash or do something stupid.

Occasionally, an overseas driver would put in an appearance on the local scene. Datsun even got Tony Pond to race for them – he was my only real competition in those days. Pond was a different kettle of fish: he was a class act. He was competing in the World Rally Championship and was one of the best drivers in the world at that point. He'd won a few world-championship events, and every time we were up against each other, it was quite a dice.

As I mentioned earlier, in 1977 we had most of the international gang here for the Total Rally, and Hannu Mikkola, a world champion, also competed in a few rallies here. Mikkola returned to South Africa in 1978 to compete in a Natal rally, and in 1979 he was my teammate at Ford for the Castrol Rally. We had one helluva scrap at that event. Mikkola really raised the bar for the South African drivers. He was something else. I remember one stage in particular during the 1979 Castrol ... it was pissing with rain and very muddy, and he passed me three times. He'd pass me, then he'd *moer* off the road; I would pass him, then a short while later he'd come roaring past me again.

On the local rally scene, though, this was the start of an era of total dominance for me. I won nine championships in a row – one with Datsun/Chev, five with Ford, and three with Audi. Interestingly, my dominance didn't negatively impact South African rallying at all – it actually had the opposite effect. These were times when the anti-apartheid boycotts resulted in South Africans seeing and participating in very few international sporting events. As a result, local rallying got a helluva lot of publicity. There would, for instance, be live coverage of the Castrol Rally – even for the middle-of-the-night stages.

The fact that I was doing well against international drivers further stoked interest, particularly in whether a local driver could claim my South African title.

Ja, those were great times for me – 1978 to 1982, five wonderful years. It would take something very special to lure me away from my Ford Escort BDA ...

Did somebody say 'Audi Quattro'?

QUATTROS – ON THE DIRT AND ON THE TRACK

The big news in world rallying in the early 80s was the arrival of the Audi Quattro. From its official World Rally Championship debut at the 1981 Monte Carlo Rally, the car was a game-changer. The Audi was powered by an inline 2.2-litre, five-cylinder turbo engine that was originally good for around 320bhp. Most significantly, though, all that power was transferred to the road surface by a four-wheel-drive system, and that combination simply blew everyone else into the weeds. Until then, all the top rally cars had been rear-wheel drives, but this new machine was in a class of its own.

My phone rang again at the end of 1982 – a sound, as you've gathered by now, that often signalled I would soon have a new employer. It was VW/Audi South Africa. They were bringing two Quattro A1 evolutions to compete in the SA rally championships – would I like to drive one? *Would I like to drive one?* I mean, does Riaan Cruywagen wear a wig? *Of course* I would like to drive one. And the fact that they were prepared to pay me a whopping R120 000 a year to do so was an added bonus. That kind of money put me into the big bucks locally – Audi SA even had to get permission from Germany to pay me that amount, as it would mean I would be earning more than the MD of the South African subsidiary.

As this would be the first time VW/Audi would ever have an official motor-sport team in South Africa, it was also an opportunity to get involved with something right from ground level. Of course there had been plenty of VWs in SA motor sport through the years. In the 1960s, guys like Gordon Briggs and Albie Odendaal rallied those fastback VW 411s with the double-oval headlights, and there were always a few Beetles around. But this was their first official entry into motor sport.

My erstwhile team manager at Chevrolet, Geoff Mortimer, was appointed as both Audi team manager and driver of the second car. Obviously, with the added traction of the four-wheel-drive system and the by-now 330bhp out of the five-cylinder turbo engine, the Quattro was a great car in terms of performance. It wasn't as spectacular as the BDA Escort as it wasn't nearly as tail-happy and there was far less sideways action, but it was certainly quicker than anything else out there. I could drive the car at any pace I wanted. Just as it dominated overseas, winning the World Rally Championship for Constructors title in 1982, it dominated here. My old teammate at Ford, Hannu Mikkola, would also win the 1983 World Rally Championships for Drivers in a Quattro.

I had to make a slight adjustment to the car, as it was a left-hand drive. The fact that the gear lever was now in my right hand didn't bother me – I actually preferred that, because it gave me a better feel for the gears – but as I was now sitting on the other side of the car, I had to get used to judging where the car was on the road. In the first couple of rallies in which I competed, I clipped the corners on the navigator's side far too often, but I soon enough mastered the car to the point where I found that I preferred a left-hand-drive car. I still do.

I was dominant in the Quattro to the point of becoming boring. I won the SA championship in 1983, 1984, 1985 and 1988. An interesting event during this period was an international rally I competed in in 1984. I'd been whining about wanting to do some international racing, like I'd done with Ford, and Audi finally relented and gave me a drive in the works team for the Portuguese Rally.

I'd initially wanted to race in the RAC Rally in the UK because, like our rallies in South Africa, it wasn't run on pace notes. The Portuguese Rally, however, was, which my navigator, Franz Boshoff, and I weren't used to. In fact, we crashed as a result. First of all, we didn't have a proper rally car in which to recce the route, which is what you normally did before a rally in order to make your pace notes. We only had a standard, road-going Quattro. And it broke.

We were near Porto when something buckled under the car – I think it might have been part of the suspension. Fortunately, we found the local Audi dealer, who, once he'd looked at the car, happily told us that it would take at least a day to fix and that we would have to stay at his house. It was probably a 10-minute job, but the Portuguese are so fanatical about rallying that he wasn't going to let the opportunity of having two drivers for company slip through his fingers. On the upside, it turned out that his family had been making port for the past 500 years, and he took us to this *cava* where the port was stored.

Obviously I asked him if I could buy a bottle. He said yes, and sold us each a bottle of 60-year-old port. Then he also gave us each a bottle of 150-year-old port. After our subsequent crash in the rally, Franz and I flattened the 60-year-old bottles, but I kept the old one and took it home with me. I even managed to hang on to it for a couple of years – until we had a big after-rally party at my house in Port Elizabeth one night. At about three o'clock in the morning, somebody said, 'Have you got any port?'

'*Port*? Boet, have I got some port for you ...'

And so we knocked back that 150-year-old bottle of Portuguese port. Man, was I annoyed with myself the next morning. But, anyway, back to the story ...

On our final recce during practice, driving our actual rally car, we had another big crash. When I say 'big crash', it was big in the sense that the car did a complete corkscrew. But it was also a pretty unusual big crash, as all we had damaged were the right-hand-side door handle – and the aerial.

Our rally car was Audi works driver Walter Röhrl's spare, and we were getting a feel for it the day before the rally started. I hit one of the big jumps at a slight angle, which caused the car to corkscrew mid-air and, as it went past a tree, a branch severed the door handle. I think we also burst a tyre when we landed. The Audi service crew wouldn't believe me when I told them what had happened. I politely asked them how else they think I could have lost a door handle and an aerial without scratching any other part of the car.

The Audi works team was packed with big names – the afore-mentioned Walter Röhrl, Stig Blomqvist, Hannu Mikkola and

Michèle Mouton – and among all this rally royalty, Franz and I were doing pretty well once the event kicked off. We were, in fact, running third on Day Two of the rally when we crashed. And we crashed properly this time. It was basically a pace-note stuff-up. Franz turned over two pages instead of one, and rather than call a 'crest 90 left', for which I would have braked hard for a 90-degree left-hander, he called 'crest flat', which meant pedal to the metal.

We were already airborne when I saw the road turn left under my side window. We *moered* the bank hard on the other side of the road, ripping off our right front suspension and breaking an oil pipe, which squirted oil on the hot turbo that ignited a small fire. On top of the bank – like everywhere else on the route – was a horde of Portuguese spectators. And because of the crowd pressure, three of them proceeded to fall off the bank and onto the roof of our car. All I could hear above me was dwah, dwah, dwah.

They then proceeded to steal the car. While we were in it.

One chap ripped off the bonnet and, as I was sitting there undoing my seat belts, someone else came around the car and actually tried to steal the bloody steering wheel. The looting continued until cops on horses arrived and chased the thieves away. But that's Portuguese rally fans for you. Complete lunatics.

In those days there was zero crowd control. People would stand in the road and only scarper when you were a few metres away … all this while the drivers were doing speeds of up to 200 km/h. You couldn't even see where the road was or where it was going. I kakked myself when I saw this on the first stage. 'Fuck,' I said to Franz, 'we're going to kill somebody.' The spectators actually used to paint their hands and hit the cars as they went past. Each person's hands would be painted a different colour so that, after each stage, they could go to the service points to see who had hit the most cars. I couldn't even hear Franz half the time with all the dah dah dah dah dah thumping by the lunatics trying to imprint their colour on our car.

But it was a pity about the crash, as we were involved in some serious dicing with Stig Blomqvist at the time. Afterwards, Walter Röhrl came up to me and said I had done bloody great. He could not believe that I was up there with Blomqvist's car.

That international rally aside, I was beginning to grow tired of this form of motor sport. Fortunately, from 1983 things started getting very interesting for me on the international track-racing front – more about that in a moment – and for the first time in my life it looked as if I could actually stop rallying altogether and focus on circuit racing. After all, I'd originally got into the rallying business only because it was the only form of motor sport I could afford. The nine national championships I had won up until then had certainly fed my ego and retained my interest, but any interest I had would come to an abrupt end during the Port Elizabeth Rally in 1986.

I was leading the championship, but halfway through the rally, something inside me simply said, *enough*. No drama, no inner turmoil, no hand-wringing angst. I just knew that that was it. At the end of the stage, I turned to my navigator and said, 'Franz, come, let's end this rally business now. I'm going to stop.'

And I stopped it right there.

I still managed to come second in the championship that year – Hannes Grobbelaar in his big 500+bhp Nissan Skyline won. He'd go on to be very successful in the SA Off-Road Championship, but it was the only SA Rally Championship he ever won. Geoff, in the other Quattro, also had a bad year. He rolled on a mountain trial and had another big incident in another rally.

Audi, of course, were upset about the turn of events. As always, the issue for me was that, even though I had had great success rallying in South Africa, I wasn't *racing*. Well, at least not officially.

Every now and again I would compete in a race under an assumed name – I'd scramble my first and second names, Sarel and Daniel: 'Leinad Lerás'. I'd obtain a competition licence under my alias – I still have the one that says 'Leinad Lerás' – and there was certainly no shortage of offers from other teams for me to choose from.

With some planning and a little luck, I was able to keep my identity a secret at these under-the-radar sorties. *I* was the original Stig. Before a race I would make sure that the car was parked some distance away from the rest of the teams, and I'd put on a full-face helmet and plain racing overalls, then drive onto the track, finish the race and disappear.

It wasn't front-of-the-field stuff – only in the lower classes – so I wasn't attracting too much interest. Group N racing was in its heyday then, with guys like Serge Damseaux in the big Ford Sierra XR8 getting all the attention. Funnily enough, many people think that I drove that XR8, but … nope.

Unfortunately, eventually my cover was blown …

Alfa Romeo's de facto motor-sport manager in the 80s, Sampie Bosman, had asked me to drive his Alfa at Kyalami – my secret racing excursions always seemed to involve Alfas – and I managed to put the car on pole at qualifying. As luck would have it, Audi team manager, André van der Watt, saw me get out of the damn car. The VW/Audi guys were attending the event only because of some silly VW Citi Golf race. Van der Watt 'requested' that I stop my clandestine racing activities forthwith.

I would win some Group N-class championships for VW/ Audi, but for me it wasn't proper racing. By now I was also competing overseas, and as I was driving serious racing cars in Europe and the US, to come back to South Africa and get behind the wheel of a Golf was not exactly the most exciting thing to do.

In fact, compared with the sports-prototype machines I was now racing overseas (patience, patience, I'll tell you all about it in the next chapter), I could do Group N racing with my eyes closed … and a cigarette stuck in the corner of my mouth.

Which is exactly what I did during the 1984 Group N three-hour endurance race at Killarney. VW had just launched the

16-valve Golf GTi, and they'd flown in German ace Jochen Mass to co-drive the car with me. As excited as the Veedub chaps were about their new hot hatch, having been in a Porsche capable of reaching 400 km/h, the GTi was going to be a bit of an anticlimax. To combat what would be a driving stint utterly devoid of excitement, I packed a few goodies to keep me occupied: three cans of Fanta, a packet of Rothmans and a lighter.

I proceeded to lead the race while sipping a Fanta and smoking the occasional cigarette. I could tell by the look on the marshals' faces that they had never seen anything like it before.

Jochen and I duly won the race, and, predictably, afterwards I was confronted by a delegation of annoyed race officials.

'Were you smoking during that race?!'

'Yes. Yes, I was. Would you like one?'

'But you can't smoke during a motor race ...'

'Why not? Does it say anywhere in the rules that I can't?'

Silence.

That Monday a fax was dispatched with an amendment to the MotorSport SA rules. It was now expressly forbidden to smoke while you raced.

In 1987 – having given up rallying – I only raced overseas. The next year, however, Audi South Africa convinced me to come back. The carrot they dangled was the mighty Audi Sport Quattro S1. In European rallying, the Group B class had basically become an arms race among the likes of Lancia, Peugeot, Ford and Audi. The Quattro had originated the competition, but it was essentially a front-engined road car that only rallied for Audi. Audi's rivals responded with limited-edition homologation cars that were out-and-out rally specials. The Group B regs stated that a manufacturer had to produce a minimum of 200 road-going cars in order to rally the model. This allowed them to build cars like the Lancia Delta S4 and Peugeot 205 T16, which might have looked like hatchbacks, but were no more than mid-engined supercars. (At least Ford's RS2000 looked exotic, though it arrived on the scene too late to be a winner.) With fancy four-wheel-drive systems and a turbo-charged engine located behind the driver and navigator, they were too good for the original Quattro in the world championship.

So Audi responded with the S1. Now *there* was a tricky bastard. Unlike the long-wheelbase first Quattro, the S1 had a shorter wheelbase and a more powerful 600bhp engine, which made it twitchy as hell. Where the first Quattro had been nice and predictable, the S1 didn't care whether it was going straight or sideways. It also looked completely mad with its massive rear wing, boxy wheel arches and chin spoiler that would have made a snowplough proud.

It was a real handful for any driver, but also helluva challenging, as you were always in the shit with the S1. And I liked that. Basically, the S1 had fantastic power, but it never handled properly. If they had put that engine in the original Quattro, it would have been a much better car.

Because it was still basically a road car with the engine up front, the S1 still couldn't beat the Lancias and Peugeots – in Europe. But here in South Africa, it was a winner. Geoff Mortimer had won the 1987 SA championship in it, and I returned to take the crown in 1988.

But it would turn out to be the last hurrah for Group B worldwide. The cars were getting ridiculously powerful – up to a rumoured 600+bhp – and a couple of horrific accidents overseas forced the Fédération Internationale de l'Automobile (FIA) to ban the class. Thirty-one people were injured and three killed at the Portuguese rally, when Portuguese national champion Joaquim Santos lost control of his Ford RS2000 over a rise and ploughed into spectators. As I mentioned earlier, matters weren't helped by the fact that there was zero crowd control in those days and that hordes of spectators – particularly in Portugal – would block the roads and only clear a path for the speeding cars at the very last second.

Then Finnish rally star Henri Toivonen and co-driver Sergio Cresto were burnt to death when their Lancia Delta S4 went off the road and down a ravine during the Tour de Corse Rally. That was the final straw for the class …

The end of the Group B era would also lead to my leaving VW/Audi. But it was only one of the factors that led to my departure.

First, the car VW/Audi had given me turned out to be easily the crappest car of my rallying career. While we could still have run the Quattro S1s for one more year in 1989, VW/Audi decided instead to enter MotorSport SA's new four-wheel-drive, 2.0-litre class along with Toyota. However, whereas Toyota had built a pretty decent car with an imported drivetrain from renowned transmission specialists Xtrac, VW decided to go with a locally developed system designed by André Verwey. Verwey was a good motor-sport engineer – he would go on to make transmissions for Indy cars in the US – but he knew nothing about this one.

Simply put, it was the biggest fuck-up I'd ever seen in my life. The gearbox broke all the time. Even though the car was built as a Class A four-wheel-drive, we actually started running it as a Class B front-wheel-drive, normal GTi-type thing. It was a little slower, but at least the bloody car would finish a rally, as opposed to this four-wheel-drive balls-up that was forever breaking down. In fact, my VW teammate Glyn Hall actually won the 1989 championship in the Class B Golf. It was a case of consistency wins out. Not only was my car always packing up, but fortunately for us, Toyota was also having some teething issues with their new car.

In the two years that I drove the Golf – in 1989 and 1990 – I posted 14 non-finishes. In my entire rallying career up until then, I'd registered only 13 non-finishes.

However, I did manage to win the 1990 Castrol Rally – thanks in large part to our mechanics. We had *three* gearboxes – none of them worked properly, but by using different ones for different stages, we managed to stay competitive. One gearbox didn't have first and second gears any more; the other didn't have fifth and sixth; and the third had lost gears in the middle. We dumped the one with the middle gears, but thanks to a million gearbox changes by my crew, we were able to use the one with fifth and sixth on the tighter stages, and when we knew it was a fast stage, we put in the other one.

As one can imagine, I really didn't like the car that much – especially after having driven the Quattro. It got so bad that I even slapped a sticker on my car that read: 'I would rather play golf than drive one.' Ja, I didn't want to drive the thing. I told VW to get the same drivetrain as Toyota, but they were too hard-arsed to comply. I was *not* happy.

Second, I left the VW/Audi mother ship because of the Audi racing car that they ran here from 1989 to 1994 for the Wesbank Modified series. The rules had changed in 1989 to allow American Trans-Am and IMSA GT-spec cars to enter. Audi saw the gap and brought out a car that had just won the 1988 Trans-Am Series in the US. It had eight races in the series, giving Hurley Haywood the title. Audi wanted to rebuild their image in the US and, with the Group B rally cars now banned, they decided to take the four-wheel-drive and turbo technology and put it in an Audi 500-shaped body. The Quattro car developed up to 720bhp from its five-cylinder turbo.

Audi brought out two cars, one for me and one for Chris Aberdein. Right from the first race it was clear that the Audis were way too good for the competition. In fact, they were so technically superior to anything else in the Wesbank series that it no longer felt like racing to me.

This will put it in perspective ...

The first race of the season took place at Kyalami and, on the warm-up lap, the turbo pipe blew off. I had to get back into the pits to get it tightened, which meant starting the race from the pit lane. The entire Wesbank field had to go off before I could join the fray. It didn't matter much. By the end of the first lap, I was in front. That's how quick the car was.

It was a magic car, it really was. The handling was incredible for a four-wheel-drive. Normally those cars don't handle that well on the track – if you start really throwing them around, they understeer a lot. But somehow Audi had managed to get it spot on. You could do anything with it – slide it, make it oversteer – and it had this incredible traction around the corners. You knew that when you nailed that car on the apex, even with the turbo lag, you could slingshot out of there. As far as its top speed was concerned, it was probably a little slower than the Fords, but because it was practically impossible to lock up the brakes – you'd have to lock up all four wheels to accomplish that – you could brake *way* later than anyone else. It just made winning so *easy*.

The series rules dictated that a winner would carry extra weight in order to slow the car down and supposedly keep the race competitive. In my opinion, it was a stupid rule at the best of times, but especially so in this case.

Even carrying up to 150 kilograms extra weight in my car, I would still win easily. It was so 'bad' that I had to 'manufacture' some excitement for the spectators. For me to just drive off into the distance would have killed the series, so I made sure that I stayed with the other guys – sometimes I'd even let one of them take the lead (if SuperVan was feeling particularly generous) – then I'd simply blast to the front on the last lap. The car was so good, we didn't even use the aero-package they utilised in the States, which would've given the car an extra second-and-a-half a lap. But we didn't need it; I could fart around the track without its help.

After waltzing away with the title in 1989, there was a bit of a balls-up in the 1990 championship. Although I was still the dominant driver in the series, winning most of the races, the utterly ridiculous handicap rules had started to make the car unsafe. Carrying extra weight when you won had been Dick Sorenson's brainchild. Dick ran the Wesbank Modified series and had decided that the best way to keep the races competitive was to make the winners carry extra lead ballast. As I've said, it was a stupid idea. Instead of, say, finding a way to limit the car's power to make it more even, he was actually penalising the driver with an increasingly heavier car.

With up to 200 extra kilograms on board, your car would handle very differently, to the point where the excessive tyre wear would make it dangerous. Needless to say, Dick and I never got on too well. To this day I tell him the only thing right about him is his name. He thinks I'm joking. These days Dick is running the Production Class series and he's still implementing his weight-handicap rules. It was bullshit back then, it's bullshit now, and bullshit it will always be.

It got so bad that, at the East London race that year, I refused to drive the car because it was carrying so much extra weight – it was patently unsafe. Then, of course, MotorSport SA convened a court of inquiry because of my decision, and I told Dick that he wasn't qualified to judge what was or wasn't safe on the track. I remember chucking my racing licence across the table and saying, 'If you want the fucking licence, take it!' And walking out. I still had my international Super Licence then – only F1 drivers have them now – so it was a bit of showmanship on my part. The result was that I was found 'not guilty' and they gave me back my licence.

We also didn't compete at Welkom that year because we didn't have the right fuel; I missed another race to do a world sports-car event in Dijon, France; and there was another incident that season that I can't remember. What I do remember, however, is that when I did race, I won. My teammate, Chris Aberdein, never beat me in the Audis, but he was consistent. He accumulated so many points coming second behind me that he took the title.

In 1990, I also competed in the Porsche Turbo Cup series in South Africa. Some privateer drivers were running Porsche 944

Turbos from the German race series. Local drivers Toby Venter and my ex–Kreepy Krauly colleague, Wayne Taylor, were the dominant drivers – until people like me, Aberdein and Nico Bianco decided to enter cars. I'd driven these cars before and really enjoyed them.

A race-spec Porsche is a wonderful piece of engineering. The German series had actually been in South Africa in previous years to run as an opener to the annual World Sportscar Championship race at Kyalami, and I'd driven one. I won the race, too. Along with Aberdein and Bianco, I'd also been invited to race in the Turbo Cup, which was also a sprint support race for the 1988 Le Mans. I came second, so I was pretty familiar with the car. It must have pissed off Venter and Taylor, because all of a sudden they went from being the big fish in the local Turbo Cup to coming fourth and fifth after Aberdein, Bianco and I entered. We pretty much dominated the series until it ended.

To finish the Audi/Wesbank saga: after two seasons in such a superior car, I was getting bored. It was an ironic situation, really. With that annoying Golf rally car and the Audi track monster, I had both the crappest and the best cars I had ever driven. I was immensely dissatisfied. It was ironic on an epic, turbo-charged, four-wheel-drive scale.

VW/Audi had got wind of the fact that I might be heading for the door, so towards the end of 1990 they called a special meeting with their marketing manager, Anthony Denham, and André van der Watt. Once again I was being called into the principal's office, but this time I wasn't quite the naughty schoolboy with cap in hand. They promised to fix the Golf, which they eventually did, but I knew it would take a while. Unlike Audi, who were involved in rallying internationally – meaning we could simply order parts from overseas – VW had to develop all their stuff locally. Even today with their rally team, everything is developed in South Africa.

So VW/Audi wanted me to stay. I said I would think about it.

And I did, briefly. But then I left. They were quite pissed off, and my departure caused something of a rumpus. They told me that I was making the wrong decision, and I guess I was, but SuperVan had made up his mind.

So back to Ford.

Ford offered me two advantages ... and one of them promised immense satisfaction. Sure, they put a large pile of money on the table, which is always nice, but they also offered me the opportunity to show my fellow competitors how good a racing driver I really was. I wanted to get into the Ford Sapphire I'd so easily beaten in the IMSA Audi and turn the tables. To take the chequered flag ahead of my vastly superior former racing car would be a definitive middle-finger-in-the-air display of my driving ability. And SuperVan liked few things better than the opportunity to flip his middle finger.

Before I tell you about that, we need to take a trip overseas to explain how I'd honed my skills to the point where I knew I could take the Audi ...

5

HITTING THE *REALLY* BIG TIME

Porsches, pool cleaners ... and a Yank rocket ship

We're taking a few steps back, to 1982. It was my first stint with Ford and it involved, of all things, an automatic pool cleaner.

South African entrepreneur and motor-sport fanatic, Danny Chauvier, had come up with a revolutionary device that would clean your pool all on its own – the now ubiquitous Kreepy Krauly. As part of his marketing campaign, he'd chosen to sponsor both our Ford rally team and the Ford XR6 Interceptors that we were racing on the track in Group 1.

In those days, each November, Kyalami also hosted a big international endurance sports-car race called the Wynns 1000 Kilometres. It was part of the world championship and, therefore, a pretty big deal. All the big international teams – mostly running Porsches – would enter. Chauvier and I were at the Friday practice before Sunday's race, walking around the pits, checking it all out. When we came to Giampiero Moretti's Porsche 935, Chauvier suddenly turned to me and said, 'Would you like to drive this thing?'

'Are you kidding me? *Of course* I would like to drive it.' I might've even mentioned Riaan Cruywagen's wig again.

The Porsche 935 – nicknamed the 'Moby Dick' because of its huge whale-like rear wing – was a 650bhp turbo-charged monster (800bhp in qualifying trim) that had double the horsepower of anything I'd driven up to that point. I would've given up women for at least a week to drive one.

But it wasn't the quickest car on the grid. The Moby Dick was a three-year-old design by then and, with its low-downforce aerodynamic set-up, was actually developed for Le Mans' superfast La Sarthe circuit. Still, it might not have been that happy around Kyalami's twisty bits, but down the track's long main straight it could do about 320 km/h – as quick as any Formula 1 car.

Chauvier had heard that Moretti would take on an extra driver provided the price was right, and that the driver holding the cheque was at least mildly talented. Although Moretti was the owner of Momo, a successful company making automobile accessories, and therefore wealthy in his own right, running your own private racing team is still a very costly exercise. And so the deal was done. Kreepy Krauly would get to slap some stickers on Moretti's car – and I would get behind the wheel of a proper racing machine for the first time in my life.

Funnily enough, I'd actually brought my helmet and overalls with me to the track – with local cars involved in the race, there was always an outside chance they may be looking for another driver. I hadn't expected *this*, though. I had also just left Ford and my contract to rally the Audi Quattros hadn't kicked in yet, so at that moment, I was a free agent.

As this all happened so near to race day, I had limited practice time in the car. Also, my co-drivers, Moretti and Formula 1 driver Mauro Baldi, were both short-arses. Baldi must've been about all of five foot tall, so the car was set for the two of them and not for someone of my more lofty stature. I'm six foot four. It was very uncomfortable, to put it mildly. Even with the seat moved back as far as it would go, I was still driving with my knees somewhere near my ears and the steering wheel up against my chest. But, hey, I was in a racing Porsche – I was going to drive this thing no matter how cramped I was.

Moretti had obviously never seen me drive, so he was taking something of a chance. His instructions to me were fairly straight-forward: 'Don' fuck uppa da car.' Chauvier had also hinted that there could be further drives down the line with Moretti, plus I didn't want piss off any of the big-name drivers in the race, so I drove conservatively and spent a lot of time staring into my rear-view mirror.

Thankfully, I didn't have to qualify the 935, but as the race progressed, my times got better and better. By the end I was quicker than Moretti and almost as quick as the more experienced Baldi. I reckon another day in the car and I would have been up there with him. We finished fifth behind winners Jacky Ickx and Jochen Mass in the factory Rothmans Porsche 956 – a very respectable result, given that we were up against these new state-of-the-art sports cars that had been developed that year for the new Group C formula.

Things were looking up … and they were about to get even better.

OFF TO THE US OF A

Danny Chauvier had big plans for his burgeoning pool-cleaner business … plans that included the United States of America. Moretti and his team were competing in the IMSA series in the US, and Chauvier wanted to carry on with our little deal. I'm pretty sure Moretti had some other driver signed up for the 1983 IMSA season, but with the kind of money Danny was offering, that poor bastard, no doubt, got shoved aside. So, with the top half of the 935 painted red, sporting the yellow Momo logo, and the bottom half the light-blue and white of Kreepy Krauly, we went racing Stateside from June that year.

Given that I was also rallying the Quattro back in South Africa, it became the start of an extremely hectic lifestyle for me – and it would last for the next eight years. My life would consist of racetracks and rally routes, interspersed with airports and hotels. As you can imagine, it wasn't very good for my personal life – at least not for my marriage. It was, however, very good for my sex life – but more about that a little later. For the moment we are sticking with internal combustion of the automotive kind.

With all of this going on, my main commitment was to Audi, as I'd signed their contract before I'd got involved with Moretti. Fortunately it didn't make a helluva lot of difference and, of the six races I was scheduled to compete in in the 1983 IMSA series, there was only one I couldn't make because of a rally back home. For that race, we drafted in South African driver Desiré Wilson, who was actually based in the US at the time – in Columbus, Ohio, if I remember correctly. To date, Desiré remains the only woman driver from South Africa to make it internationally, racing sports cars and competing in a few Formula 1 races.

Just to give you some background on the IMSA series: it developed out of the legendary, unlimited engine-capacity Can Am series of the late 60s/early 70s. Unlike the one-class Can Am series, IMSA allowed a variety of different cars, from the sports prototypes like the Porsche 962s in the GTP class to vaguely road-car-based GT vehicles like the Audi 500 Quattro I would later race during the 1989 and 1990 season back home. There would be starting grids with at least 40 cars of a quite big speed differential between the fastest and the slowest. Apart from the 24-hour Daytona and 12-hour Sebring races, the rest would last anywhere from one to six hours, so that if you were in a GTP car, you'd end up lapping slower cars – a lot.

It was a big adjustment for me – I was the big fish in a small pond who had now become the small fish in a big pond. All the big European names were in the IMSA series – Hans Stuck, Bob Wollek, Klaus Ludwig – as they were competing on the US scene as well as in the World Sportscar Championship. Apart from Al Holbert, the Americans didn't impress me much. Most of them came from a NASCAR or other oval-track racing background, which didn't seem to translate too well into proper circuit racing, where corners actually turned right as well as left.

Still, it was pretty intimidating in the beginning. Back in South Africa, there were maybe four good drivers, whereas all of a sudden, here I was up against 15 or 20. The standard of driving was just so much higher. These boys had been and done it all before. Not only were they way more experienced than I was, but the Porsche 935 I was driving – as fast as it was – was no match for the newer, low-slung, ground-effects cars.

It was your basic sink-or-swim scenario. This was what I had wanted to do my whole life. It was *haal uit en wys* time. For the first two races of the season, Moretti would qualify the car and I would race with him, but it was soon evident that I was the faster driver, and I took over qualifying duties (Moretti passed away in January 2012).

Ground-effects cars like the March 83G were quicker than us, as was Bob Tullius's Jaguar XJR-5, but we did okay. Our main opposition was John Fitzpatrick, who was running a car exactly the same as ours. The car was set up specifically for him, whereas mine was a compromise that suited Moretti as well. Fitzpatrick was usually quicker than me, though all in all we had a fair season.

The Marches were mostly powered by Chevy V8s – all except Al Holbert's. Holbert was not only a great driver, but also a brilliant engineer, and he had decided to run his March 83G with a Porsche engine. It was a smart move – one that gave him and his co-driver, five-time Le Mans winner Derek Bell, the championship that year. Moretti had a similar car, but he couldn't ever get his March's handling sorted out. These were the early days of ground-effects aerodynamics, but Moretti's mechanics didn't know enough about how they worked to get the car functioning properly. Moretti drove the March on his own for a couple of races at the start of the season, but by the time I joined him, he'd decided to drive the more reliable and predictable 935.

Of the five races I did, we retired once, got two sevenths, a sixth and, at the Pocono 500 Mile in Pennsylvania, managed to grab second place. The whole exercise was clearly benefitting Kreepy Krauly's Danny Chauvier, as not only did the marketing aspect promote his business, but he also loved the motor-sport scene and was always with us wherever we raced. For the follow-

Three generations of Sarel van der Merwes outside my grandfather's house in Malvern, Johannesburg, in 1946. That's me on my grandfather Sarel's knee, with my father, also Sarel, standing next to us

Age one in 1947. The photographer was obviously a beautiful woman, hence the ear-to-ear grin

Was there ever any doubt I'd be a racing driver? I'm three years old here ... my navigational skills were still developing

My Afrikaanse Hoër Seunsskool Standard 8 photo. If I'm looking slightly remorseful, it might be because I'd 'stolen' ... and then crashed ... my father's Porsche 356 Speedster

My father about to roll his Porsche Speedster in 1959 at the old Grand Central track halfway between Joburg and Pretoria

My father (centre) with his Auto Union/DKW 1000 and assorted trophies. This was around 1960/61

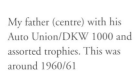

My parents, Nicolene and Sarel. Both would pass away too early, succumbing to cancer within two years of each other: my mother in 1977 at 53, and my father in 1979 at 57

My second wife, Tersia Ackerman, *circa* 1971. If you ignore the £50 English barmaid, this was my first 'real' marriage

Dorothy Bridgens, my third wife, and our two children, Sarel and Nicolene, at our house in 1981. I left my second wife for Dorothy

Me with my fourth, current and most certainly final wife, Danielle Baard, and my daughter Nicolene

A tear in my eye at my daughter Nohlene's wedding in 2009

DKW Junior I used to have the odd crash at the start of my racing career and on this occasion it happened even before I got to the track. Driving to this 1968 race at Pietermaritzburg's Roy Hesketh Circuit, I dinged the Deek's right headlight quite badly

Datsun P150 SSS My big breakthrough at the 1973 Pretoria News Rally where, in the regional Transvaal championship, I beat national champion Lambert Fekken in his modified Ford Escort BDA in my standard Datsun

Datsun 160U I won my first national championship rally in this car, my standard Datsun. I beat all comers, including multiple champ Jan Hettema in his modified car, at the 1974 Duckhams Cape Rally

The young, up-and-coming racing driver – not quite SuperVan yet

Alfetta Despite my rallying
success, I just really wanted to
race. Alfa gave me a car in 1974.
My rally employers, Datsun,
were not happy. So I left

Toyota Corolla SR5 Not a great car and not a
happy relationship with Toyota. This car exploded
and burnt off my moustache. Reason enough to
leave. This is at the 1976 Castrol Rally

Ford Escort BDA Mk II Of all the cars I
drove, this was my favourite. Rear-wheel
drive, fantastic handling – a real driver's car

Ford Escort BDA Mk II The Ford BDA and I competed
overseas a few times. Here we are at the 1978 Rally of Ireland

Ford Cortina 3.0 S My first competitive racing car. Part of my deal to rally with Ford was that I'd get a decent track car. Here we are leading the pack in a 1978 Group 1 race

Ford Escort Ian Scheckter and I sizing each other up during the 1980 Manufacturers' Challenge Saloon Car championship. Later, Scheckter brain-fade would involve the two of us in one of SA motor sport's most talked-about crashes

Porsche 935 'Whale Tail' My first adventure in the US with Giampiero Moretti's Momo team in 1983. The car behind us is a March 82G – Kreepy Krauly owner Danny Chauvier would buy the updated 83G for us to form our own team in 1984

Audi Quattro A2 When it arrived in South Africa for the 1983 season, it was so far ahead of the game, it could quite literally beat the opposition on three wheels

Porsche 956 My first Le Mans in 1984, driving for Ken Fitzpatrick's Skoal-Bandit-sponsored team. We came third that year

Porsche 962 At the 1985 Le Mans, where I was teamed with co-drivers George Fouché, the talented young South African, and the considerably less talented Mario Hytten. We think he may have been Swiss. Despite him, we came a respectable fifth

Porsche 962 Le Mans 1986 and a race I'd rather forget. My co-driver, Jo Gartner, was killed when this black Porsche 962 crashed at high speed along the Mulsanne Straight

Audi Quattro A2 I also rallied the Quattro in Europe a few times. Here I'm trying hard not to hit Portuguese spectators during the 1984 Rally of Portugal

Chevrolet Corvette GTP As a General Motors factory driver, I piloted this beast for a little over three years, from August 1985 to October 1988. At one point the car was pushing out 1200bhp from its turbo V6

Porsche 962 1987 … another Le Mans I'd rather forget. Thanks to some suspect fuel, our Japanese-sponsored car expired while I was driving it in the warm-up lap

Audi Quattro S1 More powerful than the Quattro A1, and with a shorter wheelbase, thus way trickier to drive. In any competent driver's hands, though, utterly unbeatable. This is a 1988 fly-by

Porsche 962 The start of the 1988 Le Mans and I've finally been given the nod to drive for the factory Porsche team

ing season, in 1984, he therefore decided that we should have our very own, fully Kreepy Krauly–sponsored team.

And to do that, we needed to buy a car.

FORWARD MARCH

We looked around a fair amount. We knew we had to get a car with a ground-effects aerodynamic package. Group C cars in Europe, like the Porsche 956 and Lancia LC2, had revolutionised the scene with their ability to stick to the track unlike anything before. Ground effects allowed you to go around corners far quicker and, as racing is actually all about how fast you can go around corners, you could only win if you had ground effects.

The obvious option was to buy an American-spec 962 customer car from Porsche, but they were too expensive even for Chauvier's budget. The Porsche 935s, too, were still very popular to race in the US, as Porsches are always good privateer cars to run – they're very well built and engineered and offer a lot of factory assistance. One option was to buy a 935 from the Paul Team. Father and son, John Paul and John Paul Jnr, had taken a Moby Dick 935 like Moretti's and turned it into a ground-effects car.

We nearly bought that car, but some rather odd circumstances scuppered the deal. I'll never forget sitting in Paul Snr's office in Atlanta with him telling us that he wanted to sell the team because he was – and I quote – in a spot of 'legal bother'. Every newspaper in America would soon reveal exactly what that spot of bother was – turns out that the Pauls were not only racers, but also pretty serious drug dealers. The police had discovered a massive underground facility, where these good old boys were growing marijuana.

John Paul Snr ended up spending 13 years in jail for attempted murder after shooting another drug dealer, though that wasn't the end of it. Once out on parole, his girlfriend, who was living with him on his big yacht, mysteriously disappeared in 2000.

Paul Snr was questioned about the very suspicious circumstances, but then he disappeared too … never to be seen again.

Nevertheless, John Paul Jnr was a pretty decent driver who actually won the 1982 IMSA championship in the 935, but in 1986 he was also arrested, along with his dad, on drug racketeering charges. Junior got a five-year jail sentence.

We got a March.

It wasn't just any March; it was Al Holbert's 1983 IMSA championship-winning March 83G with the Porsche engine. Along with purchasing a genuinely competitive car, we were also very fortunate to get Ken Howes on board as our crew chief. Ken had been Ian Scheckter's chief mechanic in the Formula Atlantic single-seater series back in South Africa, but he clearly had the ability to make it overseas. There wasn't much happening at home for him at that time other than saloon-car racing, so it didn't take too much convincing for him to pack his bags and join us in the States.

It was one seriously good move for Ken, too. In fact, the guy is still there and is currently second-in-charge at Hendrick Motorsports – by far the most successful team currently competing in NASCAR. They run four full-time teams that include reigning champ Jimmie Johnson, Mark Martin, Jeff Gordon and Dale Earnhardt Jnr.

Single-seater formulas and ground effects were Ken's training ground, so I'm not really sure what he makes of the NASCAR business, where all you do is go round and round a bloody oval. Obviously he must be making good money.

So there we were, back in the US for a full IMSA season with a proper ground-effects car. It being an endurance series, I naturally needed some co-drivers to share the driving duties. Along with a car now fully decked out in Kreepy Krauly colours and logos, Chauvier also wanted an all–South African driver line-up. Initially, I was therefore joined by Graham Duxbury and Tony Martin, both of whom had come through the single-seater ranks back home.

It was an incredibly exciting time, but not one without a certain element of pressure. In 1983 we weren't in a competitive car and, while I knew I could take on the other Porsche 935s, I still didn't know how I would do against the big boys in their ground-effects cars. Would I have the chops to beat them? I thought I could do it, but I didn't know for sure. I had a feeling that maybe this was where I belonged, but first I had to prove it to myself, my team and my competitors. I knew that if I missed this gap, my racing future would be back in South Africa. No question then ... even if I had to kill myself trying, I had to succeed.

The fact that the famous 24 Hours of Daytona was the season opener only increased the amount of pressure. Apart from Le Mans, this was one of the world's most prestigious endurance sports-car races.

Contrary to my preferred 'in your face' strategy back home, I decided for once to take an under-the-radar approach. So I kept my mouth shut. I've seen a lot of drivers talk themselves into drives on the international stage only to find that they don't have the game to back it up. First you need to prove that you can do it to yourself, and only then are you ready to take on other drivers. I needed to take the March to its limit to find out both how it handled and how I handled it.

Turns out I handled it pretty well. We won the race.

I'll go into more detail on how we went about it in Chapter 9, but it would be the most important victory of my career. It set me up as one of the top sports-car drivers in the world. In the early part of the race we engaged in a huge dice with Mario Andretti's Porsche 962, which was making its debut in IMSA that year, but after it retired with overheating problems, it was a case of nursing the March home to one very unexpected victory. Given my experience and abilities at the time, I was easily the fastest driver in our team – Dux was the slowest, but Martin was able to put in some steady times. Of the 24 hours, I therefore drove for all but 10.

Initially I didn't really realise what a big deal it was to win the race. Of course I thought it was a nice event to win, but it was only when I was interviewed live on ABC with about 30 million people watching that the significance of what we'd achieved sunk in. This would, without question, mean an international career in motor sport for me. It was what I had wanted from the start.

For Danny Chauvier and Kreepy Krauly, the spin-off was even better. Because of the product's funny name, people wanted to know what it was, and so, on live television at the end of the race, the immaculately coiffured ABC presenter asked me what exactly a Kreepy Krauly was. I told him in a fair amount of detail. You just can't buy that kind of publicity, and, with Kreepy Krauly in the process of being launched in the US right then, the timing was absolutely spot on. Soon, Americans were buying the pool cleaner in their droves, which set Danny Chauvier up for life. In 1999, the former door-to-door pool-equipment salesman would sell the company for many millions of dollars. I guess I should've charged him a deal-brokerage fee.

Unfortunately the rest of the 1984 season didn't quite live up to its fantastic start. First, there was a driver shuffle – we used Dux for Daytona and Sebring only, and signed up Ian Scheckter to replace Tony Martin towards the end of the season.

There was an unplanned car shuffle, too. After Daytona, we went testing at Road Atlanta, where the March completely burnt out. I was driving the car at the time, and a small leak dripped fuel onto the hot turbo, which started a fire. This set the suspension alight and, as I entered one of the corners, the car just spun. I thought I'd hit an oil spill or something, but what had happened was that one of the magnesium suspension uprights had caught alight and subsequently melted, sending me into a spin.

As I was twirling around in the car, I noticed the flames, and then the fuel tank, which was beneath the cockpit, exploded under my arse. It pinned me inside the car and I had to climb out of the other door, making my way through the flames as the car burnt to shit. Nothing was left of it.

Interestingly, in 2011 I got a call from a guy in the States who said he'd bought what he'd been told was our Daytona-winning March. He wanted to check the car's status with me, but unfortunately I had to give him the bad news. He might've bought a March 83G, but it wasn't the March 83G we'd driven to victory at Daytona.

The guy even started arguing with me over the phone. I explained to him that when one's car explodes under one's arse, one tends to remember the details very vividly. Apparently there's a big lawsuit going on there at the moment, and they even wanted to fly me to the US to testify. I declined – unless, of course, they were prepared to pay me a thick wad of dollar bills. I advised them to get hold of Ken Howes – not only was he already in the US, but as team boss, he would know exactly what had happened.

The whole mess is further complicated by the fact that we actually burnt *two* cars that year. We built up another car after the first fire and went on to win another race, at Lime Rock in Connecticut, but in Portland later that year, we also reduced this car to ashes. It happened while the March was standing on the grid prior to the start of the race. Tony Martin decided to push a valve (next to the door) that releases the fuel flap. Martin is one of those fiddlers who can't sit still and is always touching or prodding something. Anyway, we used to freeze the fuel prior to putting it in the car, as we would get more in the tank, but even though Martin closed the flap again, because the car was standing on the grid in the sun when he pushed the button, some fuel leaked out.

During the race the fuel must have got onto the hot turbo, which once again combusted. I was actually leading the race at the time, but as I sped past the pits, Ken Howes came on over the radio.

'Sarel, you're on fire. And I don't mean that you're driving really well. You'd better pull over somewhere, my friend.'

I couldn't see any fire while I was driving, as the flames were probably being blown back behind the car, but I knew it was a big one when I pulled over at one of the marshal points and all the bloody marshals ran away. I managed to get the hell out of there as the flames were engulfing the car … and once again, a March had burnt out.

So we lost a second car. And we couldn't salvage much either, as the car's suspension was made of highly flammable magnesium – when it burns, *everything* burns. Best-case scenario is that you can save the gearbox, as that sits right at the back, and in that second Portland fire, we managed to save that and a few suspension parts. But that was it.

Things were now getting very expensive, even for Danny. And we didn't have any insurance, either; you don't get insurance for racing cars. This time we couldn't even build up another car – we had to buy a brand-new one, which cost Danny $200 000. In today's money, that's probably close to a couple of million dollars.

In hindsight, I reckon we should actually have spent our money on a Porsche 962 from day one. It might have been double the price of the March, but it was just a better car. The March was probably a bit quicker on top speed because it was a smaller, narrower car and therefore had less aerodynamic drag, but, on the whole, the Porsche set-up was just so much better than what we had.

Although I could often qualify on the front row with the March and, because I had a bit more top speed, could actually get among the 962s on the faster tracks, the rest of the time they had my number. It would be close, but Al Holbert in particular was just too good in his Löwenbräu-sponsored Porsche. He was dominant in 1984, winning the championship.

In fact, I drove his Porsche in one race that year – at Sears Point. It was right after our second March burn-out, so I didn't have a car, and because of some other commitment, Holbert was unable to make the race. Rather than fly Derek Bell over from England, Holbert offered me the drive, as at least the car would then still get some constructors' championship points. The arrangement benefitted me too, as I would a) finally get to drive a Porsche 962, and b) have a chance to earn some points for the driver's championship. I ended up finishing fourth in the race.

But, all in all, it was a pretty good debut season for the Kreepy Krauly team. We came fifth in the championship despite missing two races due to the burnt-out cars. And we won two races – Daytona and Lime Rock – plus we had a few thirds and quite a few top fives.

For me personally, though, it was fantastic year – a watershed. Thanks to that Daytona win, the Fitzpatrick team would invite me to race their Skoal Bandit–sponsored Porsche 956 at Le Mans, where we came third (that's the race described in the book's opening paragraphs), which really established me internationally. I was also doing well back home, winning the SA Rally Championship for Audi and a Group N championship for VW. It was an incredibly tight schedule to manage, but, ironically, given my regular feuds with them, MotorSport South Africa actually helped me out.

The IMSA season calendar was released quite early, so I was able to persuade MotorSport SA to move a rally date a week earlier or later to accommodate my US racing. I think they knew it was good for South African motor sport not only to see me doing well overseas, but also to have me back home in front of local crowds. I was not only a big drawcard for them, but I guess I also helped to inspire the next generation of South African drivers.

Unfortunately, our third season in the US was a total balls-up.

He never admitted it to me, but I think Danny wasn't really serious about running a team for the entire 1985 season. We only competed in two races – Daytona and the Miami Grand Prix. Daytona was the season opener, as usual, and I think Danny was hoping that we could pull off another big one; and then the

Miami race was in Florida – home of his new Kreepy Krauly head office.

We were also beginning to feel some political heat in the States. Nineteen-eighty-five was an election year, and the Reverend Jesse Jackson was creating a major drama in the media, asking how they could allow a white South African team to compete in Miami, as we were representing a racist government. Citing bad publicity for his business as the reason, Danny canned our whole operation. But I honestly don't think he was ever in it for the whole year.

I felt, at the time, that our team approach in 1985 was too wishy-washy. For starters, we ran Yokohama tyres at Daytona, which in those days were quite shit. Danny either got them for free or might've even been paid to use them, but suddenly we were like a second-and-a-half to two seconds slower than in 1984. We'd actually made some improvements to the car since the previous year, so we should, in fact, have been faster.

The race itself was a disaster. We were in third early on at one point, but then a tyre blew while Scheckter was driving. We managed to get him back to the pits and replaced the tyre, but then Tony Martin – whom we'd re-hired for this race – charged out of the pits without pumping the brake pedal and tossed the car into the barriers before he'd even exited the pit. There's a sharp 180-degree corner coming out of the pits and he just went straight into the fucking barriers. That was it. The car was smashed. Race over.

Then, after Miami, Danny announced that it was all over. Suddenly, the only racing I was doing was back home. After driving these big-horsepower, ground-effects sports cars, I was now puttering around Kyalami in standard production cars. Of course I had the thrills of the Audi Quattro rally car, but it was still a massive comedown from where I'd just been.

FIRST PIET, THEN KEN, TO THE RESCUE

Salvation was at hand, though, and it came via two people – first Piet Fouché, and then, indirectly, through Ken Howes.

Piet was the wealthy father of promising young South African driver George Fouché, and he decided that George should do the world endurance championships for sports cars. What a nice dad. Piet made a deal with privateer team Kremer, basically buying the use of a Porsche 956 from April to June of 1985, and then slapped Pretoria Brick stickers – the name of his company – all over the car.

Piet then phoned me and asked me if I would go with George to teach him the ins and outs of racing at this level. Sounded like a good plan. So, with me as essentially the lead driver, George as my appy and assorted foreigners as the third guest driver, off we went and did four races – Monza in Italy, Silverstone in England, Le Mans in France and Melbourne in Australia.

I would've preferred to run as a two-man team, especially for Le Mans, but we needed a third pair of hands. Like all privateer teams, Kremer would accept someone if they brought along a lot of money, and Le Mans is one of those races where you always have a million Europeans standing around with briefcases full of cash wanting to buy a drive. Mario Hytten was our guy's name – you'll never have heard of him – and the only reason he drove with us is because he brought with him Barclay cigarette-sponsorship money. He was bloody useless. I think he might've been Swiss, but I'm not sure.

We could work around Hytten, though. He had to qualify the car as per race rules, but he didn't get much drive-time thereafter. During the race we let him drive for an hour at the start and then, because the car was still in good condition towards the end of the race, we gave him another quick stint. He didn't mind – he was in the team pictures and could boast that he'd driven at Le Mans. Anyway, apart from him we had a good race and came fifth, which basically reflected our overall season. We never managed a podium, but we were always somewhere in the top 10: at Melbourne we were fourth, and at Monza and Silverstone we came eighth.

Young George was a pretty good driver and a good-natured youngster. He was 20 years younger than me and physically quite strong. He wouldn't tire out in a race and would post the same lap times from start to finish. If we'd known of his ability a couple of years earlier, he would have been the guy to have hired on the Kreepy Krauly team. I think he'd only been in Group N production cars at that point, so we had no idea what he was like in anything with proper horsepower.

While all this was going on, I also had a phone call from our former Kreepy Krauly crew chief, Ken Howes. Ken had stayed on in America and had managed to get into the Hendrick Motorsports team, which I mentioned earlier. Hendrick was contracted by General Motors to run their IMSA Chevrolet Corvette project – something that had started the previous year, but in a fairly low-key manner. Now, with Hendrick running the show, they were ready to step it up a notch. Halfway through the season with the Fouchés, Ken called …

'What are you doing in the next few months?'

'Not much besides rallying the Audi in South Africa and racing a Porsche 956 around the world. Why?'

'Well, would you like to race in America again?'

'Where do I sign?'

My schedule would be hectic to the point of ridiculous, but I really wanted to get back into a full-time IMSA drive. The car I was being offered a drive in was the Chevrolet Corvette GTP. The chassis was a Lola T-710 series, first built in 1982, and was the first ground-effects car in the IMSA series. General Motors had bought one and clothed it in bodywork that vaguely resembled their production Corvette. It was a very beautiful car to look at, but because General Motors insisted on Corvette lookalike panels, the nose didn't give us any downforce. It was just too nice and round and beautiful to be effective.

When I first got there, the car was also totally unreliable. Quick as hell thanks to a 900bhp Chevy V6 pushrod motor with a turbocharger the size of a barrel, but not very refined. It had a gazillion horsepower, but things would go wrong – which was basically the common theme of my time with the team. Make no mistake, I had a wonderful three years with them – from August 1985 to October 1988 – but it was frustrating, too. General Motors – the epitome of Corporate America – were not the ideal motor-racing partner. They were so bloody bureaucratic, I honestly don't know how they got anything done.

My first race with them serves as an example. It was the car's first outing, at the Road America circuit near Milwaukee, and my teammate, Englishman David Hobbs, qualified 11th on the grid. Not too bad, seeing how we were up against the Porsche 962s, March 83Gs, the Jag XJR-5s, and the official Ford entry, the Mustang Probe GTP. But it fairly quickly went pear-shaped, and by half-distance the car gave up.

The next race was even worse.

By now the team had decided that I was the fastest driver, and I was tasked with qualifying the car. In my second race – the street circuit in Columbus – I qualified quite high up on the grid, but I knew that the car wouldn't last the distance. Either I could start and run the car in first for a while and at least get some publicity, or we could let Hobbs drive it more conservatively. And, yes, they went for the latter option, arguing that the car might actually finish and that Hobbs knew the circuit better than I did.

The car lasted 13 out of 139 laps. I never even got to drive my stint.

The final race of the season was marginally better. At the Daytona Finale (a short three-hour affair – not to be confused with the 24-hour season opener), I qualified the car on pole and we actually led for 10 laps. My new co-driver for that race, Bill Adams, also set the fastest lap. This time the car only broke on lap 65.

But matters improved a lot in 1986. Firstly, David Hobbs left for BMW and we signed Doc Bundy from the Tullius Jag team.

It was decided that I would be the number-one driver. Naturally, SuperVan approved. And the car also improved a lot. The team managed to develop the engine's reliability, although fuel consumption would always be our Achilles heel.

But the Corvette was fast, there was no denying that, and qualifying with boost turned up, we had something like 1200bhp at our disposal. At Watkins Glen, the speed record had been held for ages by the Formula 1 guys – they were doing about 305 km/h down the straight. I did 344 km/h. In fact, we had *too* much power. Way too much. Apart from the power scaring me out of my socks, the car's tyres sometimes wouldn't even last a single qualifying lap. You would have to decide which part of the track to write off – you were either going to burn your tyres up and battle at the end, or you were going to go like hell in the beginning and ease off at the end because your slicks had become like bubblegum.

I managed seven pole positions and several fastest laps that year. The Corvette was clearly the quickest car around. At Watkins Glen, for example, we had problems with the fuel injectors during qualifying, which put us only 15th on the starting grid. By the end of the first lap, I was leading. Apart from reliability issues and the odd accident, our main problem was the fact that the turbo-charged V6 was unbelievably thirsty, so we'd always have to make one more pit stop than the rest of the field. We were using a Bosch fuel-management system, which we could tune to a point where we weren't that far off the other guys. If everyone needed to make two pit stops in a race, we were fine, but if it was a one-stop race, we were fucked – we would have to do a splash and dash at the end, which set us back down the field.

Still, the car was really competitive, and by mid-season the mechanical failures were starting to get fewer and fewer. We even managed two wins in 1986 – at Road Atlanta and Palm Beach.

Unfortunately, at that point, Corporate America decided to stick its nose into our affairs. General Motors decided that instead of the Bosch management system that we were finally perfecting, we would be using the new Cadillac system. Cadillac was part of General Motors, which would make for good marketing. Now we had a GM management guy called Richard – naturally, we called him Dick – and a GM engineer on our team, which just pissed everyone off. Especially because the Cadillac system was complete and utter *crap*. The car's fuel consumption – something we'd worked so hard to improve – just went for a ball of shit.

I simply could not understand why General Motors wanted to do this. The public certainly didn't give a damn what engine-management system we were running – what mattered to them was how well the Corvette was performing on the track. We kakked on Dick, yelled at him, called him a *poes* and everything, but GM would not budge. Perhaps they didn't understand the word *poes*.

It wasn't the only colourful Afrikaans I taught the IMSA pit crews. I was also friendly with the Castrol Jaguar team and used to hang out with them a lot – they were real down-to-earth types – and they wanted to learn a few Afrikaans swear words. 'What,' they wanted to know, 'was a "dickhead" in Afrikaans?'

Pielkop was the most direct translation I could think of, which they naturally pronounced as 'peel cop'. They bandied the word about all the time. I raced in Le Mans that year as well, and even there I heard one Pommie mechanic tell his fellow crew mate to stop being a 'peel cop'. At one of the races in the States that year, my old Ford boss, Bernie Marriner, and Arthur Fouché – George's brother – came to visit me. My crew was always very keen to know when any South Africans were coming by, as it gave them the opportunity to use their new Afrikaans vocab.

We had this one little mechanic – Hodgie, a *moer* of a funny guy – and I primed him for Bernie and Arthur's visit.

'Two South Africans are coming to see me this morning. Both a little on the fat side. I think this might be a good time to practise that word I taught you.'

I saw Bernie and Arthur approaching and hid behind a stack of fuel drums.

'Morning,' said Hodgie.

'Good morning. We're looking for Sarel. Is he here?'

'And what would you two peel cops want with him?'

You should've seen their faces. It was flippin' priceless.

Sadly, not as priceless as some secret tech we had got our hands on … and then lost. It was race-winning stuff. General Motors had bought Lotus, and Lotus had developed active suspension for Ayrton Senna's Lotus 99T Formula 1 car. As Chevrolet was part of General Motors, we got to try the new tech as well. In testing at the Road Atlanta track, we were immediately quicker. It was incredible – almost counter-intuitive. Normally, on very fast corners, the load would be on the outside tyres, but with active suspension, you'd suddenly feel the load shift and all four slicks would grip, sling-shooting the car around.

We tested with the system for three days. To give you an idea of how much faster we were, I had set the outright lap record at Road Atlanta earlier that year qualifying for a race. It was a lap record that would stand for a number of years. With the active suspension system, I went one-and-a-half seconds quicker than my own outright lap record. And that is when I think the bastards saw us …

Somebody must have been spying on one of our test sessions, because IMSA suddenly banned active suspension before we could even use it in a race. Pity, as it was some seriously trick shit. You could make the car do *whatever* you wanted it to do. Even under heavy braking, the car quickly settled into a straight line instead of snaking around. That was probably the furthest I ventured into cutting-edge racing technology. At that point, it was the most advanced tech in motor sport.

Unfortunately, Dick and his crew continued to hang around during the 1987 season. This prompted the team's decision to drop the V6 turbo for a normally aspirated 6-litre, 800bhp Chevy

V8. There was nothing Dick and his GM engineer could really do with a V8. A V8 is a V8. A management system – even one made by those Cadillac clowns – wouldn't be much of a factor. In fact, by going the V8 route, our lap times improved at most of the tracks.

Although we had a lot more horsepower with the V6, the engine also suffered from huge turbo lag because of the big, single turbo. On tight tracks we were always at a disadvantage, because you either had no horsepower while the turbo was busy spooling up, or 900 horses, which would suddenly hit you on the back of the head. Tough to control that kind of car. With the V8 we had a steady 780 to 800bhp, which had plenty of torque throughout its rev range, and it was, therefore, a much more responsive car to drive. We'd also modified the rear bodywork, which gave us more downforce. On the negative side, we were also running the V8 at the absolute limit of its abilities, so we had a couple of blow-ups that season.

All in all, we made four pole positions, but couldn't translate any of them into a win. The best results were a second place at Leguna Seca and three third places at Mid-Ohio, Sears Point and San Antonio respectively.

By the beginning of the 1988 season, I think GM were already thinking of packing it in. With an ageing chassis and an unwilling-ness on the part of GM to do any development, we were way off the pace. A single podium – third – at Watkins Glen was the best we could do. After the last race of the season, we were informed that there would be no more. General Motors were pulling out of IMSA, and Rick Hendrick shut down his IMSA team.

It made it a little easier for me to decide what to do next. My schedule had become far too demanding – I was also racing in the world endurance championship in Europe for privateer teams running Porsche 962s … I needed to park something. The endless flying was really getting to me. Every week I would be on another flight. For a tall guy like me, air travel is very uncomfortable. Even business class feels cramped. And there's all that hanging around in airports, of course, and your luggage inevitably going missing – it always happens sooner or later. And flights get delayed and you miss your connection and … and … and.

So, after hearing that the Corvette gig was over, I phoned Audi and told them that I was available to rally for them again, and they signed me up. As mentioned, I had stopped rallying for them during 1986. In 1988, 1989 and 1990, I would continue to race in some World Sportscar Championships around the world for Porsche privateer teams like Jöest, Brün and Kremer, but my American adventure was effectively over.

6

RUNNING WITH THE BIG DOGS

Some good ole boys, several more Porsches ... and one very big wake-up call

A LITTLE NASCAR ASIDE

Actually, we can't close the book on the States just yet. I need to tell you about the few races I ran in that great American circus known as NASCAR.

Hendrick Motorsports, who ran the Corvette team, also ran teams in NASCAR, and on a couple of occasions, when one of their regular drivers was injured or ill, Rick Hendrick asked me to fill in. I competed in four races between 1986 and 1988, driving the Tide-sponsored car at Daytona, Charlottesville and Watkins Glen. And it was all a bit of a let-down, to be honest. At least in the sense of the actual driving. The tactics and tricks were another story altogether, but in terms of real car control, it was just a case of going through the gears around those big ovals and, once in top gear, just keeping it there. For the corners, you just came off the gas a little, but otherwise that was it.

Tactically, however, it was a different ball game. There were a lot of tricks, and if you didn't know them, you didn't have a chance. At Daytona I was running second behind NASCAR legend, the late Dale Earnhardt. Every time we'd come off Turn Four, I'd get a bit of a run on him. 'This NASCAR thing is a walk in the bloody park,' I thought to myself. 'I'm going to take him next time.'

As we exited Turn Four, I came out of his slipstream, dropped to the inside and ... lost 24 places. The rest of the field had seen what I was doing and just closed up behind Earnhardt. In NAS-CAR, the slipstream effect is *everything*, and a bunch of cars going along nose to tail will lap faster than some idiot going along on his own. In this scenario, that idiot was me. They simply all tucked in behind Earnhardt and hung me out to dry. In the space of the back straight, I went from second to 26th. At a superfast, big oval track like Daytona, you can really see the effects of slipstreaming. Daytona is absolutely flat out all the way, and in qualifying we were doing 43-second laps. Hooked up in the train during the race, though, we were running 41s.

It's a very strange feeling to be sitting in the middle of a 40-car train on those fast tracks. You're touching the guy in front, the guy behind you is touching your bumper, and your car is forever moving around without any driver input from you. You also quickly learn that because of the bankings on the ovals' corners, they are not actually corners at all. They're basically straights, too, and the car adopts a natural attitude of oversteer. If you try to turn, you just end up in the wall.

Your pit crew – especially the spotter – plays a major role in the race. From his perch, the spotter can see the whole track, and he'll tell you stuff, like, go wide in a particular corner because you are quicker there and the other guy's slower, or whatever. I never got used to this constant bloody chattering in my ear.

What I really didn't like about NASCAR is that you never feel as if much of anything is your own decision. If the whole train decides to move to the top, you've got to go with them or you'll get dropped off the back. And then you might be about to pass someone you've been stalking for five laps when a voice comes over the radio to order you to pit. You *have* to pit. It's like racing by committee.

The cars are also set up for either high or low, meaning that they are either set up to travel along the bottom groove of the racetrack or along the top groove, next to the wall. And you have to stay in your groove. Go off line and suddenly the car's handling goes for a ball of shit. These cars don't really have what you and I would regard as 'roadholding'. They're dialled into one line, where you've got to sit the whole day. Nope. Not for me. It bored me to death.

The only time things got a little exciting was when something went wrong. And when things go wrong in NASCAR, they really go wrong. Accidents were just a mess. Which is why you had to go to Rookie School. It didn't matter who the hell you were; you might have won Grand Prix races or Le Mans, but if you hadn't yet raced NASCAR, it was off to Rookie School with your ass. And that was the end of the goddamn story. Goddamn it.

The first thing you learnt about Rookie School was that it was run by the Bible Belt. And given my somewhat ambivalent relationship with religion, we immediately got off on the wrong cowboy boot. First of all, you had to pitch up there at 6 o'clock in the morning, upon which you were required to bow your head for the morning prayer.

Daytona was my rookie race, and there was an Australian with his girlfriend in my little school group. They were a weird couple, even by my standards. He wore a long trench coat and had funny hair. She had rings everywhere, tattoos and shit, and wore a tiny miniskirt. So things were looking up: I could sense some entertainment in the offing. In any case, there we were, praying, and straight afterwards the guy in charge immediately addressed the Aussie.

'Please stand up, Bruce.' I forget what his actual name was. 'You don't look like you belong in NASCAR, so you gotta change your clothes. And I take it that's your lady friend next to you? Yeah? Well, she ain't allowed in the pits area looking like that. She can sit on the grandstand. That's the end of the story. You don't like it, go home.'

Apart from the entertainment value, Rookie School was actually fairly useful, particularly when they told you what to do when things went wrong. And when things went wrong in a tightly packed field of 40-odd NASCAR motor vehicles travelling at 320 km/h, like I said, they tended to go wrong in a big way. During one of the practice sessions a big accident happened ahead of me, and the Rookie School headmaster's words immediately came to mind.

'Turn down, son. If there's an accident, y'all just turn down to the bottom of the track. You don't want to be turning up the bank and getting caught up on the wall.'

So I just turned down and spun for what seemed like forever. The cars are built like brick shithouses and weigh a ton, so when they start spinning at 320 km/h, they don't stop. The spin would carry on for about a mile – you'd obviously write off a set of tyres, but at least you'd save the car.

There were some real characters among the drivers, and none more so than the legendary AJ Foyt. One day, I was sitting in my racing car, waiting to go out onto the track during official practice. I was in the rookie line. If you're a rookie, you wait in a separate queue. For every three regular drivers the officials allow on their precious track, they'd allow one rookie. So, anyway, Foyt – who's like a motor-racing god in the US – obviously isn't concentrating, because he follows me out of the pits and into the rookie queue.

He parks behind me and we wait and we wait as other cars go out. I'm looking in my rear-view mirror at this lot, knowing something is going to happen. And, again, it's very likely to be highly entertaining. Foyt can't understand what the hold-up is, but eventually he twigs that he's in the wrong line. He starts yelling at a marshal to let him into the other lane, but the marshal won't have any of it.

Foyt loses it, climbs out of the driver's-side window, pushes the car back to make some space in the line, climbs back in through the window, sticks it in first gear, floors it, and charges the marshal. The poor oke kaaaaks himself, sprints to the pit wall and has to dive over to avoid being smeared along the concrete. Man, it was funny.

Obviously the NASCAR officials didn't see the humour and fined Foyt $18 000. I chatted to him later – he liked South Africans and took something of a shine to me – and asked him if it had been worth all that money.

'My friend, I woulda paid another 50 if I coulda hit the cunt.'

Foyt also took part in some races in the IMSA series with us, and after one season-ending Daytona Finale, matters got a bit out of hand. We were attending the prize giving at the hotel where we were all staying. As often happened, the event turned into a big piss-up, with an even bigger debate raging as to who could actually have won if things had only gone their way. In other words, the usual post-race-in-the-bar discussion. Foyt stands up and shouts: 'Stop this shee-it. Which of y'all have got rent-a-cars?'

So we all put up our hands.

'Grab your car keys, gentlemen, and follow me to the god-damn car park.'

We were to have a race on the public road that surrounds the Daytona Speedway. Slow cars in front, big cars at the back. I'm sort of in the middle of the pack, and Foyt's at the back in his big Cadillac. Off we go. I'm passing some guys, Foyt is passing some guys, and we are all drunk. Yes, it was all very irresponsible.

We're on what's pretty much a public highway, which has this ditch in the middle of the road. I see Foyt's Cadillac roar past me, weave a little, and then, as he takes the lead, lose it and roll into the ditch. *Right* in front of a cop. Obviously we all stop because, shit, AJ has rolled his car. By the time we get out of our cars and run over to the scene of the accident, the cop is already pulling AJ out of the car.

'And you're drunk too!' says the cop.

''Course I'm drunk, son! D'ya think I'm a fucking stunt driver?'

Even the cop had to laugh. As I said, Foyt is a god in America.

We just took him back to the hotel and that was that. He was a real character, always very boisterous, arguing with motor-sport authorities and carrying on. Naturally, SuperVan liked him a lot. Foyt retired in 1986, so I met him right at the end of his career – I think he simply didn't give a shit by then and just did whatever he wanted. As a driver, his CV is up there with the best ever. The Indy Car series was his main event, where he holds just about every record. He's also the only driver ever to have won the Indy 500, the Daytona 500 and the 24 Hours of Le Mans.

THE PORSCHES
While all this American racing was going on, I was also, as mentioned earlier, picking up drives for various privateer teams running Porsche 956s and, later, 962s, in the World Endurance Championship (called the World Sportscar Championship from 1986). I'd done Le Mans in 1984, coming third, and I did those races with young George Fouché in 1985 (described in the previous chapter).

I should, in fact, have won Le Mans in 1984. Driving a Skoal Bandit–sponsored Porsche 956 with David Hobbs and Philippe Streiff, I picked up a noise towards the end of the race and made the decision to radio it in. Other drivers might not have registered it, but I did, and the team called me in.

Unfortunately, they then took a bloody age to find the problem. And when they did, it was just a small chip on one of the valves. It would have made no difference to the car's performance – shit, we could probably have run for another 24 hours. But with the time spent in the pits, we went from leading by three laps to third place. And there wasn't enough time to make up any positions from there. Man … do I regret opening my mouth … It's something that will hound me for the rest of my life.

I was back at Le Mans in 1986, but I wished I wasn't. It was a tragic race for our team and one I'd sooner forget. I was driving for the Kremer team, and my Porsche 962 teammates were

Japan's Kunimitsu Takahashi and Austrian Jo Gartner. Gartner was a very good driver – he'd done a season in Formula 1 for the Osella team in 1984 and he was also doing the IMSA series with me in 1986. Successfully, too. His Bob Akin Motor Racing team and their Coca-Cola–sponsored 962 had won the 12 Hours of Sebring in March of that year.

Our Le Mans car was black that year, sponsored by Japanese electronics giant Kenwood. I'm generally not superstitious, but I remember thinking that the car looked particularly morbid the first time I saw it. We weren't great in qualifying – 15th, I think – but we were doing okay in the race. We got up to around eighth. Takahashi kept to himself – a language issue, I guess – but Gartner and I got on well. I wouldn't say that we were buddies, but we had quite a lot of chats during the IMSA series.

During the race, Gartner came in for an unscheduled pit stop and said that something was wrong with the Porsche's handling. Turned out that a suspension wishbone had broken on the rear right. It was fixable, and off he went again. We'd dropped back a few places because of the pit stop, but managed to move up as the race wore on into the night. On lap 168, I came in for a scheduled fuel stop and driver change. It's a compulsory two-minute stop at Le Mans, so there's no real rush – they enforce the two-minute pit stop to reduce any chance of a fuel fire that the crew might cause because of trying to speed things up.

Gartner jumped into the car and headed out into the night. But he never came around to complete his lap. I remember George Fouché and I were standing in the pits, talking – Kremer ran two cars that year and George was driving the sister car. We were in number 10 and he was in number 11. George and I presumed that something had broken on the car or Gartner had gone off the track. Quite a lot of time passed, and finally we realised that something serious must have happened.

Eventually team boss Erwin Kremer came up to us – his face absolutely ashen – and simply said, 'Jo ist tot.' Jo is dead.

I saw the car later – lots of blood everywhere – and even though it was completely stuffed, you could see that the left rear suspension was broken. We presumed that that had caused the accident. Coming down the Mulsanne Straight, the left rear wishbone had probably snapped, causing the Porsche to swerve left, where it must've dug in on the grass and flipped. The car went over the barrier upside down, which sliced off the top half of the car ... and cut Jo in half.

This happened no more than 45 seconds after I had handed the car over to Jo – it could so easily have been me in the car when that wishbone broke. It's difficult to blame anyone when something like that happens in motor sport, but during my time as driver for privateer teams like Kremer, Jöest and Brün, it was the Kremer team that would skimp now and again. Whereas Jöest and Brün would always run brand-new parts, the fact that we'd already broken a suspension part earlier in the race suggested that the Kremer team had perhaps been using parts that were not brand new. In a 24-hour race like Le Mans, you have to start with everything new on the car.

That said, I raced for Jöest the following year at Le Mans and our car broke on the warm-up lap. We were in a yellow, white and black 962 sponsored by a Japanese retail clothing-chain company called Taka-Q, but my co-drivers, Chip Robinson, and my old mate from the IMSA Corvette team, David Hobbs, and I didn't get very far.

There was some drama at Le Mans that year about the fuel. You know what the French are like – they decide to make some stupid rule with which all the teams have to comply, even if it's the daftest thing since drowning a snail in garlic butter and eating it. That year they insisted on all of us using a lower-octane fuel, and unfortunately our car didn't like it.

I was doing the first driving stint and, while following the pace car on the warm-up lap, the Porsche burnt a hole in the cylinder ... and that was it. I never even started the race. I just got out of the car and headed to the nearest bar to drown the whole experience in whatever overpriced liquor they were selling there.

Actually, before that, I had to walk back through the sponsors' area and, as I did, all the Japanese turned around and faced away from me. I was like, 'Hey. To hell with you guys, it wasn't my fault.' Later I found out that this was, in fact, a sign of respect, as they don't want to look at you in your hour of grief.

That's the Japs for you. Interesting bunch. I not only raced for a Japanese-sponsored team, but I raced in Japan a couple of times too, in World Sportscar Championship rounds. I got used to the Japanese's social etiquette, like bowing when you greet each other. You must always bow a bit lower than your boss, too ... which is not easy if you're six foot four and he is four foot six. It got bloody complicated sometimes. You've got to figure out things like, even though this guy is high up in the company, maybe he considers you to be higher than him. Eventually you'd break your back trying to out-low-bow the guy.

Weird shit. But the Japanese are a very organised and clean nation. I never saw any rubbish lying around; everything was in its place. I guess you have to be organised if you're living on such a small island with so many other people. The traffic was incredible. I once drove 200 kilometres to the circuit in Fuji, which took me three hours. The next time I decided to take the bullet train – the only problem was that all the signs were in Japanese and I couldn't figure out which platform I had to be on. Eventually I went to stand on some steps and yelled, 'Does anyone speak English?'

Fortunately some guy helped me out. He took me to the right platform and said, 'The next train will be here in six minutes. Get onto that train, and then one hour and three minutes later, get off and you'll be in Fuji.' And that's exactly what happened. I even timed it. One hour and three minutes later we stopped, and there was Fuji. That sort of thing really impresses you.

In my experience, this has never happened to me in South

Africa. But what occurred during practice for that race wouldn't happen in South Africa either ...

It was absolutely pouring with rain during the first practice session at Fuji. I mean, pissing down. Water was cascading across the track – it was like one big river, and none of the Western drivers went out. It was suicide. But all the Japanese drivers were out there. Apparently it was all about showing how brave you were.

In reality, it was all about showing how quickly you can slide off a track.

The okes were spinning off all over the circuit, or slamming into the barriers, or, if they were lucky, getting stuck in the gravel traps. But they were all out there. It was ridiculous – you couldn't possibly have learnt anything. I'd always fancied myself as a bit of a rain expert on the track, especially with my rallying experience, but not even I would have ventured out onto that water-soaked circuit.

Nevertheless, I got on quite well with the Japanese – in fact, I get on well with most people – and the Japs must have liked me too, because they gave me all sorts of presents. They might have driven me nuts if I'd lived there all the time, but for business purposes, it was a wonderful set-up.

There was, however, one benefit to the debacle on the track in 1987. Before the Taka-Q Porsche ate its own cylinder, I managed to qualify it in fourth position among the factory Porsches and Sauber-Mercedeses. That made the big cheeses at Porsche sit up and take notice, and in 1988 I was offered a drive in one of the Shell-sponsored official-works Porsche 962s. The factory entered three works cars at Le Mans that year: their regular drivers – Klaus Ludwig, Hans-Joachim Stuck and Derek Bell – were in the number-one car; Mario, Michael and John Andretti were in the number-two car; and Bob Wollek, Vern Schuppan and I were in car number three.

The invitation had come out of the blue. I got a call asking me if I was interested in joining the team for Le Mans, and of course it wasn't very difficult to say yes. This was the really big league and easily the most professional outfit I'd ever been a part of. When I arrived at Charles de Gaulle airport, for example, I was greeted by a woman who had been waiting for me. She asked me to follow her outside, and there a Porsche 911 turbo awaited me. She gave me my hotel address and handed me the car keys.

But, overall, the set-up wasn't too intimidating – I had been around for a while by then and knew how good I was, and I knew my fellow drivers well. I was mates with Ludwig, Stuck and Bell, and I knew the Andrettis too, having both co-driven with and raced against them in the IMSA series. As it was the Porsche factory team, they were using the very latest technology, of course. It would also be the first time in my racing career that I would come across Big Brother.

The team sat us down in the pits and Porsche's chief engineer got up and gave us the rundown as to exactly how we should drive the car. Using one of those telescopic pointing gadgets, he starts prodding an image of the circuit projected up on a screen. This is what you do here, and this is what you do there, and these are the revs I want you to use and, and, and …

Then he shows us this little red button on the right-hand side of the steering column. If you pressed it, you got more boost in the turbo – instant extra power. He was at pains to stress that it was only for overtaking when we were in a dice situation, and maybe at the start of the Mulsanne Straight so that we could carry extra speed all the way down. We most certainly shouldn't press the button all the time, as it would put extra stress on the engine and kill our fuel economy. Four, maybe five times a lap was the officially recommended dosage.

So off we all went to try it out, and it was bloody wonderful. Press the button and you got a big wallop of extra power. After the first session, they called everybody back into the room with the white screen and the pointing gadget, and Mr Chief Engineer asked us all how many times we had used the boost button.

'Herr Stuck?'

'Um … I think maybe four … ja, four.'

He asked all of us and we all gave him a number.

Then all of a sudden, the actual numbers appeared on the screen. The bastards had had an engine telemetry system hooked up and they could tell exactly how many times each of us had thumbed the little red button.

'Herr Stuck, you said four. It was, in fact, 13!'

Turns out we had *all* lied. All of us had initially mumbled a number between four and six, but it had actually been more like 10 or 13. All except Herr Schuppan. He had pressed it 16 times.

Our main opposition was the Silk Cut Jaguar team with their hi-tech, carbon-fibre-chassied XJR-9s. Thanks to the turbo-boost buttons, though, we out-qualified them, taking the first three places on the grid. Klaus, Hans and I were within one second of one another, which, over a 3-minute 15-second lap is pretty close to bugger all. The Andrettis and Bell were a little slower, and Schuppan the slowest.

But the works Porsches could never sustain that pace in race conditions, and a series of mishaps put the brakes on any chance of victory. Four or five hours in, all three cars were called in for a refuel, but Ludwig said no, he had enough for another lap, and he just raced right past the pit. Turns out he didn't have enough. I came in, with the Andrettis right behind me, but Ludwig came to a spluttering halt out on the track. One of his co-drivers ran out there with a can of fuel to get him back to the pits. His mistake dropped them to fifth or sixth – out of the running for the lead.

Our car was now the Jags' main challenger, and I had a big dice with the leading Jag – we probably had something like 35 seconds on the rest of the field. It was very exciting, almost like a sprint race and not a 24-hour endurance run. We took it to the limit on every lap. At least, Wollek and I did. Schuppan was off the pace. Eventually the team manager kind of sidelined him, and Wollek and I did all the driving.

In a long-distance race like Le Mans, where you need three drivers, all of you have to put in lap times that are no more than a second apart, or you start losing out. Which was why Porsche management quietly told Schuppan that he could go and put his feet up and they'd let him know when he could drive again. Which was never. He was two seconds off the lap times Wollek and I were posting and that, over the entire race distance, was way too much. A guy like Bell, for example, was always a little slower than Jacky Ickx or Stuck, but he had won three Le Mans crowns with them. The time difference between him and them, though, was marginal. Bell was consistent, and he'd drive the car conservatively, which is what you needed from a driver in an endurance team.

That year, the main problem with the Porsches was that in order to stay with the more sophisticated Jags, we were relying on that boost button, which meant we were using more fuel than their normally aspirated V12. Which meant more pit stops. Which meant we had to push harder to stay in touch. Eventually, our engine gave in. It was about 4 a.m. and I was lying in the pits waiting for my stint when Wollek came in and said that it was all over – there was a major problem with the engine. Porsche never told us exactly what it was, but that was it for us.

The Andrettis were never in contention, which left the Dummfries/Lammers/Wallace Jag to take the marque's first victory since 1957. It was still a close affair, though. The Jag had gearbox problems in the closing stages and Jan Lammers had to keep it in fourth gear to make sure they endured to the end. The Ludwig/Stuck/Bell Porsche made a storming come-back to finish second, just 2 minutes 30 seconds behind the ailing Jag. The Andrettis ended sixth.

And so Porsche's seven-year winning streak at Le Mans ended and, realising that their car was too old-school to be competitive any more, they pulled their works cars out of the event for the next decade. Until now, there's only been one official Porsche entry at Le Mans, and that was 1998's winning effort with the 911 GT1.

Even though we didn't finish, being part of Porsche's ultra-professional set-up remains a career highlight. Their attention to detail was unbelievable – from making sure you had a Porsche road car to drive, right down to reserving a parking place for you, with your name signposted, at the track. We even had a nutritionist to look after us. It's obviously commonplace in sport these days, but back then, it was unheard of. But it wasn't my scene, I can tell you. I'm a very fussy eater. I gave their food a miss and, when I was feeling hungry, just wandered past the million restaurants and food stalls they have at Le Mans and went in and ordered a steak.

The team also had a masseuse. Every time you got out of the car, you could have a little bit of a rub- and a lie-down. That was nice. Obviously this is all par for the course for today's Formula 1 prima donnas, but even Ludwig and Co., Porsche's normal team drivers, said that things weren't normally *this* good.

For the 1989 Le Mans, I was back in a Brün privateer 962, with co-drivers Harald Grohs and Akihiko Nakaya. I'd never heard of Nakaya before, but he brought along the sponsor, 'From A', who provided the money and the colour scheme for our bright-yellow car. He was another one of those Japanese drivers who kept to himself. Unfortunately, he was also another Japanese driver who was crap at driving. He crashed on his first stint. We qualified 10th that year and were probably running around 6th when Nakaya put the car into the barrier at the Porsche Curves. We all pissed off back to our hotels as soon as we heard the news. In fact, the last time I saw Nakaya was when he left the pits to start his stint.

The other driver, though, was a real character – a wonderful guy who owned a bunch of brothels in Frankfurt. Apparently Harald's helpful staff earned him the kind of money that allowed him to go racing.

My swansong in international motor sport happened in 1990. Not only was the travelling really getting to me, but I was tired of all the ducking and diving I had to do with a South African passport.

My final season was really nostalgic for me. I signed up with Kremer to be their number-one driver for what would be almost a full season of the World Sports Prototype Championship. Kremer weren't the best of the privateer teams – unlike Brün and Jöest, they would take on less-talented co-drivers if they had enough bucks – but it did give me an opportunity to drive all the great tracks one more time … Spa, Monza and Le Mans, among others. These were tracks I grew up reading about as a kid … how could I not go for it one more time?

A young Bernd Schneider was my co-driver in most of the races. Our car wasn't very competitive, but one could tell Schneider had talent. He had raced in Formula 1 for Zakspeed and Arrows (without scoring any points), so he wasn't exactly a nobody, and he would go on to win six German Tour Car titles for Mercedes. But the best we could do in the Kremer Porsche 962 was three ninth places at Monza, Spa and Donnington. Which was good compared to Le Mans that year, which was shit. And that's no metaphor. It involved actual shit …

The Friday night before the race, my then girlfriend and now wife, Danielle, and I went out for dinner. I can't remember what I ate, but I woke up at 5 o'clock on the Saturday morning of the race with terrible stomach cramps. I could barely make it to the bathroom before it started coming out both ends. I was pretty sick, but I wasn't going to let some stupid little French bug spoil my final Le Mans. I started to feel slightly better later in the day, but I still shat in my racing overalls during one of my driving stints.

It couldn't have been too pleasant for my co-drivers – Hideki Okada and my old mate from Le Mans 1986, Kunimitsu Taka-hashi – but racing is a tough business and if you can't take the shit, stay out of the bathroom. Or something to that effect. They never mentioned anything to me, being such polite okes, but no doubt some opinions were shared in private.

Eventually, at about 3 a.m. on the Sunday, the team doctor – also Japanese – wrapped me in a blanket and put me on a drip. Within minutes, I had recovered. It was nothing short of a miracle. I don't know what was in the drip – clearly some highly illegal brew – but I would have loved to have bought a 44-gallon drum of the stuff.

Our actual race that year was just as crap. One of my talented co-drivers put the car into the barriers, and we eventually finished 24th. It was my worst-ever finish at Le Mans.

And not the greatest way to bow out.

7

BACK HOME

Ford-shaped revenge, a Korean surprise … and my
final race

GOOD FORD, BAD FORD

The move back to Ford in 1991, as mentioned at the end of
Chapter 4, was a SuperVan-driven desire to show how good a
racing driver I really was. If I could beat the Audis in the Ford,
I would be making one sizeable, unchallengeable statement. But
as much as it would satisfy my ego, SuperVan didn't drive for
peanuts, and it also took an equally sizeable cheque to get me to
change the colour of my overalls.

The money came via Sasol. In fact, the petroleum giant was
behind the whole thing from the start. They were sponsoring the
Ford Sapphires that Graham Duxbury, George Fouché and Ian
Scheckter were driving in the Wesbank Modifieds – the cars I
was trouncing in the Audi. Enough of that, though. Sasol put up
the money for Ford; I think it was even a Sasol representative who
first approached me. And the offer, if I remember correctly, was
around R380 000 for the year.

Having banked the cash and climbed into my new blue uniform, I now had to produce the goods – my reputation was on
the line. SuperVan had made it clear to his fellow drivers exactly
why he was leaving VW/Audi, and, in addition, I needed to show
the suits at Ford and Sasol that I was worth all that cash.

I did have one advantage. The year before, Bernie Marriner,
who was running the Ford team, and whom I knew well from
my rally days with Ford, had asked me to do a few covert laps

in the Sapphire. I was killing his drivers on the track and Bernie wanted to know if it was the car or just inferior driving talent. Scheckter was bitching and moaning about the Ford's performance, so at his home circuit in East London I hopped in and took the car out. I was immediately quicker than him in a car I'd never before driven.

I therefore knew that the Ford Sapphire had the speed; it was just a matter of fine-tuning the handling. The car was powered by a four-cylinder, 2.0-litre, turbo-charged Cosworth that had originally been developed for Ford's Group B rally monster, the Ford RS200. On the downside, while the trick engine was imported from Europe, the chassis was locally made. And it was heavy. Like the Audi, we also had 720bhp and accompanying lag from the turbo, but the Ford was only rear-wheel-drive. Being four-wheel-drive, the Audi could get away with the turbo's characteristic delay in power delivery, but the Ford was tricky.

You were always busy in it. You had to anticipate when the power would arrive and make damn sure that you were in the right gear by the time it came on song. That wasn't so easy to do around the corners. There were also some issues with the car's aerodynamics, but I'd learnt a few tricks in the States and, with one or two tweaks, we managed to get a little more downforce as well. Once the car was sorted, I was confident my driving ability would do the rest.

Obviously, the Audis were the cars I wanted to beat. Chris Aberdein and Terry Moss were in their two cars and both represented the next generation of South African drivers. There's no doubt they wanted to take me out and so make their names. And I was equally determined to show them that they had a long way to go before they could match me. Ben Morgenrood was the other main threat. He was in the quick-but-fragile triple-rotor, rotary-engined Mazda MX-6 – the same engine Mazda had used at Le Mans the year before. It was the noisiest flipping thing you ever heard, but let me tell you, it was one very quick little car.

Kyalami was the venue for the first race that season and the big showdown. Qualifying didn't go too well – a turbo pipe blew off – and I started seventh on the grid. I made up a few places at the start and was soon behind Aberdein in the first Audi in front of me. I managed to squeeze past him and then set off after Moss in the leading Audi. I outbraked him going into Clubhouse Corner, took the lead and managed to hang on for the win.

There was some very enthusiastic celebrating in the Ford pit after the race, as you can imagine. Ironically, the extra weight that had pissed me off so mightily at Audi would then be bolted into my Ford. It seemed that wherever I went, I was closely followed by a few hundred kilograms of lead.

The weight turned out to be more of a problem in the Ford than it had been in the Audi. Because the Ford's rear-wheel-drive handling wasn't a patch on the Audi's, the extra weight affected the car a great deal. For one thing, the tyres would go off quickly. Because of the Ford's rear-wheel-drive and big turbo motor, the power was like an on/off switch, and the rear tyres would wear out by half-distance, whereas the Audi's power was to all four wheels, so the tyre wear wasn't nearly as bad. We also couldn't get the balance of the Ford right – the extra weight always made it understeer. Remember also that, in the Audi, I was driving well within the car's capabilities, so we could carry the weight and still be competitive.

It didn't help that I was the only Ford up against two Audis very keen to do whatever it took to beat me. One would give me a nudge and the other would go through to win. It was tough to compete against that, but I did manage to – accidentally, by mistake, in error – take both of them out during one of the heats at Kyalami.

In my annoyance, I had made the error of uttering the following, all-too-public statement …

'Bugger this. If those idiots keep penalising me, I'm going to fucking well take both Audis out of the fucking race. Fuck.'

And I did. Though I didn't really mean it.

The incident happened at Kyalami, and we're talking the original track here – it still had the long main straight that dipped down before going into Crowthorne Corner, a fastish right-hander, followed by two flat outs: Barbecue Bend and Jukskei Sweep. It was a fantastic track. But that's all gone now after they built the business park and changed the track's layout. I could never figure out why they didn't just keep that part of old Kyalami and construct the business park on the lower side. It would've made for a better track and probably saved them a whole lot of money. Anyway, back to the little 'accident' …

After declaring my intentions, I did, indeed, manage to end the race swiftly for both Audis, at the very first corner of the very first lap. My former teammate, Chris Aberdein, led off the start line, with Terry Moss in the other Audi right behind him. And at this point, I'll hand you over to SuperVan … He swears that what happened next is a factually accurate version of events.

Thanks. Ja, we were going into Sunset and, being as good as I am on the brakes, I got on the inside of both Audis. Chris closed the gap, and even though I rode the kerb trying not to hit him, he drove into me. I hit him. He hit Moss. And all three of us went off. Naturally, there were a lot of very unhappy people at Kyalami that day, especially because I had predicted that this would happen. There were courts of inquiry and God knows what else, but if you look at the video replay, you can see that I was trying to keep out of the way. Unfortunately, given what I'd said earlier, I couldn't have orchestrated things any better had I intentionally tried to run them off the track … Everybody out of the race in one go, and at the very first corner, too.

But whenever I managed to keep out of trouble, I won races – I won a couple more in the Sapphire that year, and I kept the Audis honest enough. Moss went on to win the title, but I can't remember where I ended – either second or third. I tend to not remember the details of a season in which I don't win the title. Funny that.

I had made my point, though.

The Sapphire got totalled in a big crash at Welkom early the following year. I'll discuss this incident a little later, but suffice to say that the accident was instigated by Terry 'Subtle' Moss. It was a massive shunt that meant we needed to find a new chassis, and find one quickly. The solution was to buy a Mercury Cougar that had run in the IMSA series. It had a better chassis than the Sapphire, but we didn't run the IMSA V8 engine, which was a mistake. Because we had a whole lot of 2.0-litre turbo engines left over from the Sapphire, we continued with those. And because these engines would deliver their power in one massive surge, it would again light up the rear tyres and the performance would fall off as the race went on.

We should instead have bought the whole Cougar package with the V8, which would've been a lot more competitive. The situation was similar to the one we'd had with the Corvette GTP in the US. Its original V6 turbo had monumental power, but once we switched to a V8, the 'Vette was quicker despite having less power. The V8 offers you more tractable power with strong, predictable delivery right through the rev range.

Moss won the title again that year – this was 1993 – and in a new car. Audi had once again imported a couple of fancy Audis from the IMSA series – two Audi 90 GTO cars. But because we didn't sell the 90 locally, they were re-bodied as an Audi S4. As with its predecessor, which I had driven, this new car was also a four-wheel-drive with a 2.2-litre, five-cylinder, turbo-charged motor.

Towards the end of the season I was putting a lot of pressure on Ford to sort their shit out and get me a better car. I didn't merely want to win the odd race – I now wanted the championship. And I knew just the car in which I could deliver it. I phoned my mate Jack Roush in the US. Roush ran teams in IMSA and NASCAR, and he'd won the 1993 IMSA GT series with a Ford Mustang. When I say Ford Mustang, this wasn't *actually* a Mustang. It looked a little like one, but it was a space-frame race chassis wrapped in a fibreglass body and powered by a Ford racing V8. I had met Roush during my days in IMSA and I knew him to be both a builder of quality racing cars and an upstanding guy. I picked up the phone.

'Jack, Sarel. Those championship-winning Ford Mustangs ... what are you doing with them?'

'Well ... Mr van der Meer! I was planning to race them again. Why?'

'Would you sell us one?'

'Hmm ... yeah, okay, I could let one go.'

And that was that. I think we paid about R500 000 for the car and engine, which was a total bargain. It arrived on the ship just ahead of the final race of the 1993 season in Port Elizabeth. I mean, it had literally *just* arrived. We didn't even have a chance to test it. The car was still wearing its US stickers and the same set of tyres it had last raced on over there. First I went out in the Cougar and qualified it on pole, then I decided to take the Mustang out to see what it could do. The car immediately went quicker than the Cougar, even on old rubber. I knew then that we were onto a winner.

With that car in my hands, we finally turned the tables on Audi in 1994. Apart from the power – a 6.0-litre V8 good for somewhere in the region of 700bhp – it had a great chassis, and I kicked some lederhosen-wearing Audi butt to win the title ahead of Moss and Aberdein. I was either first or second throughout the season and always in the comfortable position of being in control of the championship.

In the last race of the season – out of the two heats – I only needed third place to win the title. In the first heat, I took it easy and came third, and then I won the second heat just to show them who the big dog really was. The V8 that we had brought in actually changed the ball game for Wesbank Modifieds, as it became a V8 series after that. A V8 is still the cheapest horsepower you can buy.

Everything changed again the following year when Ford moved into the Super Touring Car formula. Bad idea. Very bad idea.

South Africa's Super Touring series had started in 1993 and was based on the British Touring Car rules and specs. As the cars actually looked like sedans one could buy off South African showroom floors, the series proved popular with manufacturers, and just about everyone who was making cars in this country suddenly had a Super Touring Car entry. I never cared too much for the whole shebang. A fact exacerbated by the two lemons Ford bought to compete in the series.

For the 1995 season, the bosses at Ford decided it was high time the brand made its presence felt in the series and entered two Ford Mondeos.

But as I said, I thought Super Touring Car was a bad idea. They were just too expensive, which had a negative impact on motor sport in South Africa. Because all the manufacturers felt that they needed to be represented, they pulled money from all other formulas. Even South African rallying suffered as the manufacturers poured their cash into this new series. As it turned out, only two manufacturers were successful – initially Michael Briggs won two championships (1993 and 1995) in the Opel Vectra, and later Giniel de Villiers dominated in the Nissan Primera, winning the series from 1997 to 2000.

I know Giniel and the Nissan, having won four titles in a row, are often blamed for killing off the series. But I don't blame him. I was glad that he killed it. Total waste of bloody money, *and* it left the rest of SA motor sport in ruins. Everything just got wiped off the board. The Wesbank series hovered with a few wrecks running around, and the rally scene all but died. You really can attribute it all to Touring Cars.

Its legacy is still felt in SA motor sport today. The only formula where big money is being spent is in the Production Car class. But, again, they're making the same mistake they made with Touring Cars. Some of the teams' budgets run into the millions, and they're approaching Touring Cars in terms of their sophistication. I watched a couple of races at Killarney recently. There were only 10 or so cars on the grid and virtually no overtaking. What another bloody balls-up.

Admittedly, my somewhat unenthusiastic attitude towards Touring Cars might also have something to do with the absolute lemon Ford gave me to drive. Because Ford were doing pretty well in the British Touring Car Championship in their Mondeo – Kiwi Paul Radisich had come third in the 1993 and 1994 series – one of Ford SA's directors went over to see if he could buy a car or two for us. Man, did they see him coming. Ford UK did sell him two cars, but they were total crap.

Sure, the technology in these Mondeos was only two years old, but they were still suspiciously slow and unreliable, even for two-year-old cars. We even had Radisich out here for a race or two and he couldn't figure out why our Mondeos were so bad. It was only after one of our gearboxes ate itself and we phoned one of the motor-sport guys in England that we realised what had happened.

'One of our gearboxes has disintegrated – has anything like this happened to your cars?'

'What? You can't break those boxes, mate. They're practically bullet proof. What's the serial number?'

The number was duly given … and a somewhat surprised and embarrassed voice came back on the line.

'Yeah … um … how did you get hold of that box? It was one of our original test prototypes and should never have been sold.'

Turns out we'd basically been sold a bunch of spare parts that were masquerading as a racing car. They were just fucking useless … old scrap. Yes, you're thinking, 'How could Ford shoot itself in the foot like that? Surely we were all part of the same company? Group hugs all round, etc.'

Well, that's what I'd thought, too. Perhaps it had to do with the fact that Ford SA was now part of SAMCOR with Mazda, and Ford UK saw us as just another customer. Well, not just another customer – that would've meant halfway decent service. Instead they saw us as a bunch of wet-behind-the-ears idiots from the southern tip of Africa. We had a shocking season. I have no idea where we ended. My brain has chosen to delete the information.

In January the following year, Ford decided to cut its losses and informed me that they were no longer racing. This was interesting to me, as I still had a contract with them for the 1996 season. They could pull out of racing, but they still had to pay me. I even kept the two company cars. Rather than sit on my arse twiddling my thumbs, I competed in a couple of Touring Car races in a privateer car that I was offered. The car was way off the pace, but at least I was out on the track.

I suppose that's the other side of me – the *Not SuperVan*. For all SuperVan's swagger and attitude, he's raced cars for the simple reason that he loves racing cars. The public image, the demands for big pay cheques and the big ego all have, at their core, a simple desire to be on a track in a car, having a dice. (That said, the BMW wasn't a great car. In fact, it even overcame my desire to race. After three races, I handed the keys back to its owner.)

While I was at Ford, I also did a bit of rallying – not terribly successfully, though. Probably because the car was actually a Mazda. Back in those dark, badge-engineered days of the SAMCOR mess, Ford and Mazda would simply stick badges on each other's cars and call them something else. The Ford Lazer, for example, was really a Mazda 323. And it was in one of these that I would compete in the SA rally championships in 1992 and 1993.

We were up against Serge Damseaux and his Toyota Conquest with its Xtrac drivetrain. We also had four-wheel-drive on the Lazer, but Toyota had a handbrake system on their car that allowed them to engage the brake and release it quickly. The Ford was a good car, and I won quite a few rallies in it, but the handbrake factor gave the Toyotas a real advantage. On the tight stages with that system, you really got it lined up to go around the corners, and Damsie would always take me on at all the tight moments. The Toyota had also had a bit more horsepower, but that wasn't really the key issue – on the fast stuff you could run with them. I ended up coming second in the championship for both those years, so we did win our fair share.

By the end of 1993, I decided to call it quits in rally driving. I had just had enough. I went to Ford and said, look, we can win the odd rally, but the car just isn't good enough to win a championship. I'm not doing the job you're paying me to do in the rallies, so I think I'm going to stop rallying. We got young Enzo Kuun to drive the rally car and I kind of managed him in the rallies. I still went on all the rallies, and in fact Kuun won his first national championship event with me – the 1993 Sasol Rally.

But as it turns out, I wasn't quite finished as a rally driver. One night I got drunk and ended up in a Daewoo. As one does...

EVERY DOG HAS HIS DAEWOO

After Ford quit racing in 1996, I happened to be staying with my buddy Johan Evertse, who owned a big Daewoo dealership. This cheap Korean brand was still relatively new in South Africa, and it didn't exactly have a reputation for cutting-edge automotive technology. Over one or two glasses of fine Scotch whisky, Johan not only floated the idea of starting a rally programme, but also suggested that I drive one of the cars in the upcoming Castrol Rally.

Naturally, I told him to piss off – I had had enough crap cars for one year, thank you very much, and, besides, I had quit rallying three years earlier.

We carried on drinking.

Then, at some point in the course of the evening, I somehow must have agreed to Johan's hare-brained scheme. I know this because I woke up the next morning with a bit of a hangover and a vague recollection of shaking Johan's hand and uttering the words, 'Yes, I'd love to go rallying in a Daewoo.'

At breakfast the following morning I did what any sane rally driver who'd won 11 national rally championships would do ...

'Listen, Johan ... that bullshit about the Castrol, forget about it. It was an interesting idea, we drank whisky, we had a laugh. But seriously, I'm not doing it.'

'Ja ... about that ... thing is, you see, I've already told the press. It'll be in tonight's papers.'

'You bloody bastard ...'

Not that Daewoo South Africa had anything close to a rally car. Turns out the only other Daewoo being rallied anywhere in the world was a Daewoo Cielo in Kenya. Two Indian chaps were running it, and Daewoo SA managed to secure it for the Castrol. The thing about the Daewoo Cielo was that it's actually an Opel Kadett with a slightly different grill and different badges. With Opel rally parts behind the Daewoo tappet cover, it was actually a fairly decent car. So we shipped it down to South Africa, stuck on some new stickers ... and my old mate, navigator Franz Boshoff, and I rocked up at the start of the Castrol.

Of course there were a couple of sniggers from the other drivers, but it didn't bother me too much. In the past, that kind of behaviour would've seen SuperVan lace up his boxing gloves, but I was fairly relaxed by then. I'd been off the scene for a while and I had no expectations at all, especially in this car. On the other hand, it was a long way from the start in Pretoria to the finish four days later in Mbabane, Swaziland. Anything could happen.

It took me the first couple of stages to get used to rallying again, but then I gradually started to push as I began to feel more comfortable. We stayed in the top five – I mean, this was me, after all, not some palooka – but then all of a sudden the big guns like Kuun and Damseaux started to fall away because of mechanical problems and crashes. At the first overnight stop, we were third. Suddenly, the race was getting quite serious. And it would get even more serious. Halfway through the next day, we were in the lead ... and we sort of hung on there until the end. So we won the bloody thing!

Naturally, SuperVan dusted off his party shoes for the prize giving at the Mbabane Holiday Inn. And, naturally, it turned into one helluva bash. It was my 11th Castrol Rally title and the 25th anniversary of South Africa's premier rally event. There was no way SuperVan was going to let the occasion pass without a comment or two – especially as I was to make a speech at the function.

The Koreans were with us too, and they couldn't believe that they'd won a rally at their first attempt. They'd also entered cars in the lower classes and had won some of those too, so it was a massive event for Daewoo. Even the Koreans were letting their hair down – which wasn't easy, as their hair mostly seems to grow up – and by the time I had to go on stage and make my speech, I was pretty pissed. So not only did I have a dig at my fellow competitors ...

'How many times do I have to walk up here before one of you arseholes can actually win this thing?'

But I also managed to get my Koreans mixed up. Which, come on, be honest, is not difficult.

'And of course I couldn't have done it without my team. To win first time out is an incredible achievement. Thank you ... Hyundai!'

And that set the tone for the kind of evening of which one remembers only bits and pieces.

We competed in one more rally in 1996 – the Sasol – and I think we came fifth. As I recall, we had engine trouble. We were running top three most of the time, but eventually dropped down. Based on our early successes, Daewoo decided to give rallying a full go. On my advice, they hired Enzo Kuun as another driver and entered two cars in the 1997 SA championship. Enzo was, and is, a very good rally driver, and we'd been mates. I knew his parents well, too, and I'd witnessed his arrival on the rally scene as a youngster.

But we didn't have cars. The one in which I'd won the Castrol had been returned to the Indians, and with the new season imminent, we needed to make a plan ... and quickly. I knew a guy called JoJo somebody or other who had an Opel Kadett rally car that we could upgrade and slap a Daewoo grill on. We got some trick shit from Opel Germany, which I used until we could get our own works cars built. Again we basically created top-spec Opel rally cars with Daewoo bodywork. The cars were great and we were pretty dominant. I won four rallies, Enzo won another two, and Serge won two or three.

And I should've won my 12th SA championship. Unfortunately, I got banned ...

Enzo and I were observed driving the route of one of the stages in the upcoming Cape rally when the rules were clear that no competitors would be allowed to do so prior to the rally, but we were trying to make some pace notes. Ja, it was wrong, 'rules is rules' and all that, but we were only trying to level the playing field a little. Damseaux, our big rival that year, was from Cape Town and he drove those roads all the time. We had therefore decided to sneak in to make a recce.

Despite our notes, Serge still won the rally – I came second and Enzo third – but before the final results could be announced, our illegal excursion was brought to the organisers' attention. I think a local farmer must have seen and reported us. The Kapenaars didn't like this at all, and we were not only excluded from the results, but MotorSport South Africa also banned us for the next rally. Missing those events opened up the way for Damseaux, who managed to overhaul my points tally and win the championship. If I had just finished the Cape Rally, I would've been champion for the 12th time. Man, was I annoyed. Sure we broke the rules, but the two-rally exclusion was very heavy-handed. Not that it was totally surprising – SuperVan had never missed an opportunity to tell MotorSport SA how crap they were, and their 'punishment' had the unmistakable whiff of revenge.

For the 1998 season, Daewoo built new cars based on the new Lanos production cars. But we only competed in two rallies with these cars before our aspirations came to a sudden halt with some major upheaval in Daewoo's management. I think the big boss in South Africa was shown the door or given a very sharp sword, but they just pulled out of rallying overnight. Fortunately I still had a contract, so I got paid out again, but Enzo got dropped in the kak, as his contract hadn't been as watertight as mine. Daewoo also kindly gave me a road car as part of the severance deal: a bright-yellow Cielo. Ja ... I gave it straight to the wife.

And that was it as far as rallying and SuperVan were concerned. The curtain had finally come down on a sport that had initially established me as a player in SA motor sport and given me a career as a professional driver. But somehow it wasn't such a big deal. As I've said, I loved track racing more, and I still had a few years left on that front.

I very rarely get the desire to drive a rally car these days. The only time I might feel a bit of a twinge is if I'm driving through the Nelspruit area of the Lowveld. If God were a rally driver, he'd spend his time blasting through these mountains and forests. They are *the* most beautiful rally roads you'll find anywhere in the world. They just naturally lend themselves to this form of motor sport, and I had most of my big wins in this neck of the woods. I grew up rallying here. The Castrol and the Sasol Rallies went through the Lowveld, so I won a helluva lot of stages in these forests.

PEDAL TO THE METAL WITH SASOL. AGAIN

Someone shut up those bloody violins so that we can get back to racing cars.

Not much else happened for me in racing until about halfway through 1999. Then George Fouché bought a Ford Mustang from Jimmy Price and entered the car in the Wesbank series. It wasn't an actual Mustang, but a space-frame chassis with a 6.0-litre V8 engine and a fibreglass Mustang body shape. Jimmy was a very good car builder; he had a factory in Port Elizabeth and was building replica AC Cobras and Ford GT40s. They were high-quality replicas and Jimmy did well selling them in the US.

For some reason, George had decided to retire at the ripe old age of 32, and he asked me to drive the car. I ran a few races in the Mustang and got some seconds and thirds, but I never won anything. But that would change at the end of the 1999 season, when my old benefactor, Sasol, came knocking at my door. They were once again keen to run a proper two-car team in the Wesbank series, but this time with the added aim of developing and promoting a black racing driver. Sasol wasn't too fussed about what cars we chose to drive, though obviously we needed to be competitive; they just wanted to have a team in the Wesbank series. And so the Sasol SuperVan Racing team was born.

I wasn't doing anything else at the time, so I was an obvious choice as a driver. Or, to put it slightly more accurately, I was the only decent driver not involved with another team. I then managed to secure the services of an up-and-coming youngster called Gugu Zulu, and with a bag of cash courtesy of Sasol, went about buying two cars and a transporter. Zulu is a talented driver who'd done well in the Vodacom Isondo Sports 2000 national championships, and he has since gone on to carve a successful rally career for himself with the VW team.

The proper Ford Mustang racing car with which I had whipped the Audis in 1994 was now owned by multiple South African powerboat-champion-turned-race-driver Peter Lindenberg. I knew how good that chassis was, and in the right hands I thought it could still compete at the front of the field. Sasol and I made Peter a good offer, which he accepted. The second Mustang was basically a locally made copy of that car – similar chassis and the same engine.

For two reasons, I was really motivated to win the title that year. Firstly, if I won, we'd get sponsorship money for the following year. And, secondly, I wanted some more championships in a formula I felt I should've won many more times in my career. Sure, I'd won all those rally championships, but a combination of stupid weight handicaps and overseas travel meant that SuperVan had far less Wesbank-shaped silverware than he wanted.

I therefore decided to drive for the championship – which meant often settling for seconds and thirds instead of risking a big overtaking manoeuvre to steal the win. My tactics paid off. In a very competitive field of V8s, I won the Wesbank title in 2000, and again in 2001.

It was tougher for Gugu, though. He was thrown in at the deep end, and he struggled with the extra grunt of the big V8s. As I said, Gugu had cut his teeth driving underpowered little 1.6-litre, open-cockpit sports cars in the Vodacom Isondo 2000 development series. So ja, he took some time to get used to the Mustang's 600bhp and messed up quite a lot of my machinery in the process.

By the end of 2001, the Mustangs were a little long in the tooth, and we needed some newer machinery. As it happened, Opel announced that they were pulling out of Wesbank – they had been running two V8 Astras – so their cars were up for grabs. With their short wheelbase, they were twitchy little bastards and not easy to drive, but with some aero tweaks, I knew that they could be winners.

A million rand bought us both cars, as well as their fancy transporter. Sasol and I deemed it a good deal, and so for 2002, we had two new cars on the grid – with Gugu and me driving. But things would soon change. One of us would be sidelined ... and two new drivers would turn our outfit into a three-car team.

Surprisingly, the guy sidelined was me.

In between Wesbank races, I was also doing some rally commentating for the TV channel SuperSport. I attended all the rallies and was basically their resident expert, discussing the ins and outs of the various events and cars, and conducting interviews with the drivers. Anyway, we were in Badplaas on some rally and I woke up one morning as sick as a dog. I was not only puking, but weirdly I had no sense of balance. I couldn't walk straight. I was either walking into things or falling over.

I was staying at Schalk Burger's house – the rally Schalk, not the rugby Schalk – and I lay there for a couple of days thinking that I had some kind of bug that was messing with my inner ear. No such luck. This was clearly something a little more serious. Eventually I said, no, bugger this, take me back to the airport, I need to go back home to Cape Town to see a specialist. I remember walking through the airport using my luggage trolley like a zimmer frame. As I went through security, I got the predictable, 'Sir, you can't go through with a trolley' line.

'Fine. But if I let go of this flippin' thing, you had better get me a wheelchair.'

I managed to get back home and went to see a few specialists. In between lying flat on my back in bed, I had to undergo brain scans and God knows what else. In the meantime, I still had a Wesbank team to run, so I had to find another driver fast – there was no way I could drive a 1.3-litre rental, let alone a V8 racing car. Young Johan Fourie was the obvious choice. He had real talent – he was a fast but smooth driver who knew how to look after a car. Johan also brought sponsorship with him in the form of MD Transport – his dad, Mike's, company.

By this stage, my back was also pretty sore. With all the falling around, I had somehow also stuffed up my back. So I went to see a chiropractor, a genius called Rob Beffa in Cape Town, who took one look at me and said, 'Tell me, how's your balance?'

'Terrible! How did you know?'

'Well, for starters, you nearly took out the door frame when you walked into my office.'

Well, it turns out that it was all due to a pinched nerve in my neck. I must've slept with my neck at a funny angle while in

Badplaas. One session with the chiro and R500 later, I was cured. This was after I'd spent in the region of R30k on specialists and brain scans. A pinched nerve that had originated in my ear ... All these fucking superstars and their fancy fucking machines who thought I'd had a stroke or something. Their misdiagnosis cost me a bloody championship too. Fuck.

Yes. SuperVan and I were both somewhat displeased.

In the meantime, I still had a team to manage and, if I couldn't win the title myself, I wanted one of my drivers to win it. Fourie was our best bet, but coming into the season late, he had some ground to make up. I took him out of the MD Transport Opel and stuck him in my Sasol-sponsored Opel. Sasol were, after all, paying for all of it, and we needed a car with their stickers on to win the championship. I took Gugu out of the other Opel and put him back in the Sasol Mustang – he was happier driving that car anyway – and hired Shaun Watson-Smith to drive the MD Transport Opel.

It all went according to plan. With Shaun and Gugu as his wingmen, Johan managed to win the title on the final day. By now I had sufficiently recovered from the pinched nerve to get back in the driver's seat for the final race. It would be not only the final race of the season, but also the final race in SuperVan's career as a professional racing driver ...

ONE LAST CHEQUERED FLAG ...

At the beginning of the 2002 season, I had begun to think that perhaps this should be my last. A number of factors contributed to cementing my decision – the pinched nerve being one of them. Hanging up my helmet was finally beginning to make a lot of sense.

I was getting on by now – even SuperVan had to admit as much. I was on the wrong side of 55, and I'd had 35 great years as a professional driver. I don't think there's another South African who could say the same. I also had a very good reputation and I didn't want to damage it with a slow and sad decline. If you carry on for too long – as a certain German Formula 1 driver has made the mistake of doing – you inevitably start to lose out to the hunger and razor-sharp reflexes that the next generation of youngsters come armed with. Or in my case, at 55, the next generation's next generation. The golden legacy you'd like to leave quickly loses its lustre.

I could also see the writing on the wall for the Wesbank series, as it was becoming really expensive to compete in it and wasn't getting the kind of press attention it used to get in the past. And it wasn't as if I really wanted to drive in another formula either. I could have gone into a Group N, but to be competitive there, you either had to get a factory drive or spend a whole lot of money setting up your own team, and I didn't feel like going through all that shit again.

A few weeks before that final race at Kyalami, I announced in the press that I had decided to retire. And on the Wednesday before my final race, they arranged a retirement dinner for me at the track's Wesbank Boma.

It was a lovely affair, emceed by Roger McLeery, and we auctioned off some of my memorabilia – overalls, gloves, racing boots and whatnot – and some of the guys made speeches. Most notable was Jan Hettema's speech. He'd been my big rival at the start of my rally career, but over the years the two of us had become good friends. While we had been fierce rivals for a time, I think he had known that I represented the next generation and would be the one who would dethrone him, and in his speech he acknowledged me as a worthy successor. I felt honoured.

Some of the younger guys also said a few words, including Michael Briggs and Enzo Kuun, the next generation after me. They thanked me for the support I had given them in their careers, saying that rather than feel threatened by them, I had given them valuable advice and encouragement. Very kind words from both men ...

Of course, I also had a few words to say. I'm buggered if I can remember what they were, though. Danielle says I said something about all the friends I had made and talked about the many sacrifices my family had had to make. SuperVan denies it all.

I didn't get too emotional that night – I don't think my retirement had quite sunk in yet. That would happen on race day.

A lot of people turned up to watch the race. They had also named the main pavilion after me – 'The Sarel van der Merwe Grandstand' – and shit like that, so ja, it turned into quite a *snot en trane* day. Before I could cry into my hankie, though, there was still some business to take care of – Johan needed to win the championship.

As always, there would be two heats on race day, and Johan only needed to finish in the top three in Heat One to clinch it. He did it, but not before almost giving me heart failure. Instead of driving conservatively and coming third, he got into a scrap with Roelf 'Red Mist' du Plessis and his Camaro …

Driving the MD Transport Astra, I was sitting in third position, shaking my head as I watched these two idiots banging doors all over the show before Johan eventually got past him. But knowing Du Plessis, he'd try a suicidal overtaking manoeuvre somewhere in the closing laps that would inevitably take both of them out. I had no choice. Muscling past Du Plessis, I spent the remaining laps riding shotgun for Fourie to protect his lead. After 35 years, I knew well enough how to make my racing car as wide as a bus, and Du Plessis had no chance of getting past me. Johan Fourie won the heat and the championship.

But Heat Two was SuperVan's. With the 2002 Wesbank championship in the bag, nothing but victory would do as a fitting full stop to his career. I was determined to win that race, even if it meant taking out the whole field in the process. It was just one of those deals.

And win it I did. I put Roelf du Plessis in his place one last time, taking him out in grand style by bumping him off into the sand trap. I was classified first overall for the day as well.

Du Plessis was beyond annoyed.

It was a bittersweet last lap, though. I knew I had the race in the bag, but I also knew that this would be the last time I would take the chequered flag as a professional. So I crossed the line to win … and left a major part of my life behind. Racing cars was all I'd done for 35 years, and now it was all over. Although focused on driving the car during the race, when I crossed that finish line, the reality of it all really hit me. It was a very emotional moment. I suspect even SuperVan had a tear in his eye, though he would obviously flatly deny it.

You can cue those violins now. And … cut.

After the race, we took the driver's door off the car and I sort of sat on the sill and drove it around Kyalami one last time while I waved at the fans. That was followed by the obligatory rubber-laying doughnuts in the pits and the inevitable piss-up in the bar afterwards. It was great and heartsore at the same time. Retiring from the rally scene hadn't been nearly as emotional. Besides, I'd retired twice from rallying – once on the spur of the moment and the second time because Daewoo had pulled out. Racing, on the other hand, was my first love, and there had also been the big build-up to my retirement. There was a finality to it that the rally thing never had.

Sixteen South African National Championships later, and finally I was done.

But I wasn't done with motor sport. The Sasol SuperVan Racing team were dominant in 2002, recording 30 podium finishes, including 15 victories, in the 22 races. It would've been silly to put a stop to that kind of momentum. So, for the next two years I continued to run the team in Wesbank. With more success, too. We developed a new Opel Omega that gave Johan two more championships – one with me and one after his dad bought one of the cars the following year and started his own team.

It was a great car with proper ground effects and it blew everyone else away. So much so that they had to change the rules the next year because the Omega was too good. By then I'd had enough of team ownership. To be honest, I was never cut out for that kak – as a team owner you have all the pain-in-the-arse nonsense of motor sport but none of the fun. Drivers would bugger up your cars, plus you had to deal with all the in-fighting among your drivers, the other teams' bickering and protests to the race stewards … ja, no, enough of that.

These days I still compete in the odd race here and there – just because I stopped driving as a career doesn't mean that the kick I get from driving a racing car has disappeared. I still love racing as much as I did when I first started. I miss the thrill of it every day, and if I could roll back the years by four decades, I'd do it again in a heartbeat. But I'm also aware of my legacy as a driver and I've made sure that the races I compete in only maintain or enhance my reputation.

So I'll take part in races like the Citi Celebrity Challenge, held in 2009 to mark the end of the Citi Golf's 25-year production run in South Africa. VW honoured this bestselling car with two race meetings – one at Kyalami and one at Killarney – and a grid of standard Citi Golfs was packed with drivers who'd been associated with VW and Audi through the years. Among them were the likes of Giniel de Villiers, Terry Moss and Chris Aberdein – except for De Villiers, they were all *laaities* I'd put in their place back in the day.

In a slow, one-make race like the Citi Golf challenge, I knew I'd still have the chops to mix it with the younger guys. Besides, it was a fun experience. I would've naturally lost a little outright pace, but I was confident my experience would make up for it. Despite his retirement, SuperVan could still be a wiley old bastard. In one race, I got taken out by Moss – no surprises there – but in the second race I managed to out-think young Giniel and won.

These days, whenever the opportunity presents itself, I'll accept a drive in the Historic Saloons series, mostly behind the wheel of the big red Ford Galaxie, as described in the SuperVan chapter. I don't know when I'll ever stop. Look at the Brit David Piper. He still brings his historic racing crowd to South Africa each year – putting on one race at Zwartkops and another at Killarney. Piper is in his 80s now but he still drives his irreplaceable fleet of classic sports cars with as much enthusiasm as he did when he was younger. I love this form of racing. Not only do cars like the Porsche 917, Ferrari 250 LM and assorted Lolas, Chevrons and Ford GT40 replicas remind me of my younger days, but the racing is hard – although responsible, given the machinery we're driving.

Ja. Old but responsible. That's SuperVan these days.

Not.

8

THE WOMEN

There were a lot. And quite a few of them I married

By now you may have picked up on the fact that I like women. A lot. So much so that some decisions I made in the course of my life might perhaps have bypassed my brain. Or, more accurately, bypassed my entire upper body. These very often spur-of-the-moment decisions not only had a significant impact on my personal life, but on my bank account too. Sex, I learnt soon enough, is a very expensive business.

I blame it all on school.

In the late 50s and early 60s, South Africa was a conservative place, and nowhere was more conservative than the boys-only Afrikaanse Hoër Seunskool. As an Affies scholar, I wasn't exposed to real life, especially in the way of girls. They were around when I was in primary school, but after Standard 6 (now Grade 8) they just disappeared off the radar. Besides, I was far more interested in sport than anything I thought girls might have to offer. They might as well have been from another planet.

Ja. I was something of a late starter.

Acceleration, however, has always been a strong point of mine, and it didn't take too long for me to get up to speed. I started my journey in Mozambique, of all places. I was with family friend Coenraad Spamer, who, remember, was a well-known racing driver. I was one of his support crew. I had just finished matric, so I must've been 18, and I was dead keen to be part of motor sport in any way I could. Mozambique seemed like a bit of an adventure. And it was – though not entirely in the way I had anticipated.

132

Spamer, God bless him, took me to a brothel, where, to my complete and utter astonishment, this woman took off all her clothes and whispered the kind of invitations that were surely illegal back in Pretoria. To cut a very short story even shorter, about 20 seconds later, I understood with complete clarity what all the fuss was about. This, I thought to myself, was most definitely an avenue I planned to pursue.

Sadly, that avenue wasn't always open to traffic in my younger days. I had to go back home, to the air force, where, as one of many thousands of young South African men in uniform, I was hardly a stand-out prospect that appealed to the nation's young women. I had the occasional girlfriend, but I never managed more than to cop a feel. As with my career in the air force, I was battling to get off the ground with women, too.

But things changed at varsity. Educational institutions tend to be filled with young men and women eager to discover all that life has to offer, and what a wonderful culture of learning it was. I enjoyed slightly more success there, but, even so, I was still fairly conservative in my approach to women. Only in my early 20s did that avenue, which I was so very keen to explore, become more of a busy street. And it was all thanks to motor sport.

Simply put, it made a *moer* of a big difference. Chicks were always hanging around the rallies and racetracks, and when I started shaping in motor sport, I really started shaping in the chick department, too. By 1969, I even had a steady girlfriend. Her name was Tersia Ackerman, though I didn't meet her at the track. I was having lunch with a friend in a restaurant one day when I saw this pretty blonde at a table with her parents. I didn't speak to her, but we exchanged a couple of looks, which was like a green light to me. As I really liked what I saw, the next day I hotfooted it back to the restaurant to find out who had sat at that table. The restaurant manager could only tell me that it was the Ackermans. So I phoned every Ackerman in Pretoria. There were 23 of them. Eventually I got hold of the right girl and asked her out. Our date went rather well, and we started seeing each other regularly. And so forth …

Then, foolishly, I went and married someone else. In my defence, it was for practical purposes. As you'll remember from Chapter 3, I'd gone over to England at the beginning of 1970 on a three-month tourist visa in the hopes of breaking into one of the local racing teams. The endeavour was less than successful, and I soon faced the prospect of having to return home. Thanks to – let's call her an entrepreneurial barmaid – and £50 in cash, I was able to get married and stay in Britain. Unfortunately, no racing deal was forthcoming and I eventually returned to South Africa at the end of that year.

Tersia – ever faithful – was waiting for me, and I decided to get married for the second time in the space of a little more than a year. This time, it wouldn't be for money. Not that it made any difference – marriage and me were a bad combination, no matter what my motivation was for walking down the aisle. If I have to be honest, I think guilt, more than anything else, played a role. Tersia had waited for me, and she was by now very friendly with my parents. And everybody seemed to like her. Marrying her seemed like the right thing to do, and what everyone expected.

However, I wasn't expected to start fooling around with a girl I worked with at Datsun. Over the next three years, my Datsun *skelm* was supplemented by a number of young women who also didn't seem too bothered about my marital status.

Not surprisingly, by 1974 I was, once again, divorced. Tersia hadn't suspected anything, but I'd eventually owned up. I told her about my mistress – her name was Dorothy Bridgens – and made it clear that I would probably mess her around for the rest of our lives, so it would be best all round if we called it quits. So I moved out and left her with everything – except, of course, my car. Naturally, I had bought Tersia her own car – what kind of a heartless bastard do you think I am? – and I let her have the flat and its contents. I didn't have too much back then, but I gave everything to her.

My confession had come as a bit of a shock to Tersia, but she was more disappointed than angry. She was a decent person who certainly didn't deserve what she got with me. I have no idea where she is now. It's been 30 years since I last heard from her. The last time I spoke to her was in 1982, when I was given a high-profile drive in a Porsche 935 at Kyalami. She phoned me. I had always told Tersia that I'd give my right ball to drive a Porsche, and she called on the Monday after the race to see if I still possessed both testicles.

To get back to the 70s, though: things were starting to happen for me in motor sport. Datsun had made me a works driver, and it seemed as if women liked nothing better than a works-team racing driver. Even if it was only for Datsun. I was still seeing Datsun Dorothy, but by no means exclusively. As far as women were concerned, I was a free agent. I was a night owl then, who would get up at four o'clock in the afternoon and then play all night – which is probably why I was so good at night rallying. I had my own apartment, but I also used to stay with Dorothy.

Dorothy didn't know about my other women, although she must have been stupid if she didn't suspect something, as I was always out. There seemed to be a *lot* of eager women in Pretoria, which included other men's wives.

Pretoria wasn't a big place back then, and I was now something of a public figure with a growing reputation both inside the car and out of it. To the extent that one husband even had a private detective follow me. I did happen to know his wife – pretty well, actually – and the guy was quite rightly starting to suspect something. Having a private dick follow me in a car, however, wasn't the smartest idea. I tend to drive pretty fast, which made the one other car on the road trying to keep up with me pretty easy to spot.

When I noticed this guy trying his best to stay on my tail, I purposefully drove up a dead-end street, did a handbrake turn and, as he came around the corner, accelerated right up to him. I asked him politely what he thought he was doing, but he got such a huge fright that he ducked.

I knew exactly who had hired him – I can't mention any names because the guy is still involved in the motoring industry – but the husband never took it any further and he never confronted me himself. He and his wife subsequently got divorced.

I, however, got married. Again. Dorothy was pregnant.

There I was, having a wonderful time, playing the field, and suddenly I find out I'm going to be a father. So, in 1977, marriage was on the cards again. My mother was also dying of cancer at the time, and she wanted to see me settled down. And she wanted grandkids, so getting married seemed the right thing to do. Which, of course, it definitely wasn't.

Dorothy and I went on to have two kids – Sarel, born in 1977, and Nicolene, born in 1982 – but marriage and fatherhood did nothing to curb my nocturnal activities. I was now doing well on the rallying scene, which just seemed to attract women even more – especially the married ones. They knew I was always available for some no-strings-attached fun … though there was the odd instance when a couple of the strings hadn't quite detached themselves. On one or two occasions, I had an irate husband to deal with …

I was having some fun with a woman who'd recently separated from her husband. They weren't quite divorced yet, but the deal was about to go through. Her husband decided to follow me one day, but not to her place – I was on my way to visit yet another chick. So the husband found out that I was also 'cheating' on his soon-to-be ex-wife, and he and a buddy confronted me in front of this other chick's place. They were pretty *hardegat*, but I could handle myself if they wanted to slug it out. I knew I could take both of them on, and I suspect they knew it too, because after a few threats and accusing me of being the cause of the divorce – which was bullshit – they eventually buggered off.

It wasn't pleasant, but I guess you have to be philosophical about the situation and take the bad with the good. Women were targeting me, which I didn't mind at all. As far as I was concerned, it wasn't too bad being a target, even if it meant putting up with a pissed-off boyfriend or husband now and then. It wasn't as if I was going out there to steal their women ... their women were coming to *me*.

Dorothy had no idea what I was up to. I always had some motor-sport function to attend – be it a rally prize giving or a sponsor's dinner – so I had a helluva lot of excuses. Coming home late was sort of an accepted fact, so my lifestyle simply carried on as before.

At one particular street race in Durban – it must've been in 1983 – these two girls were hanging around me. They were both very attractive young ladies, and I just couldn't make up my mind which one I should invite back to my hotel room. 'Fuck it,' I thought to myself, 'why not invite both? You never know, Christmas could come early.' I duly extended the invitation and, to my surprise, it was very quickly accepted. I love Christmas in Durban.

But then it all got very complicated. Apart from all the dalliances, in the late 70s I also started another relationship, with a woman called Barbara Mitchell, which carried on for many years. I now had a bit of a juggling act going on, because often I'd be at social functions that both women would attend. Barbara obviously knew about Dorothy, but my wife had no idea about my mistress. Ja, I'll admit this did add a certain element of excitement, but it was tricky. Whenever I went overseas and was expected to return with presents, I always bought the same gifts for both women so that I wouldn't slip up. If I bought perfume, I'd buy two of the same perfume, which I thought was pretty smart thinking – I'd never be accused of smelling of another woman's perfume.

But Dorothy eventually began to suspect that something was

up, and she began stalking me. She found out where Barbara lived and started hanging around the place, waiting to see whether I would pitch up. I realised what she was doing when I spotted her yellow Renault 5 in the area.

Then Barbara fell pregnant too. One could make a whole lot of SuperSperm jokes at this point, but we'll just let it go, shall we? In 1984 I became a father for the third time, to another girl, Nohline. Incidentally, both of my daughters were named after their grandmothers – my mother in Nicolene's case and Barbara's mother in Nohline's.

Obviously, I had to tell Dorothy – a conversation that understandably left her deeply upset – but we nevertheless decided to stay married. In 1981, Dorothy and I had moved from Pretoria to Port Elizabeth, mostly because Dorothy, having discovered Barbara's address in Pretoria, was putting pressure on me to leave town. I was driving for VW/Audi at the time, and their headquarters were in PE, so it made sense.

But what about Barbara? Well, SuperVan had that base covered, too. Prior to relocating Dorothy and the family to PE, I had secretly moved Barbara there too. Unbeknownst to my wife, my mistress was still living in the same postal code.

I was quite open about the situation with the motor-sport fraternity. Dorothy wasn't really into motor sport, so I'd often take Barbara along on the rallies. I suppose my behaviour put some pressure on everybody else in the team, as they obviously knew that I had a wife back home and the crew would also attend parties at my house quite often. So ja, we were a weird couple for Port Elizabeth, but at least I wasn't trying to hide anything. In fact, I was flaunting my affair, to be honest.

Today, with cellphone cameras and everybody tweeting this or face-bloody-booking that, it would've been a lot different, but it was such an open secret – even to the press – that it was hardly newsworthy. The whole rally scene, including the press, was quite close-knit. Although they didn't exactly protect me, they seemed to accept that that was just how SuperVan was – a bit of an arse-hole. Nothing new there, nothing worth writing about, end of story. I reckon if I'd pitched up at a rally *without* a chick, that would've been *real* news.

Racing drivers attract women – it's a fact, trust me. And just like I was leading the points table in the rally and race championships, I was also pretty much leading the 'Notches on the Bedpost' championship too. SuperVan does not like second place.

Franz Boshoff, my co-driver on rallies, actually kept a tally of my conquests, and when I hit 100 in the early 80s, he sent a telegram to my house that read: 'Congratulations on your ton. R10 000 says you won't repeat it in the same order.' Dorothy read the telegram and, not knowing what Franz was referring to, was keen for me to do whatever he was on about, as R10 000 was good money.

I don't know what the actual number was at the end of the day – I never kept score in a little black book – but I think the figure was fairly impressive. My success rate really took off once I started racing overseas.

As a big-name driver in the US and Europe, whole new continents of women opened up to me. Especially in the US, there were always groupies at the racetracks – something I have always regarded as a wonderful social phenomenon. One particular race stands out – it was in Del Mar, Texas – and one of the sponsors was a guy in his late 70s, or even 80s. Nice enough chap, but he wasn't nearly as nice as his 30-year-old wife. At the after-race party it was clear that she was up for some action, and once the old chap had had his glass of warm milk and had retired to bed, his wife and I ended up on his yacht anchored in the bay. It was a very memorable evening. Wonderful times.

I'm not saying I could have had any woman I wanted, but I never lacked for company. Wherever you went, there were always chicks around, and I even had some steadies in America as well. They were often married women whom I would hang out with on a regular basis. Whenever I was in town, I knew I could give them a call for some dinner and sport.

My behaviour might have been motivated by the fact that I didn't really have many friends to hang out with other than the people in the motor-sport world. All the guys would scatter back to their own houses after a race and I would be stuck there on my own. SuperVan certainly wasn't going to sit on his arse, twiddling his thumbs – that's for sure. Because I was in the States for such long periods of time – for months on end – I rented an apartment in Indianapolis, which was fairly central for me. This allowed me to develop a network of lady friends to help pass the time.

Occasionally I would take an American chick with me to Le Mans, because I'd fly to France straight from the States sometimes. My fellow drivers often referred to me as a man-whore. And only half-jokingly as well, the bastards. Jealousy, nothing more. I was getting more action than they were and, besides, I never accepted a goddam cent.

The great thing about the States, of course, was that there was little chance that news of my escapades would make it back to South Africa. This was before the days of digital media, and I knew it didn't matter whom I was photographed with, it would never see the light of day back home. Because of the apartheid-induced political pressure in those days, I never promoted my international racing exploits in the South African press, and most South African motor-sport fans didn't know how much overseas racing I was actually doing.

The status quo suited me just fine. It generated less political heat and I could indulge my other 'interests' too. America is also such a big place that the chances of running into anyone I knew who would spill the beans were extremely slim. It really gave me a wonderful sense of freedom.

American women really amazed me, I have to say. I had come

to know some fairly forward women in South Africa, but they were nothing compared to the ones Stateside. Maybe it was because Hollywood movies were often about affairs or scandals, but it certainly made the women pretty assertive. No complaints from my side, of course, as it made it even easier for me to operate. The chicks would just come up to me and say, 'Do you want to go to dinner?'

Of course, the subtext – if you could even call it a subtext – was, 'Okay, first you buy me dinner and then we'll have sex, okay?'

Yes sir, ma'am.

But back home, things weren't going so well. As these situations always do, my little threesome finally imploded in 1990. I was, of course, still enjoying the company of women other than my wife and mistress, but it got to a point where neither of them was prepared to put up with my shit any longer. They had both caught me out with other women on a couple of occasions. I remember one instance where I was due to drive a Porsche 962 at Kyalami and Dorothy surreptitiously followed me to the airport to see if Barbara would be with me. Turns out I wasn't taking Barbara but another woman.

Dorothy then gets on the phone to Barbara and says, 'Guess who your boyfriend is taking to Kyalami this weekend...'

When I arrived in Joburg and checked into my hotel, two phone messages were waiting for me – one from the wife and one from the mistress. The first one said, 'I hope you're enjoying your weekend with that slut,' and the second one said, 'How could you do this to me? Just stay out of my life.' Imagine the poor hotel receptionist fielding those two calls.

I'd been busted. What could I do? I mean, I was already in the shit, so why not spend the weekend doing the two things I enjoyed the most?

So by 1990 both Dorothy and Barbara had had more than they could take. Barbara had caught me in a restaurant with another woman, and Dorothy had instructed her lawyers to issue me with a divorce letter. It couldn't have been too pleasant for Dorothy, but I made no excuses about how I lived my life. She was certainly never short of anything; in fact, she had collected a nice little stash for herself. Whenever I went overseas, I used to just leave her a bunch of signed cheques, and a lot of those cheques found their way into her personal bank account. No doubt she was padding herself for the shit to come. Divorce was inevitable, and I think she was just biding her time. If it weren't for the kids, we would've split up way earlier. To be honest, if it weren't for the kids, we would never have married in the first place.

A long and pretty acrimonious divorce started when I got a letter from Dorothy's lawyers in 1990. According to the contents of the letter, because of all my philandering, Dorothy wanted some security in her life and demanded that I put the house, and everything we owned, in her name. Like *that* was going to happen. It was a predictable ploy – aim high and settle for a little less – but I wasn't biting. I ignored the letter, and eventually the lawyer phoned me to enquire whether I had received it.

'Yes, I have.'

'Oh. Okay. And what did you think?'

'What did I think? I think you, my friend, have taken leave of your senses.'

And with that we went to court.

Dorothy moved out of the house, back to Pretoria where her parents lived, and our bitter battle continued for two more years before we settled in 1992. She played the long-suffering wife with aplomb and spent most of that time telling anyone who would listen what a fucker I was. At the end of the day, Dorothy got a bit less than I had offered on day one, but the lawyers got about three or four times what she got. A two-year legal battle costs a *lot* of money.

Ja, it was a fuck-up. No other way to describe it. And of course, the kids suffered the most. Although I had access to my kids, with me in PE and Dorothy in Pretoria, I only got to see them on holidays. When I was up there racing, I would fetch them for the day, but as it wasn't a weekly event, it was hard for them.

So there I was. Three marriages, three divorces (let's not forget the barmaid). And a severely depleted bank account. You'd have thought I'd be more than a little reluctant to get involved with all that shit again.

Not … exactly.

A few months after my divorce was finalised, I got married for the fourth time. And, you'll be happy to know, I'm still married to her.

I first met Danielle Baard in 1988 at the Toyota Dealer Rally in the Western Cape. Her boyfriend was sponsoring the rally, but nothing happened between her and me, and I didn't contact her again until after I got the lawyer's letter from Dorothy's attorneys the following year. There was another race in Cape Town and I still had her number somewhere. So I phoned her, invited her out for dinner, and after that we stayed in regular contact. Danielle and I got on very well right from the word go, and it just felt like a fresh start for me. I could wipe the slate clean and begin all over again.

Dorothy had moved out of the PE house in November 1989, and that Christmas I had the kids with me for the annual holiday down at Nature's Valley. I flew Danielle up from Cape Town for the second part of the holiday. She wasn't the only surprise for my kids, though. They also met their half-sister for the first time. Nohline wasn't a secret, but Sarel and Nicolene had never met her before. Their mother had obviously fuelled a dislike in them for their sibling and, of course, there was a new woman too. It wasn't the most relaxed holiday I ever had.

Afterwards, Danielle moved to PE to be with me, and in September 1992 we got married. As I've said, we're still married today. I've got to give Danielle a lot of credit for that – she's made it work. God knows, I'm not marriage material. I think the odds on two people finding each other compatible enough to spend their entire lives together are practically impossible. I mean, there are seven bloody billion people in the world – how do you know you've found the right one?

Or, to put it another way – men make better friends with men than they do with women, right? Now imagine living with your best buddy for the rest of your life ... he'll inevitably piss you off, it doesn't matter how well you get on. How on earth are you expected to make it work with a woman?

I guess you've just got to graft really hard at it. But, even then, I'm still not convinced. Maybe polygamy is the answer. You might laugh, but look at old Walter Brün, the owner of the Brün Racing team, for whom I drove many a Porsche. Now there's a guy who has the best set-up I've ever come across. He owns a big property in Switzerland, on which he has two houses. At the top of the hill lives his wife ... and at the bottom of the hill, his mistress. When one of them pisses old Walter off, he simply goes and stays with the other.

Marriage is tough. And sometimes you have to try three times before you get it right.

Danielle knows my history with women – I've told her most of it. Clean slate and all that. The result is that she'll often meet women with whom I've been 'acquainted'. Sometimes we'll arrive at a motor-sport function and there'll be two or three women I'd previously been involved with. But it helps that Danielle grew up in the local motor-sport environment and had a fair idea of what went on when she met me. It's not as if I've gone into great detail about my life before I met her, but Danielle's pretty much up to speed. In fact, she's actually friendly with some of my exes, and sometimes they even enjoy a joke at my expense. Despite it all, I'm still mates with all the women I've been involved with. Except for Dorothy.

I'm still in touch with her – it's unavoidable with the kids –

but a fair amount of bitterness still exists and we keep our communication as brief and infrequent as possible. My son Sarel is close to his mother, so he's not as involved in my life as I would like, but I'm close to my two daughters. In the last 10 years, the two girls have actually become quite big mates. Nicolene is the link that keeps us all together. She's sort of my soul mate – we discuss everything, and she fills me in on all the family problems.

And that folks, is the story of me and the many women who have moved in and out of my life. I admit that I'm a bit of a fuck-up as far as the family-man ideal goes, but I'm getting better at it. Like I said at the beginning, as great as sex is – and it's bloody marvellous – it's also a very expensive business.

My first marriage cost me £50, my second everything I had except my clothes and my car, and while I managed to hang onto my house when my third marriage ended, it still hoovered up a large part of my bank account.

I'm definitely sticking this one out. It's cheaper that way.

9

THE GREAT CARS

The best cars we ever drove

When people ask me what my favourite racing cars were, they generally expect to hear about the all-powerful Porsches, Corvettes and Audis that I'd driven over the years. Sure, they were all great and they're all on my All-Time Best list, but there are also a number of lesser-powered racers that have given me as much pleasure.

The thing about racing cars is that it doesn't really matter how powerful the cars are or how fast they can go. Speed is relative, and if the rest of the field is doing similar speeds to you, you're going to have as much fun in a 100bhp car as you would in a 1 200bhp one. And I should know – I've raced both.

Here they are, in order of appearance...

THE DKWs

It was the car in which I started my motor-sport career, and the car in which I won that very first event I ever entered in Lourenço Marques. Not surprisingly, I've got very fond memories of this little German model.

The first Deek I raced was my mother's car – an 889cc DKW F12. It was a pretty little cream-coloured coupé that looked more part of the 50s than anything else on the track in 1967, when I raced it. It was fairly square in shape, with two round, eye-like headlights above the grill, and little fins at the back. DKW, along with the old car brands Wanderer, Horch and Auto Union, are the common ancestors of the Audi brand... hence the famous four rings.

My father had imported the car to South Africa because they weren't available here. My parents had travelled to Germany, where they bought a DKW, had then enjoyed a little road trip around the continent and afterwards shipped the car back home.

Despite being a bit long in the tooth, the Deek was still able to give the much younger Ford Anglias, Mini Coopers and Renault Gordinis a run for their money right up until the late 60s. Other than a bit of porting, we didn't have to fiddle with the engine to get more power out of it either. In those days, you just stuck on a set of Michelin X tyres and went racing. That was it – no tweaking or fettling whatsoever. And these weren't even racing tyres. The Michelin Xs were top-quality road tyres – basically the Pirelli tyre of their day – and they were both quick on the track and long-lasting – a crucial factor for cash-strapped privateers like myself.

We couldn't even change the suspension settings on the car, mostly because there weren't any suspension settings to change. The only thing you could do on a Deek was to adjust the torsion bar settings. The car had a torsion bar suspension up front, and you simply turned a nut to lift or lower the nose a little. That was the sum total of our 'modifications'. As long as the car didn't have any oil leaks, you were cleared to go racing. Not that this was ever a problem for the Deek – it didn't even have an oil tank. Instead, it had a two-stroke motor, so you just added a little oil to the petrol and that was it. The scrutineers didn't even bother to check for oil leaks and would just wave the Deek through.

Of course, safety wasn't much of a concern back then, so there was no roll cage inside. And even though you had to wear a helmet, seat belts weren't compulsory. I used a lap strap, which was basically just a belt that went around my waist and then around the back of the seat. It wasn't even attached to the car's chassis.

As the Deek was a front-wheel-drive car, understeer was its predominant characteristic, which meant you had to manage the throttle quite carefully. Asking the front wheels to turn in and also to put down the power was often one request too many, and the car would run wide. It did have disc brakes up front, which was quite an innovation compared to the Ford Anglias – not that you ever needed to use them much. The Deek had inboard disc brakes right next to the gearbox, but the car was so slow that to post a competitive lap time, you had to carry as much speed as possible through the corners. You hardly ever touched the brake pedal, so a set of pads would last a year. We didn't even bother fitting special racing pads – the Deek's original pads were good enough.

Besides that first hill-climb in Lourenço Marques, the first actual track race I raced in the Deek was a club event at Kyalami at the end of 1967. It was a handicap race, meaning the slowest qualifier starts first and, at timed intervals, the quicker cars follow. Eventually, the fastest car would leave around a minute and a half after the first guy. The theory was that everyone should arrive at the finish line at roughly the same time, making for some exciting racing.

And, as first races go, mine was certainly exciting – mostly because it rained. I was one of the faster qualifiers and thus started near the back. Also in his first race that day was Eddie Keizan, who went on to race many cars in South Africa – most notably in the local F1 series driving team Gunston Lotus 72. He would also start the motor-accessory business Tiger Wheel & Tyre. Eddie and I had a big dice that day, and I think I came sixth in the end.

I'd also compete in some races with my dad's friend Coenraad Spamer. Yes, that's him, the guy from the whorehouse in LM. He raced a Deek, and for some of the long-distance stuff, like the six-hour race in Maritzburg and the Springbok Series, he'd ask me to be his co-driver. In fact, the first time I raced at Killarney was in 1968, driving Spamer's DKW. It was an Index of Performance handicap race, so cars of all types could enter and have a chance of winning, based on a calculation related to engine capacity versus time taken. In the field were supercars like the Ford GT40, which would hurtle past us – SuperVan didn't mind, though. It gave him something to aim at.

I'd love to know where my mother's F12 is now – it would be nice to restore that car and keep it in my garage. Not that it's a car I'd like to drive nowadays. Despite my nostalgia, compared to today's cars, the DKW – like most cars of its day – was a pretty crap vehicle to drive. The car had a terrible gear linkage and, with all that understeer, it didn't handle well. I laugh when I see these classic car magazines go on and on about how great the old cars were. Some idiot writes a glowing piece on how sweet the handling of a car like an Alfa GT Junior was. *Please*. One of today's bakkies can out-handle it by miles.

I remember, for example, having had the opportunity to drive a 1950s 300SL 'Gullwing' Mercedes some time in the mid-1980s. The Gullwing was *the* supercar of its time, and it was basically a legalised version of the W194 300SL racing car that competed in the famous Mille Miglia and Carrera Panamericana road races. It was the car I had dreamt of as a young boy, and while racing in the States, I'd seen one for sale in California. The owner wanted $120 000, and I went to look at it. It's a beautiful car, and given its $1.5 million to $2.5 million value today, I should've bought it. But I didn't ... mainly because it was just so kak to drive.

For starters, its driving position was so cramped that the steering wheel – so big that it looked as if it had come from a bloody truck – had to tilt upwards just so that you could get in. Then you had to drive with this massive steering wheel that came right up against your chest. Ridiculous. The car also had this notchy gearbox, drum brakes with very little stopping power, *and* it was slower than a Golf GTi. I could drive it down to the shops to buy some cigarettes, but a long trip would have been a total pain in the arse. Old cars might be great to look at, but trust me, compared to today's vehicles, they're not that great to drive.

With the exception of the D-Type Jaguar. Now there's an old car that's fun to thrash around in. South African businessman Johann Rupert has one in his collection at the Franschhoek Motor Museum, and I've had the opportunity to get behind its wheel a couple of times. Rupert's car was the last D-Type that ever raced at Le Mans, and although it's also a surprisingly small little thing – with a huge steering wheel – that you don't really fit into, it was an exciting car to drive. It had a solid rear axle, which meant that it was always up for some sideways action, *and* they say the thing was capable of 280 km/h at Le Mans, so it was very quick.

But back to the Deeks. In 1968, a new 750cc championship for saloons was started in Natal – there were a lot of 750cc-engined cars like the NSUs around in those days – and I sold the DKW F12 and bought a 600cc DKW Junior from Spamer. The Junior was essentially the same car as the F12, just with a smaller engine – same shape, same gearbox, same handling. It wasn't that much slower than the F12, either – probably a second or so slower per lap – and, as always, the nice thing about the DKW is that you could do everything yourself. The three-cylinder engine was so small and light that, once you'd disconnected everything, you could lift the engine out on your own. The engineering was also pretty simple, so maintaining the car was easy to do yourself.

The Deek had forced me to become a proficient mechanic, as there was no money to pay a professional. My buddies and I did all the maintenance on the car. Everybody would pitch in, so there was a nice camaraderie around the little car as well.

The Deek and I won the Natal championship that year, which was something of a last hurrah for the car. It really was starting to get a little old by then, and cars like the Renault R8 were beginning to dominate the lower classes. You needed a real sports car to be competitive, and I just didn't have the money to buy one. So I turned to rallying and bought a second-hand Toyota. Yup, about as far from a specialised sports car as one could get. Still, it allowed me to rally over the weekend and still drive it to work on the Monday.

Deeks are few and far between now, but you can still pick them up if you look long and hard enough. I'm an honorary member of the DKW club, so I get their newsletter every three months. These days, though, it doesn't do much besides remind me of how old I'm getting. There's always news of some or other member who's died.

DATSUN SSS

Again, not a particularly powerful car, but another important car for me in terms of my career. The Datsun 'Triple S' is the car that put me on the rally map.

I drove more than one SSS – remember, I had the expensive habit of crashing my own cars early on in my rally career – and I bought the first one in 1972. That car didn't last too long, and then, pushing my credit limit to the max, I had to buy another. After my standard SSS and I beat national champ Lambert Fekken in his modified Ford Escort at the 1973 Pretoria News Rally, I was given an official factory drive by Datsun – again in a SSS. It was in this works car that I'd win my first national rally – the 1974 Duckhams Rally in Cape Town.

The car first came out in the 510 body shape – which was sort of square-ish – and later as the more round-backed 160U. The mechanicals were basically the same, though with a single over-head cam 1 600cc engine fed by two SU-type carbs. It was a very easy engine to tune and also very easy to work on. Which was great, because as a privateer I had to do it all myself.

It was ultra-reliable too, and although you could only rev it to about 7 000rpm, it didn't mind if you spent all day at those revs. There weren't gadgets like electronic rev limiters in those days, so you could over-rev the car if you weren't careful. But that wasn't too much of an issue. The car ran out of power high up, so it was always a natural gear change, as you'd sense that it didn't want to go any more. You didn't even need to glance down at the rev counter to know that you were close to 7 000. The power band was probably between 4 000 and 6 000rpm, but you needed to work the four-speed gearbox to keep it in that range, as the SSS didn't have much low-down torque.

In the works cars I drove later, we had a bit more power, thanks to two side-draught Weber carbs and a five-speed gearbox that was more like a close-ration racing gearbox as opposed to four long gears. Whatever the 'box, though, the SSS was an easy car to drive – it had a lot of traction at the back, which made it a naturally understeering car. This was a good feature on a rally car, as it meant you could really use the throttle to set the car up for corners. It also had a great suspension set-up, which was a big bonus, as in the standard class we had to use the same shocks and tyres with which the car came off the production line. This all made the SSS a much better rallying proposition than anything else available off South African showroom floors.

That ... and the price.

In those days, a new SSS cost something like R1 600 – about R1 000 cheaper than the other 1 600cc cars like the Alfa Giulietta Super and the Fiat Abarth, which were the other rallying options. With about a million Datsun dealers around the country, getting hold of spares was always cheap and easy. Plenty of spares were also available from the scrapyards, which was fortunate for me, as even though the SSS was super-reliable, during my privateer years I was still very much in the crashing phase of my rallying career.

The crashes were nothing too dramatic, and I'll tell you all about the big ones later. More often, it was a case of just going too fast, falling off the road, hitting trees, breaking the suspension and smashing the nose. I must have had at least seven or eight crashes in my own cars. They hurt my wallet more than anything else, and I always had to find someone to help me get the smashed car back home. I recall a particular instance during the BNU international rally when I crashed the SSS somewhere on the far side of Nelspruit. I lived in Pretoria, which meant that I had to go back by train, mobilise a rescue team consisting of all my buddies, get a bakkie, find the car, and then get it more or less mobile so that we could tow it back home. It was a pain in the arse, but the thrill of racing more than made up for it all.

There was one thing the Datsun SSS wasn't, though, and that was cool. By the early 1970s, Japanese cars had lost their cheap-and-nasty stigma and, like the Korean cars of today, South Africans began to regard them as reliable, value-for-money automobiles. Still, they never had anything close to the street cred of the European cars. But they won rallies. And for young SuperVan, nothing was cooler than that.

ALFA ROMEO ALFETTA

This is an especially important car for me. My motor-sport ambitions lay first and foremost on the racetrack, and, even though I was the national rally champion by this stage, it was the Alfetta that first verified my racing credentials.

In the history of South African motor sport, no one from the rallying fraternity had ever crossed over onto the track with much success. Guys like Jan Hettema would occasionally dabble as co-drivers in endurance events such as the Kyalami Nine-Hour, but none of them had established themselves on the track. I suppose it's much like current multiple world rally champ Sébastien Loeb. He's entered Le Mans a couple of times, but he hasn't actively pursued track racing much further than that.

Being the first to cross over successfully, however, was precisely the kind of goal that got SuperVan out of bed in the morning. Besides, there were so many nose-in-the-air, single-seater racing drivers – the likes of the Scheckters, Dave Charlton and Tony Martin – whom I was just itching to put in their place.

Aside from their little single-seater group hugs, these guys also raced in the saloon classes, which gave me the opportunity to go up against them. Being as tall as I am, it was never possible for me to race an open-wheeled, single-seater racing car. I simply could not fit into the cockpit. It always pissed me off that these guys reckoned they were the superior drivers just because they were in single-seaters. The Alfetta was the car that would help me readjust their world view.

Halfway through my second season as a works rally driver for Datsun, Alfa came along and offered me not one, but two racing cars: one to drive in the national Group N production-car class, and another in Class B of The Star Modified series. It led to all sorts of drama with Datsun, and despite accumulating the majority of my points in the Datsun SSS, I concluded the 1974 rally season rallying in an Alfetta ... and winning the title.

As a rally car, the Alfetta was kak, but as a racing car it was another story altogether. Racing two Alfettas in separate classes involved two sets of qualifying and races each race weekend. It wasn't a hassle – it was my idea of heaven. A whole, entire weekend filled with motor racing. *And* they were paying me. There was quite a big difference between the two cars – both in the way they looked and the way they performed. The standard Alfetta was, well, pretty much standard, with that beautiful-sounding, four-cylinder 1800cc Alfetta engine and road tyres. The other Alfetta was a different animal altogether ...

Aside from the flared wheel arches and front/back-end body mods for better aerodynamics, the modified Alfetta had up-rated brakes, a better racing suspension and a trick 1750cc motor supplied by Alfa Romeo's racing partners, Auto Delta. Compared to my standard Alfetta's motor, this one's power came from racing cams, special pistons and higher compression – in other words, a whole lot of expensive Italian shit; it all added up to going eight or nine seconds quicker per lap than the standard car.

This was also the first time I'd ever raced on slick tyres, and the amount of grip you had through the corners blew me away. I remember getting a massive fright the first time I drove shod with those grippy slicks. In a Group N car, you were forever hopping over the kerbs in an attempt to cut corners and set faster lap times. This was standard practice, and the cars just skipped over them. But when I tried it on my first lap in the slick-wearing modified Alfetta, the car reacted violently, ripping the steering wheel out of my hands. All that sticky rubber hitting a kerb was not a good idea. Instead of skidding over like the production car, the modified's tyres would grip and steer right up the kerb.

Once I'd sorted my lines out, and with the help of the car's superb brakes, I could jump on the anchors about 15 metres later than usual. And, with the extra grip the slicks provided, the modified Alfetta would blast out of corners faster than anything I'd been in before.

For once, I was also physically comfortable behind the wheel. The previous year, my car had been raced by team leader Arnold Chatz (he was now racing the Alfa GTV in Class A). And because he was also quite a tall chap, the seat position in the Alfetta was perfect for me. The only bad thing I remember about the car was the gearbox. For optimal balance, the 'box was located at the back of the car, with the gear lever up front. So the gearbox felt a little vague, because of the long linkages, but it never cost any time, as the 50:50 weight split that resulted from sticking the 'box at the rear of the car more than made up for it. Overall, the Alfetta was wonderfully driveable.

Its neutral balance made the Alfetta do anything you wanted, whether it was to oversteer or understeer. This even applied to the standard car, but on the modified version, it was all amplified. Ja, it was a wonderful experience driving that car. For the first time, SuperVan was in a piece of hi-tech automotive machinery and, with this superior handling machine, I was able to beat bigger-engined Class B cars, like Hennie van der Linde's V6 Capri and Ben Morgenrood's 4.1-litre Chev, on a regular basis. The Capris were my biggest competition, but with the big, heavy V6 in the nose of that car, their handling was always compromised.

By beating some of those recognised motor-racing names, the Alfetta also confirmed SuperVan's personal opinion that he was a racing genius. Finally, here was a car that could back up what SuperVan's mouth had been saying all along.

FORD ESCORT BDA MK II

This, by a Lowveld country mile, is my all-time favourite car. Not because of its power, or how quickly it went, or what it did for my career, but because of the way it handled.

I suppose it's ironic, given my love of racing, that a rally car would be my favourite, but the Ford Escort BDA was the ultimate driver's car. You could simply make it do whatever the hell you wanted it to do. You could manhandle it and chuck it around, but it always remained entirely predictable. It was almost as if it welcomed the abuse. I could spend the whole time driving on or over the limit in the BDA and not worry about anything – I knew that even if I overcooked it, with the right corrective inputs, the car would respond immediately. It was also a tough little bastard, and even if I hit a rock, I knew that the suspension wouldn't break or that anything dramatic would happen to put an end to my rally.

As I've said, I'd been desperate to get a Ford works drive just so that I could drive the Escort BDA. The Mk I BDA had been on the local rally scene since 1972, with Albie Odendaal and Lambert Fekken in the team. After that it was Hergen and Roelof Fekken, as well as the then reigning top dog, Jan Hettema, who enjoyed its favours. Many of the world's top rally drivers – the likes of Björn Waldegård and Hannu Mikkola – had all driven it, so it was an established and well-sorted car by the time I strapped on its seat belt. Fortunately, my two SA championships had convinced Ford that I was the future star to back, and they kicked Hettema off the team and offered me the drive.

Initially, it was a case of 'be careful what you wish for', and it took me a couple of rallies to familiarise myself with the Ford. Remember, I had finished the previous season driving a Chevrolet Chevair, which was a longer, heavier car that required much cleaner lines to be quick. The Escort was the complete opposite. I still recall the moment it all clicked. Interestingly, it was the moment the car fell over. I had cut a corner a little too closely, which bounced both inside wheels off the ground. I immediately lifted off the throttle – an instinctive response, but also the wrong one in the case of the Escort. The lack of power flipped the car onto its side.

At that moment, I understood that I simply needed to stay on the gas with this car. I would do it a million times in the following years – clip the corner but keep my foot planted on the gas. The car would simply slide out of the turn with one wheel in the air. The BDA was a very small, narrow car, so it fell over quite easily. I'll never forget one rally in the Lowveld – I can't remember which year it was – but I was having a pleasant dice with someone and the car again fell on its side ... but the momentum just kind of swung back and the car righted itself. It was as weird as it sounds, believe me. I got going again and won the stage. When I got back to the service area, Bernie Marriner, the team manager, wanted to know why there were so many dents on the side of the car. He thought we'd rolled it. When I explained what had happened, he told me that I was talking bullshit. I had to assure him that, while it was certainly true that I did sometimes try to bullshit him, this wasn't one of those occasions.

Once I'd got to grips with the Escort, it was as if the car had been made for me. Once you got used to driving it on the throttle, you could control everything with it, as opposed to using the brakes. You could set the car up for a corner and then control its entry angle purely by flexing your ankle on the gas pedal. If you wanted to turn a bit sharper, you just gave it more gas and it would turn in quicker. If you wanted to straighten it out, you simply lifted off a little. And then, by using the handbrake, you could basically turn the car within its own length, which made hairpin bends a breeze.

In later years, when I saw footage of the Scandinavians driving the Escort, doing their famous 'Finnish Flicks' to line the car up for corners and drifting it sideways around every bend from here to Helsinki, I realised I had been doing something similar. The local guys who'd driven the car before me hadn't cottoned on to the right way of driving it and didn't use the throttle as much as I did. I knew this for a fact. I had some of my mates record the sounds of our cars during night stages through the forest and it was unmistakable. You could hear when I was driving because my car was always in the rev power band. And given the twists and turns of a forest stage, that could only mean that I had the car sideways and was controlling it with my right ankle rather than with the steering wheel.

While the BDA had the same two-door body shape as the popular Escort 1600 Sport road car, the similarity ended there. Whereas the racing Alfettas I had driven – even the modified ones – still felt a bit like souped-up, road-going Alfettas, the BDA was nothing like its road-going siblings. This was an out-and-out rallying machine.

To give you an idea of just how good a car it was, I held the record for a stage that went down the Otto du Plessis Pass between Ida and Clifford in the Eastern Cape for nearly 30 years. I set the record during the 1981 Border Management Rally, and I think Enzo Kuun managed to better it only in 2009. Obviously, going uphill, a car like the Audi Quattro would've caned it with its four-wheel-drive traction, but downhill, the nimble BDA could outdrive even an Audi …

At the heart of the BDA was its wonderful 2.0-litre engine – the so-called BDA – which loved nothing better than to gulp air through two massive Weber carbs and scream abuse at its competitors to the tune of 9 000 to 10 000rpm. At first we had about 250 to 260bhp on tap, but towards the end we had 2.1-litres and closer to 270bhp to counter the power of the Opel Asconas. The Opel was more powerful and had more torque, but it was also a bigger, heavier car. The Escort only weighed about 1 000 kilograms. And we even managed to bring that down to 900 kilograms for the final lightweight version.

The car's power band ranged from about 4 000rpm to whatever you wanted. It could even rev to 11 000rpm if that was what you needed, though I'd usually never require more than 9 000. At the Reno Rally in the US, we crossed a dead-flat, seven-mile salt pan and I kept it on 10 200rpm the whole time. The car never even blinked. It also had an indestructible five-speed gearbox with a brilliant short-throw action that would keep you hooked into the ideal rev-range all day long.

There was one thing you had to watch out for, though: the kickback on the steering wheel. The full turn of the front wheels was from lock to lock, so if the wheels hit something at the wrong angle, the resultant whip-around of the steering wheel had been known to break drivers' thumbs. Obviously, SuperVan never hit anything at the wrong angle. When he hit something, the angle was exactly as he'd intended.

I drove that car for five very happy years, and our relationship only ended when Audi offered me the Quattro drive. The big German car with its four-wheel-drive system signalled the future of rallying, so I couldn't pass up the opportunity to drive it. Still, I can honestly say that I loved every second I spent in the BDA, right from day one. And I can't say that about any other car.

Of course it was easier to win in the Audi, and it was a more dominant and even a better car. And yes, if I was in an Audi and SuperVan was in the BDA, I'd kick his skinny arse. But I know he'd be having a lot more fun than me! Testament to my love for this car is the fact that I've just gone and bought one. I recently found an immaculate Mk II Escort for sale, and also managed to source an ultra-rare BDA engine. I still need to find a few other parts – the steering rack and gearbox – but once I've got those,

I'll have the car repainted in the Southern Sun livery of my original car. Then it's off for some fun in a couple of historic rally events!

AUDI QUATTRO

Ja, it's an iconic car, ja, it was a brilliant piece of automotive design, and, yes, it's probably the car most closely associated with me. And … and … and. There's no way I cannot list the Audi as one of my great cars. But I can't say that I loved it. In fact, I hold a bit of a grudge against the car. You see, the Audi Quattro screwed up rallying.

Make no mistake, the car was an engineering coup – within the existing World Rally Championship regulations, Audi had come up with what was essentially a four-wheel-drive road car adapted for rallying. It was the first turbo car in rallying, too. But the problem was, it forced everyone else to change to four-wheel-drive too, and with all this new grip, spectacular rallying went out of the window. If you think the WRC provides spectacular sliding, you should've seen what is was like when we only had rear-wheel-drive machines. Now *that* was spectacular. It's thanks to the Audi Quattro that the spectacle all but disappeared.

Still, one can't deny the Audi Quattro's iconic status. When it appeared at its first WRC event – the 1981 Rally of Monte Carlo – it was ahead of the game, and even though it would soon be superseded in Europe by the out-and-out rally machines developed by Peugeot and Lancia for the new Group B regs, in South Africa it remained utterly untouchable from the time I first rallied it in 1982 until Audi SA retired it in 1988.

It was just *too* good. I didn't have to work hard driving it, either. Whereas the BDA was exciting and you had to sit on the limit all the time to make it go fast, with the Audi everything sort of happened by itself. This was the first car that started to eliminate the driver from the equation – in a BDA, SuperVan was probably responsible for 75 per cent of the time it would set.

In the Audi, his contribution probably dropped to 60. He didn't like it much.

Perhaps I'm being a little too revisionist with my history. The Quattro wasn't totally brilliant; it did have its idiosyncrasies. Its main problem was its turbo lag. Those big, single turbos were nothing like the modern ones that are around today. The Quattro had serious lag, so you had to pre-plan every corner, as the power would arrive about a second after you summoned it. This was especially the case when you were gearing down for a corner – you'd stand on the gas and wait for the horses to arrive. You had to learn to anticipate the turbo lag, and in the beginning it was a bit disconcerting, but then you just adapted to it. Eventually, of course, it became second nature.

My approach with the Audi was to keep everything neat and clean – much the same as the tactics that international drivers Walter Röhrl and Stig Blomqvist used when they rallied the car. Like any 4×4, the Quattro had a natural tendency to understeer, so you had to set it up for corners, pointing the nose in early and then using the four-wheel-drive grip to pull you through. If you drove it like that, the car was very easy to control. On the odd occasion when, in a moment of BDA-like exuberance, I turned the car sideways, it was easy to correct. I simply had to feed in a little more power and the 50:50 power split between the front and rear wheels would straighten the car up faster than you could say 'lederhosen'.

Like the works team in Europe, through the years we were also given the various evolutions of the Quattro models. We started with the original 'A1', which was closely based on the actual road car, and ended with the winged S1 monster. The original 2.2-litre turbo engine was gradually persuaded to increase its original output of 320bhp to around 600bhp.

The car was immensely strong – you could hit a fridge and not really notice it. Perhaps its only weakness was some of the trick bits, like the turbo or the cranks, or the engine-management system that could play up. The Bosch management system was pretty finicky, and if we were competing in an event that included high mountain stages, we'd have to get there a day early to set the car up for the altitude. For the first time in my career, we had a computer expert on our team.

Driving such a dominant car would not normally have been tolerated by SuperVan for too long. As with the Wesbank series Audi I had driven on the track in 1989/90, competing in a car that was so obviously superior to the competition only provided him with short-term satisfaction. Yes, SuperVan loved to win, but if he was driving a car so good that anyone else on the grid could also win in it, then what was the damn point? No, being outshone by a car was not in the script.

However ...

I had had a change in attitude to rallying during that part of my career. SuperVan's main focus was now mostly overseas, so rallying had become of secondary importance to me. But the fact that I could pop back to South Africa and race in a rally suited me. It was a nice relaxing little break that almost always included a victory. If rallying had been my prime concern then, there's no doubt I would've left Audi and moved to another team with a lesser car. Personal satisfaction would have demanded it.

To give you an idea exactly how dominant the Audi was, during the 1983 Castrol Rally, I lost around seven minutes when the car had a turbo problem. To get back to the top of the leader board, SuperVan had to haul out his A-game. Seven minutes was a helluva gap to make up, even in an Audi Quattro. And remember, too, that the drivers ahead of me included teammate Geoff Mortimer in the sister car.

No problem. Game face on, no fucking around, right on the limit ... job done.

Although I enjoyed being in those situations with the Audi, they were, unfortunately, few and far between. In fact, so few and far between that sometimes I'd go balls-to-the-wall just for the hell of it. To spice things up a little, I'd throw in some ridiculous stage times that would just blow everybody's minds. The car could do it – especially the S1 – and it felt good to give it free rein for a bit. I was anything up to two seconds a kilometre faster than the rest – light years in rallying. During one 50-kilometre rally stage that included the Prince Alfred Pass between Knysna and Uniondale, I took a minute and 41 seconds off the next guy. A minute 41 … now that's really getting your butt kicked.

I nearly bought the last Quattro I drove. And I would have done so had I not suspected that I was being shafted. Audi initially offered the car to me for R125 000 – a lot of money then, but I was keen. Before the deal could be finalised, though, I had to race overseas, and when I came back, Audi had changed their tune. Apparently the car had been sent back to Germany because they wanted it in Europe. Understandably, I thought – it was an important and rare car, so of course they wanted to hang onto it as part of their history. But then, about three or four years ago, an Italian contacted me to say that he had bought the last Quattro S1 that I had driven for $250 000. Hmm. Now how the hell did that happen, I wondered …

So, ja, I have mixed feelings about this car. Although it was great to drive a machine at the cutting-edge of motor-sport technology – and from that point of view it will always be special to me – from a driver's point of view it certainly wasn't as great as the BDA. The Quattro could simply do too much on its own. And for SuperVan, that was the problem.

THE OTHER AUDI QUATTRO

Different Quattro … same issues. Again, I have to include the Audi 500–based Quattro that we drove in the Wesbank series on my list of great cars. But, again, I had a love-hate relationship with this car. It was an incredible piece of technology at the cutting-edge of racing development, and it won me plenty of races. But it also masked my abilities as a driver and, while I would tolerate that in a rally car, it would not pass muster with you-know-who on the track. Before this thoroughbred German – sourced from the American IMSA series – arrived on the scene, the Wesbank Modified class was a pretty close-fought affair, with the likes of Ben Morgenrood and Willie Hepburn in their Mazdas, Tony Viana in his BMW and Hennie van der Linde in the turbo-charged Nissan 300Z.

Audi were keen to establish their brand as a competitive alternative to BMW and Mercedes, which remained the car of choice for South Africans who wanted to buy luxury cars. With the technology that had been developed in racing and rallying now starting to filter down into production cars, Audi were beginning to make the kind of inroads that sees them – at the very least – on par with the other Germans today.

Their ambitions were obvious when they developed the race Quattro for the IMSA series' GT class. Although the US had a strong rally series, it was pretty small compared to Europe. All the marketing success and PR Audi had built in Europe with their Quattro rally programme meant bugger-all Stateside. You know what the Yanks are like – standing around somewhere in the countryside watching the odd car blasting past, covering you in dust, is not their idea of a good time. But sitting in your recliner in your underpants and string vest with a beer in one hand and a doughnut in the other, watching cars doing one big left turn around an oval racetrack ... now *that's* some damn fine motor racing right there.

Audi realised that they had to build a car that would catch these folks' attention – hence the Quattro. They dominated in the States right from the start. Their in-line, five-cylinder turbo engines made the Yank Camaros and Mustangs with their big V8s look positively antiquated.

When they first uncrated the car at Audi's Uitenhage HQ, its quality was immediately obvious. Everything just looked right, and so well put together. In fact, it looked very un-American for a Yank racing car. The Americans' cars were (and actually still are) not what you'd describe as cutting-edge. Aside from a couple of freaks here and there – the revolutionary ground-effects Chapparals of the 1960s, for example – American racing cars were built for reliability more than anything else. The Yanks' thinking never went further than 'V8' and 'build it like a brick shithouse'. The Audis, with their fancy flat-disc wheel covers and low side-skirts, must have induced plenty of cussing and spontaneous tobacco-spitting at racetracks across the Land of the Brave.

The Wesbank series' fairly liberal rules meant that we didn't have to change much on the Yank Audi for it to conform to local race regs. It did come with a six-speed gearbox, which was one cog too many for Wesbank, so we had to blank off the first gear to make it legal. In the States, they race on 115-octane fuel, but in South Africa it was 102 octane only. But because the Wesbank hierarchy realised the kind of interest these exotic machines would spark among local racing fans, they allowed us to run the 115 brew until the team could re-map the car for the 102.

Right out of the box, the car was a winner, as I mentioned earlier. A loose turbo pipe on the warm-up lap forced me to start from the pit lane in the car's very first race, but I still managed to pass the entire Wesbank field over one lap of the Kyalami circuit. Although the car's performance wasn't totally mind-blowing – I was racing far more potent cars overseas at the time – it was very, very quick for a saloon car. Add to that the superb balance and traction allowed by the four-wheel-drive system, and it was simply unbeatable … especially in the hands of SuperVan.

Even when the organisers started adding weight to slow the car down, I still had enough in my pocket to toy with the rest of the field and pretend to have a fairly close race. On occasion, some of my competitors suffered under the delusion that they could actually beat the Audi. It was my fault. I'd allow a guy like Tony Viana to take the lead a couple of times to make the race more exciting for the fans. Tony would think that he was now actually in the mix, but then down the main straight, or under braking,

I'd just blow right past him. Most of the time I found the drive a bit boring, to be honest. I couldn't ever unleash the car during a race – it would have given the game away.

I'm not saying that the Audi didn't have the potential to be exciting. During testing, when no one else was around, I could go flat out during a lap, and the car was then another beast altogether – it was hugely exciting when the massive four-wheel drift slid around the corners. Driven to its limit, it was plenty exciting ... I just couldn't drive it like that in a race. If I did, I would have disappeared into the distance.

The Audi was probably three seconds a lap quicker around Kyalami than any other car, though the others would eventually catch up. Audi dragged the whole Wesbank circus up to a new level. Ford upped their game with the Cosworth Sapphire, Ben Morgenrood then pitched up with the multi-rotor Mazdas, and after two seasons everyone's average lap times had gone up by five seconds.

As boring as it may have been to drive most of the time, you have to give this Audi its due – it did a lot for South African motor sport. Morgenrood has even said as much. He told me in later years that the Quattro and SuperVan's appearance in Wesbank had done a helluva lot to raise the bar in a very short period of time. And the local scene had got a little incestuous by then – all the cars were evenly matched and content to play with each other every second weekend. Local racing needed new blood, which the Audi certainly provided, and more. First one manufacturer responded, then another, and the next moment we had some real action taking place.

By the time I left Audi for Ford, their Sapphire was close to taking on the once unbeatable German. I doff my pom-pom-adorned, tartan flat cap in the Audi's direction ... the car had a major influence in this country. And it burns SuperVan's balls to say this, but it would've had a big influence with or without me.

MARCH-PORSCHE 83G

Up until 1982, the fastest racing car I'd driven was the modified
Ford Escort V6 in the Manufacturer's Challenge series. However,
thanks to Danny Chauvier's forward-thinking marketing plan
for his fledgling Kreepy Krauly pool cleaner, I would get my
first taste of serious, underpants-staining horsepower. Chauvier's
sponsorship initially got me a ride in Giampiero Moretti's wild
Porsche 935 Moby Dick at the 1982 Wynns 1 000-kilometre
World Sportscar Championship race at Kyalami. With its flat-
six turbo engine, long rear bodywork and huge whale-tail rear
wing, this was easily the most exotic piece of machinery I had
ever driven.

Based on SuperVan's driving ability and some good press coverage, Chauvier extended my stay to a full season in 1983, when
I competed in IMSA's GTP class. And, based on my performance
there, in 1984 we bought the car that would really make my name
among the elite of world sports-car drivers ... the March 83G.

The British-designed March had first appeared in 1982, where,
powered by a Chevy V8, it came second at the 12 Hours of
Sebring in the hands of Bobby Rahal and a couple of other drivers
(whose names I could never remember. Google them. I did. They
were nobodies.) In 1983, at the hands of the very talented Al
Holbert, the March won the IMSA GTP-class championship –
it was this very car for which Danny Chauvier would stump up
the cash.

The March 83G gets a place in my 'great cars list' for two
simple reasons: first, it introduced me to the amazing handling
characteristics of ground-effects aerodynamics. On its underside,
the March had a tunnel running the length of the chassis, which
was typical of ground-effects cars. It was just incredible around
corners – the faster you went, the more downforce it produced
and the better it stuck to the asphalt. A car like the 935 Moby
Dick would start sliding as you dialled in the corner, which
would make you come right off the throttle. But with the March,

you'd still put foot to pedal and the car would simply stick to the ground and bullet through the turn. I am talking about speeds in excess of 20 km/h faster than what I was used to in the 935 Moby Dick.

Going around bends at that speed required two elements: a different mindset and a big pair of balls. It was counter-intuitive entering a corner at that speed, and everything I had learnt about racing up until that point told me that the March would slide off into the kitty litter. During my first practice in the car, I latched onto the back of another March out on the track and stuck to its bumper around the twisty bits. It really accelerated my learning curve.

The best tactic was to pick a driver you knew – one who was normally a little slower than you – and follow him for a lap or two to see what he did. If he went through a corner flat out, then it must be okay to follow suit. From there I would find my own cornering limit in the car. Initially I tried to keep my exit line as tight as possible so that I would still have plenty of track in hand, but I'd gradually increase the corner speed and brake later, which pushed the March wider and wider each time I went through. Eventually I'd know exactly what the car's limits were.

I've always thought that this method was the quickest and safest way to learn both about a new car and a new track. It took no more than one practice session before SuperVan knew exactly what the March could do.

The second reason why the March 83G makes the list is that this car, more than any other, established my name as a racing driver. And it took just one race – the 1984 24 Hours of Daytona – to do so. This was also my first race in the car, and it didn't take me too long to get the hang of it. I qualified second on the grid without taking any major risks, and then, for the first hour of the race, had a full-on dice with Mario Andretti. Andretti was the superstar of Yank racing at the time. He'd won the Formula 1 crown with Lotus in 1978 and remains one of only two drivers to win races in F1, IndyCar, the World Sportscar Championship and NASCAR.

It was a massive moment in my career, not only because it put me in the spotlight, but also because, in my own head, I now realised that I was at least as good as the big boys. Obviously SuperVan always thought this was where he belonged, but thinking it is one thing and proving it another altogether.

In the Moby Dick Porsche, I'd felt that I could compete with all the other guys in similar cars, but in 1983, the ground-effects cars would just blow by me. I wasn't completely sure how much of their success was down to the car and how much to the driver. A guy like Al Holbert, who won the IMSA championship in 1983, would pass me whenever he felt like it.

Until then, SuperVan had also – uncharacteristically – taken a back-seat approach to racing in the US. Back home it was fine to make a helluva noise and remind everyone of just how good I was, but in the States, I had yet to produce the goods.

With my first race in the March, however, I staked my claim in no uncertain terms. In that first hour, swapping the lead with Andretti, I wasn't really thinking about what was happening, as I had so much to do behind the wheel, but once I got out of the car following my initial driver's stint, I thought, 'Fuck me, I'm *here*. I can take all these guys.'

My feelings were confirmed once I got behind the wheel again later. By this time, my colleagues had dropped the car back down to ninth, but once I was strapped in again, I got us back into the top three, and then in my final stint, into the lead, which I held until the chequered flag…

At the time we bought it, the March was a very good car, and it remained so until halfway through 1984. That's when Porsche got their 962 sorted, which then dominated the IMSA. Our March was also powered by a Porsche flat-six turbo engine, but being smaller and narrower than the big Porsches, it was actually quicker in a straight line. Where the Germans had our number, though, was in the handling department. Their ground-effects aerodynamic package was more advanced, and the 962s could not only out-brake us, but their mid-corner speed was superior too.

PORSCHE 956/962

It wasn't the most powerful sports prototype I ever drove – that honour goes to the Chevrolet-Corvette GTP – but it was the closest thing I'd experienced to the perfect endurance racer. The 956, for the non-petrolheads, was the first generation of Porsche's new closed-cockpit, twin-turbo World Sportscar Championship race car. The 962 was the revised and updated version. I only raced the 956 once, and that was at Le Mans in 1984 – the 962 made its debut that same year.

The transition from 956 to 962 came about when the IMSA crowd in the US banned the 956, as it didn't meet their safety rules. The foot box and the driver's feet needed to be behind the car's front axle – pretty much standard practice in race cars these days – and, as a result, the 962 had a slightly longer wheelbase. Unless you knew what to look for, though, you could barely tell the difference between the two cars. The most obvious difference was the turbo exhaust outlets, which were just behind the doors on the 956. The 962 also had a slightly elongated nose compared to the 956, but there were many front-end bonnet and wing incarnations in the 962 through the years, depending on which series the car was being driven in.

Whatever designation you were driving, there were two things that made this car stand out above all others: the build quality; and the handling.

Like any other Porsche – whether my father's old 356 or the current 911 – the 956/962 gave you that special Porsche feeling. It felt bomb-proof. The quality of the Porsche's build was the result of the finest automotive engineering. It wasn't some fast-but-fragile thoroughbred that needed to be treated with kid gloves – it was a rock-solid car that was so well designed that it could idle away all day like a diesel saloon but also do 385 km/h down the Mulsanne. No starter button here either … you started the engine with a key.

And this build quality was not enjoyed by the factory Porsches only. Oh no. Aside from the 1988 works drive I'd experienced at Le Mans, I spent my career in privateer Porsches, and they were equally well put together. And Porsche was also always ready to help the privateers. Spare parts were readily available if you needed them, and the Porsche guys were happy to give you information on what the factory team was running. They would tell everybody what settings their team was planning to run for a particular track and, using that as a base, everybody would then fine-tune their set-ups. And then there was the handling …

Although it was right up there with its rivals in brake horse-power, the Porsche wasn't necessarily the most powerful car on the grid. The 956 started life with a 2.7-litre, twin-turbo engine, good for around 620bhp, and it eventually morphed into a 700bhp, 3.2-litre, twin-turbo in the 962C. The real difference between this car and the rest of the cars on the track was the way it went around corners.

The way it handled the corners was a combination of the chassis' wonderful ground-effects aerodynamics and the drive-train's locked differential. The ground-effects downforce was just phenomenal. The car was literally sucked to the track with such force that they reckoned you could drive it upside down at 165 km/h. Whereas the Kreepy Krauly March would start to get a bit twitchy when you really laid on the power, the Porsche exited a corner like it was on rails. When I was driving the March, I'd closely follow a 962 into a corner only to see it turn on the power five to 10 yards ahead of me and create an instant gap. Not much one could do about that.

Then, of course, you had the locked diff, which made both back wheels turn at the same speed. This was ideal for high-speed action and made the car very stable. But in tight corners, you had to be sharp. All the traction at the back had the potential to over-whelm the front wheels' ability to turn and you could get under-steer if you applied the power too easily.

It was something you had to get used to, which wasn't too difficult, considering that the ground effects allowed you such higher-than-normal entry speed into corners. You didn't need much throttle until you were on your way out of the turn. The Porsche was also a pretty physical car to drive – it generated high G-forces as a by-product of the grip it had through the corners, which didn't only make it tough on your neck, but also made the car heavy to steer through the bends. And the car wasn't equipped with power-steering, so it was tough on your hands, forearms and shoulders.

All of the above was entirely manageable, though. Endurance racers were a tough bunch, and SuperVan was one of the tough-est. Seriously. I had a rep as one of *the* tough guys on the circuit. In that first year at Le Mans, in 1984, I ran over some debris on the track belonging to an Aston Martin. I was in the 956. The press had made a big hoo-ha about the legendary British marque's return to Le Mans that year, but both Nimrod-Aston Martins failed to finish. One of the cars, driven by Brit John Sheldon, came off through the Mulsanne Kink, smashed into an Armco, killed a French marshal and burst into flames. Although he survived the accident, Sheldon was badly burnt.

The debris I ran over was from this crash. A shard of metal sliced through the Porsche's floorboard ... and my leg. It hurt like hell, but this was my first Le Mans and nothing was going to get me out that car. I finished my stint, coming into the pits with blood all over my overalls.

Some years later, racing at Dijon in France, we were struggling in qualifying. Hoping that one last, kamikaze-style effort would move us up a little further, I was sent out for a flyer. Unfortu-nately I spun the car, which went backwards into a barrier. It caused so much damage to the car that it had to be repaired before qualifying was over, which meant that the rest of my team didn't get to qualify. And that meant they couldn't race. If the team was to rack up any points, I'd have to drive the entire 1 000-kilometre race on my own – which I proceeded to do.

That was me and the Porsche 956/962. A bit like Clint and his horse ...

Actually, I might be selling the car short. Testament to the Porsche's greatness was how competitive it was over its long lifespan. When it first arrived on the scene in 1982, it was a game-changer, and it remained competitive right up until the mid-90s, when a 'road-going' Dauer 962 (based on the Porsche racer) exploited the new Le Mans rules to win the race.

As a proper race car, the Porsche 962 didn't really have any competition until 1990, when Mercedes-Benz came on the scene with their C11. Yes, Jaguar's new-era, carbon-fibre XJR series cars did win a couple of Le Mans in that period, but they were never a consistent threat. For over a decade, the Porsche 956/962 was *the* car to beat ... and in motor-sport terms, that's phenomenal.

FORD MUSTANG

This is one car I really regret selling. Of all the cars I've raced in my career, I actually only owned a handful – and of that handful, it's the Mustang I wish I'd kept.

When I first drove it in 1994, I didn't own the car. I'd persuaded Ford that in order to put those damn Audis in their place and win the championship, we had to stop farting around with turbo-charged nonsense and get ourselves some honest horsepower. We needed a V8. And not just any V8, but one that gulped gasoline, smoked cigars and laughed in the face of the newfangled European 'hairdryers'.

I've told you about my conversation with US team owner Jack Roush, and it was thanks to that chat, and a trip to see him in Detroit, that for once we had ourselves a real Wesbank contender. Sure, we'd win races in the Cosworth Sapphire, but with the weight penalties Dick Sorenson and the other geniuses running MotorSport SA added onto it, the Sapphire couldn't string enough wins together for a proper run at the championship. Its turbo just didn't have the balls to deal with the extra weight. Yes, it gave you a lot of power, but you only had that power for a short space of time, and the delivery of said power was usually preceded by the Big Lull that is turbo lag.

The Yank V8, however, was definitely not lacking in the testicular department. You had a truckload of horses that rang your doorbell from as little as 3 500rpm right through to 8 000rpm. And that equated to real, usable, tractable power. This amount of torque also meant that the inevitable weight penalties old Dick would hand us didn't really cause a problem, as the car had the power to shift it.

These V8s were also bomb-proof. In all the years I ran these engines, I only ever blew up one. And it wasn't so much a detonation as a mild seizure – I suspect the engine hadn't been screwed together properly. As long as you did the proper preventative maintenance, like changing valve springs and rockers once or twice a year, the car won us races in the day and fetched our slippers at night. It was a Wesbank racing driver's best friend. Engines cost about R100 000 each back then, which might seem pricey even today, but given the bang for your buck it delivered, the racing V8 remained the cheapest source of horsepower out there.

The construction of the chassis also mirrored the engine's 'no fancy shit' approach. It was an aluminium space-frame with a couple of carbon-fibre bits here and there, but that was all. Besides the fact that carbon fibre cost the earth back then, there was little point in using this exotic light-but-strong material on the car. Dick et al were only going to fill it with lead anyway.

We saw the car for the first time when it arrived ahead of a race at the East London circuit. It was still wearing the battle scars of its final race at Daytona, where the Roush team had won the IMSA GT class championship. We didn't even have time to re-map the engine so that we could use the 102-octane fuel the Wesbank rules decreed. I hadn't planned on racing the car that weekend, but after putting our usual car – a turbo-powered Cougar – on provisional pole just 0.1 seconds ahead of Terry 'The Muppet' Moss, I decided to take the Mustang out for a little lap or two to see what it was capable of.

Fortunately MotorSport SA, in a rare instance of actual assistance, agreed to let us use 115 octane, as they did in IMSA, and with the car's worn US tyres, and only on my second ever lap in the car, I posted a time a full second ahead of Moss's effort in his Rothmans Audi. You should've seen his face.

And you should've seen SuperVan's face.

Right then, I knew we had their number ... and so did the Audi boys.

I have to credit the Sasol team at this point. Our sponsors' technical department then worked miracles to brew some 102-octane fuel that would still make the car run at the same speed as if it were drinking 115-proof. I don't know how they managed it, and we didn't want to ask, but let me tell you, it did the business.

I won the championship that year despite all the added weight we had to carry through the season because of our strong results. As I'd predicted, the V8 could more than handle the 250 kilograms of lead we were saddled with. Naturally, the Audi contingent couldn't help themselves and moaned plenty about how the car was just too fast for the formula, or that there must definitely be something illegal about it.

The only illegal aspect of the car was its 46-year-old driver who had 'SuperVan' stitched on his underpants.

To counter the whingers, SuperVan issued a little challenge. And I quote ...

'Okay, you arseholes with your Audis – yes, *you* – let's take all the weight out of all the cars and have a proper dice. There's a club race in East London coming up; bring your German autobahn cruisers and we'll have a free-for-all. Being the big-hearted guy that I am, you two can start at the front of the grid, and I'll start behind.'

No one wanted to take me on.

The downside of our championship win was that suddenly it looked as if the Wesbank crown might have been a one-hit wonder when Ford made the unfortunate decision to enter the SA Touring Car formula. Audi had earlier announced that they were moving across, and I guess Ford didn't want to stay in Wesbank without some real competition.

Peter Lindenberg bought the Mustang from Ford. Although he didn't win any championships in it, knowing the Mustang's potential, I kept my eye on its whereabouts. Lindenberg had re-bodied the car with a later Mustang silhouette, but it was still the same chassis underneath the new clothes. When I finally returned to Wesbank in 2000 as the owner of my own team, I knew there was only one car I wanted. With Sasol's backing, I had the cash to persuade Lindenberg to return the Mustang to its spiritual home, and back behind the wheel, I won two more titles, in 2000 and 2001. Not bad for a nine-year-old car.

I never really get emotional about the cars, but I was quite sad when I sold that Mustang at the end of 2001. It wasn't even starting to feel its age, either – the chassis felt as tight as the day we first got it – but I needed money to help finance the two Opels I wanted to buy for the 2002 season.

I think I sold the Mustang for something like R300 000, which was a bargain, considering that the engine alone was worth R100 000. I don't know what happened to the car; I hope somebody had the sense to keep it. As I mentioned earlier, that person should've been me.

CORVETTE GTP

Perhaps not my favourite car, but the big 'Vette was certainly the most impressive car I ever drove. In fact, I'm still not entirely sure how I got to drive it in the first place. My ability as a driver was not the issue – the previous year I'd won two IMSA races, including Daytona – but politics and public relations were in the mix. And they are not exactly two of my favourite things.

These were the dark days of apartheid, remember, and it wasn't easy for South African sportsmen and women to compete overseas. Corporate America was very aware of its public image, and for them to have a South African driver leading in a General Motors factory effort was pretty brave of them. The Corvette team had earlier hired my ex–Kreepy Krauly March crew chief Ken Howes – also a South African – which probably helped pave the way for me.

Whatever their reasons, there was no denying that Super-Van was one of the quickest guys around. So in late 1985, the deal was done without the team, or indeed the US press, mentioning any political issues for the duration of my three-and-a-bit-year tenure in the team. GM even used me for the public launches of their new Corvette road car, and various American books and magazines published some of the articles I wrote. So it wasn't as if they were trying to hide me away.

There was certainly no hiding the car's horsepower. In qualifying, under full boost, the V6 turbo engine was good for 1 200bhp. To put that into perspective, a current Formula 1 car has in the ꞌ of 780bhp. That's around 40 per cent less horsepower ᴛ ꞁ ꞁᴇ 'Vette. There are only a handful of racing drivers in the world who have ever had that much power under their right foot. Aside from the legendary 12-cylinder turbo Can Am Porsche 917/30 of the 1970s, and possibly the Brabham BT52 turbo F1 car in 1983, nothing else has come close.

The actual V6 was quite a small engine, pretty much dwarfed in the engine bay by the huge turbo and all the plumbing required to make it work. As you can imagine, getting so much power from such a small engine meant putting the engine under huge stress. That Can Am Porsche, for example, is always held up as one of the most powerful racing cars ever built, but its 5.4-litre

German engine only produced 222bhp per litre. Our little Ryan Falconer–designed V6 managed 353bhp per litre. The only way Falconer could prevent the V6 from blowing its own head off was to literally clamp the thing together with long bolts that ran from top to bottom.

With that engine, the Corvette was a tough bastard to drive. At 1 200bhp, the tyres couldn't cope and, especially on tight US circuits like Sears Point with its many corners, they wouldn't last one qualifying lap. Seriously. You'd lose so much rubber on the rear tyres that it was a case of deciding which part of the lap to save them for.

I often get asked if being behind the wheel of a car like the Corvette was intimidating. Not at all – for SuperVan, it was a huge amount of fun. Especially qualifying. At the time, there would be a first qualifying session where everyone would go out and set times, and then the top 10 would go out and battle for pole position. To up the ante, there was always a nice carrot in the shape of a wad of dollar bills for the top time.

The top 10 would go out in reverse order from the times they'd set in the initial qualifying session, so most of the time I would go out last. The 'Vette was the most reliable car in race trim, but in qualifying it was one of the quickest in the field. I loved the tension of those qualifying shoot-outs. The spotlight was on you, and you knew you had to go out and produce something special. At the time, as I was sitting in the car, I would be thinking, 'What the hell am I doing here, putting myself through all this stress?' But as soon as I was out on the track, the adrenaline rush would make it all worthwhile.

Another factor that didn't help the 'Vette's handling – and this is a fairly strange thing to say about a racing car – was its looks. The GM marketing idiots were hell-bent on the Corvette actually looking like a Corvette ... even if it compromised its handling. You could just see what they were thinking: 'We want people to recognise the car going around the track as a Corvette, because then they will walk into the dealership on Monday and want to buy one.'

Right. That seems like good, solid marketing philosophy – if such a thing exists – but what happens if the road car's body shape was actually preventing the racing car from doing well? By insisting on the 'Vette-shaped schnozz, we were stuck with a pointy-nosed car that developed precious little downforce. Not great when you have 1200bhp harnessed to your arse. We tried to persuade GM to slope the bottom of the nose inwards, like the Porsche 962, but they would have none of it. We tried all sorts of little winglets to generate every gram of downforce we could, but it never made a big enough difference.

Staggeringly stupid. I mean, it's not as if the car actually looked anything like a road-going Corvette in the first place. Go and look at the picture in the photo section of this book.

See? It looks nothing like a 'Vette.

According to the marketers, though, the American public reckoned our racing car did indeed look like the road car. Yanks … they're not the brightest. If you told them the car looked like a Beetle, they'd probably also nod their heads in agreement.

Still, SuperVan shouldn't be dismissive; it was nice to have their support. As an American outfit, we were definite crowd favourites. So what if most American motor-sport fans were fat, red-faced, beer-drinking good ole boys only marginally slimmer than their wives – it was great to hear them roar from the stands whenever we passed a German Porsche.

That Corvette really had championship-winning potential – it's a real pity that GM got their marketing types involved and never chose to develop the car. Nissan essentially took over the development of the Lola chassis, and it underpinned their GTP ZX-T car that would give Geoff Brabham a hat-trick of championships between 1988 and 1990. Worst of all was GM's insistence on using that useless Cadillac management system. It just made a very thirsty car even thirstier. I tried to point out that even NASA had used German management systems when they went to the moon, but that didn't seem to go down too well.

You're right; I do have a funny relationship with the Germans. When I'm in one of their teams, benefiting from their cutting-edge automotive technology, I get pissed off because winning comes too easily. Yet when I'm in other teams, I try to convince them to get the German goods. It's tough to read SuperVan's mind. Especially when it's hidden behind that black visor ...

10

THE SORRY STATE OF AFFAIRS THAT IS MODERN MOTOR SPORT

It's the chapter where I have a really big moan. I like this chapter

The main problem with motor sport these days is that not enough people are dying.

Let's face it, racing is a fundamentally hazardous activity. It's a blood sport. In its pure form, you have a swarm of cars driving very fast around a racetrack, piloted by a bunch of A-type personalities more than happy to take a risk or two. Under these circumstances, Death often buys a ticket to the grandstand. The drivers know it and, most importantly, the spectators know it. It's why they join Death in the expensive seats.

Along with the excitement of watching these modern-day chariots charge around an asphalt arena comes the added spice of a potential crash and the associated drama. I'm not saying that race fans actually want the drivers to die, but they certainly do want to see the kind of close, committed racing that will probably result in an accident. Of course, it's sad if a driver does get seriously hurt and, occasionally, require Death to leave his seat, but that comes with the territory. To be quite frank, if somebody dies on a racetrack, at the next round there are twice as many people.

As least that's how it used to be.

Nowadays I think everyone's forgotten why they are racing in the first place. It's become like Scalectrix. In the grainy, black-and-white old days, the guys were driving around in cloth caps and short-sleeved shirts. Then came helmets, followed by roll cages, and now there are carbon-fibre safety cells.

It seems as if there are a helluva lot more rules, and it's making everything more expensive – to the point where you can't even wear an overall that's older than three years without the authorities running through the pits waving their clipboards in the air. These things cost thousands of rands, and all they do is keep adding to the cost. Add to the cost and you have fewer competitors. Fewer competitors equals less excitement, which means fewer spectators. And without them, the sponsors pack up their tents and move on. And when that happens – as it has in South Africa – you might as well park the cars in the garage and take up bowls.

Consider the polar opposite of South African motor sport – NASCAR. This American series is massively popular. On the face of it, going round and round a banked oval track doesn't make for an exciting prospect. That's certainly true from a driver's perspective, too. It doesn't take too much skill to turn left for 500 miles. But fans love it. It's the number-one spectator sport in the US and attracts more fans to its races than any other sport in the States. Yes, even more than the numbers attracted by that odd game the Yanks play with the helmets, padding and small rugby ball.

The reasons are simple: first, the racing is very, very close. Several cars will lead proceedings throughout the day, and it's rare for anybody to win two races in a row; second, there are crashes. Lots of them. Even SuperVan will grudgingly admit that that's some exciting shit right there.

The NASCAR cars are relatively simple machines – no more than a steel-tube, space-frame chassis, aluminium bodywork and a big V8 engine up front. Built for strength more than anything else, they're heavy and unwieldy when they get off the racing line, and they'll spin for a couple of kilometres should the car's butt overtake its nose.

The upside of their burly construction means that, unlike F1 cars, they can kiss the wall without disintegrating in a shower of carbon fibre and, more often than not, carry on with the race. And then, of course, when things really get out of hand – which is not unusual when a field of 40-plus cars is driving nose to tail at 320 km/h – there can be an almighty pile-up from which drivers usually walk away with a smile and a wave to the crowd.

And that's the other thing about NASCAR – the crowd can get a lot more involved. Sure, you can sit up in the stands with your tray of supersized fast food and watch the cars, but you can also walk down to the pits where (and the F1 crew might want to avert their eyes at this shocking revelation) you can actually talk to the drivers.

Drivers in most of the world's top formulas are removed from everything. They're removed from the fans and, worst of all, they're removed from their cars. And what I mean by that is that technology has played an increasing part in the overall perform-ance package of car and driver. Winning a championship used to be mostly about the driver's ability, but these days it's all about the car.

Look at F1 at the moment – sure, Sebastian Vettel is a very talented driver, but the only reason he is dominating Grand Prix at the moment is Red Bull Racing's technical guru, Adrian Newey. Newey is a genius when it comes to F1 car design, so Red Bull is just streets ahead of the rest. Vettel himself isn't streets ahead – I reckon Fernando Alonso's probably the pick of the bunch – but Vettel's car certainly is.

On the two occasions where I was behind the wheel of a car far more advanced than the competition – and I'm talking about those two Audis – I began to resent it. People couldn't see how good *I* was; they only saw how good the Quattros were. In F1 these days, it's the battery of engineers behind the pit wall who are making the real difference out there on the track. Every season it becomes less and less about the driver and more about the tech. At the end of the season, the big, shiny trophy should go to the designer of the car, not the driver.

I know that everyone's saying how exciting the 2011 F1 season was with all that overtaking, but I think it's utter bullshit. For one, no one was overtaking Vettel, and, secondly, F1 supremo Bernie Ecclestone and his cronies resorted to artificial means to make racing closer. Instead of a set of rules that would put the focus on driver ability, we have regs that allow for these incredibly sophisticated chassis that cost millions of dollars to develop as designers try not only to stretch the existing rules as far as possible, but to develop innovations Ecclestone hasn't even conceived of yet.

What we should have is a list of regs that outlines an aerodynamically straightforward, single-seater car. Instead, to combat all the fancy stuff the teams keep coming up with, Ecclestone creates silly rules like the new adjustable rear wing that you can use for overtaking ... but only at certain times. I mean, what the hell is that all about? When exactly those times are remains guesswork for most of us who are watching, and I'm willing to bet the majority of F1 fans don't fully grasp the rules.

F1 is still not about the driver – and that's what pisses me off. The excitement generated in the 2011 season was due to the Pirelli tyres, which were specifically designed to provide optimum performance for only a handful of laps. During that window, you cannot pass anyone with fresh tyres on his car, but as soon as the tyres wear off, it's open season. The tyres, therefore, are handicapping the driver. This should never be allowed to happen, especially in a formula regarded as the domain of the world's best racing drivers.

Ecclestone has even floated the idea of artificially dampening the track to create rain-like conditions during certain times of a Grand Prix, presumably because wet races are closer affairs. Pirelli came out in support of the idea, which makes me really nervous. This nonsense could actually be on the cards. Imagine that ... track sprinklers at Monza. Enzo Ferrari would spin in his grave. Actually, he'd probably get up out of his grave and kick Ecclestone's arse.

Something else that burns my butt is the fact that race stewards are so pedantically strict. We've got to a state where, if two cars touch, you know one of them is going to get a drive-through penalty or some other punishment. So drivers are now too shit-scared to do anything even remotely aggressive, making actual passing manoeuvres less likely. Get anywhere near another car and every marshal on the track is waving a flag of some colour or other. Ridiculous. Let them hit each other without all the penalties, for goodness' sake – at least there'd still be an incentive to try to pass.

I appreciate the fact that wizardry puts F1 at the cutting-edge of motor-sport technology, and that it's an attractive proposition from a fan's point of view, but I think the engineers are messing with the wrong things. Let me tell you what I would do ...

First, all those fancy wings, winglets and other stupid airflow-management devices on the car would end up in the bin. Not only do they make the cars look ugly, but they're making overtaking impossible by scrambling the air for the car behind them. At the moment you have one car in front with its aerodynamics working, but the one behind can't generate the same downforce because of the messed-up air. No downforce, no pass. Unless, of course, they are allowed to open that adjustable rear wing ... but remember, they can only do that at specified times. *What*? Exactly ...

You have to allow some aero downforce, so basic front and rear wings are necessary, but my second big change would be that all the wings on the car would have to be non-adjustable parts of the body shell. Plus, they would have to be non-adjustable from day one. In other words, at the beginning of the season, a team would have to decide whether to design a car that'll be fast on slow tracks or fast on fast tracks.

Third, I would ban carbon-fibre disc brakes. The problem with carbon-fibre brakes is that they're just too damn good. Braking zones have now shrunk dramatically. Whereas in the old days of steel discs you'd have to start braking 150 metres before a corner, it's now down to something like 50 metres. And the stopping power is so good that they're only on the brakes for a second. Out-braking your competitors is the classic way to overtake. It's a major indicator of a driver's ability if he can brake very late, control a squirming racing car, and still turn in early enough to control the car on exit without running wide and losing the lead he's very briefly held. You simply can't out-break someone when all you have to play with is 50 metres and one second.

It's not as if carbon-fibre brakes would ever work in the real world, either, so you can throw the bullshit theory that 'F1 technology will one day trickle down to your own car' right out of the window. Carbon-fibre brakes only function properly when you can generate the kind of heat in the discs that a racing car does. Braking from 320 to 60 km/h generates the requisite heat. Slowing down from 60 to 40 km/h won't. Which means that some old granny in her new carbon-brake-shod Honda Insight2 Hybrid CVT i-VTEC Limited Edition trying to slow down at the red light is going to sail straight through the inter-section and get flattened by a wide-eyed truck driver who'll need to spend the rest of his life in therapy. And we can't have that now, can we?

Something else I would ban are those stupid contraptions that pass as steering wheels in a modern F1 car. Not only are all those buttons and switches the visible representation of the technology I think is ruining the sport, but they just *look* kak. Yes, the drivers' ability to operate the many buttons when they're travelling so fast is very impressive, but it looks more like a Sony PlayStation console than a steering wheel. And I'm sorry, but as a driver, that just offends me. Besides, I'm really crap at PlayStation.

No. I'm not all that enamoured with F1 any more.

But I do enjoy watching MotoGP these days. I've always liked bikes and I've owned quite a few road bikes in my time, as well as off-road enduro machines. I even competed in a couple of enduro events around Port Elizabeth when I was living there. I had a Honda 200R and then, later, a KTM 250 and a 495 that I used in races like the Winterberg Enduro, which was part of the national series. For the more technical enduros I'd use the smaller 250cc KTM, and then the 495cc for the more open, faster events. That big KTM was probably the scariest thing I've ever been on – and I include all the cars I've been in. The KTM had a tiny power band, with the result that you either had no power or the bike would want to wheelie in any gear.

MotoGP always gives fans a good dice and, even though there are big factory teams present, the machines are still very closely matched. MotoGP is all about the rider.

As far as four-wheel motor sport goes, I reckon the Le Mans Series for sports cars is the best. And I'm not talking about the top-tier LMP1 class, either – the only way you can tell those Audi prototypes from the rest is because they've got four *moer* of a big rings on their noses. No, I like the GT Endurance class. At least they're closely based on their road-going siblings. Plus, all the traditional rivals take part in it – Porsche, Ferrari, Aston Martin, Corvette, and now BMW – which provides some very close racing. There's just something about watching a souped-up Ferrari F458 Italia fighting it out with a Porsche 911 GT3 RSR that stirs a racing fan's blood.

DTM – German Touring Cars – is also great. Even though it has only been a two-marque series for the past few years, with Mercedes-Benz and Audi, it's very competitive, with multiple winners each season. BMW are making a comeback too, which should make DTM even better.

I just wish we had something exciting to watch in South African motor racing (this is the part where I *really* start to complain).

At the moment, the most exciting form of four-wheel motor sport in this country is the Engen Polo Cup. At this point, all the Clubman series drivers will be waving their hands and jumping up and down, but I'm talking about a national series here, gents. Yes, you guys produce some very exciting racing and you're a vital supply line of South African racing talent – and it's essentially where I got my start – but privateer racing unfortunately doesn't attract many spectators. Fans want to see the big names and the factory teams. And in that regard, South African motor sport has *very* little to offer.

Those little VW Polos might not exactly be quick, but the racing is tight no matter what circuit they're dicing on. It's mostly populated by up-and-coming youngsters wanting to make a name for themselves, and the near-standard Polo series is perfect for this. The cars are very similar in terms of performance, allowing the driver's ability to be showcased. I've even been a guest driver on the odd occasion when VW have offered me a car to drive. Most recently it arrived with the words '"Oom" Sarel v/d Merwe' emblazoned on the side. The cheeky bastards.

The Engen Cup is so enjoyable because any one of up to eight drivers could win a race, making it the place to look for new talent. The sad thing is, once you've found it, what the hell do you do with it? Where do you take the talent next? There are no big works teams that they can aspire to join. Sure, there are overblown, big-budget production cars, but because they're so expensive, the Group N field is very small. How many Engen Cup drivers will actually make it to Group N? Very few, obviously, so motor sport really is in a sad state.

To understand how it got to this point, we have to take a few steps back.

Motor sport in this country was originally run by the Royal Automobile Club. The name precisely explains the kind of people who ran it. The RAC then became part of the Automobile Association, which then took over the show. Right from the start, the gentlemen of the AA and SuperVan did not see eye to eye.

As far as I was concerned, these people weren't really elected to the position to which they were appointed, especially when motor sport became professional. Suddenly I was being told what to do by a bunch of tie-wearing, old-boys-club farts who were more interested in promoting their own welfare than anything related to the good of SA motor sport.

The AA was made up of all the regional motor-sport clubs, and there was also competition between the English and the Afrikaans members back then. On the one hand, you had the Sports Car Club (SCC) – the English crowd who controlled circuit racing; and on the other, the Pretoria-based Suid-Afrikaanse Motorsportklub and the Pretoria Motor Club, which focused on the rally scene. No prizes for guessing what cultural group they represented.

As a young Afrikaans *seun*, it was virtually impossible to get a drive in one of the works racing teams. Ja, I could enter the races, but even though I was better than some of the other drivers, I knew I'd have to find an alternative route into a competitive car. Which is exactly what SuperVan did, using his rallying successes to move up to the Alfa drives, and then with Ford when they built the modified Ford Escort for the Manufacturer's Challenge.

In the 80s, I would make sure I got onto these committees in an attempt to fight from the inside, but in my early years of racing I was the archetypal outsider/rebel/young gun. There was no doubt that the AA committees were packed with SCC members who didn't like my surname. And I didn't like them back even more. I saw the motor-sport controlling body as the enemy. Not only were they pulling the strings – strings that afforded very little benefit to the competitors – but they were, in my young, hot-shot opinion, also a bunch of idiots.

This was how a race meeting would work: the SCC would 'rent' Kyalami for the weekend from the South African Motor Racing Club, who owned the circuit. SAMRC would take the gate, but SCC would organise the event with their own track marshals and clerk of the course running the show. It was still an amateur scene back in those days, which would often lead to the organisers favouring their own club members should any on-track argy-bargy result in a formal protest. The inter-club rivalry was pretty fierce.

When SAMRC sold Kyalami in the early 80s, it essentially kicked off the professional era of motor sport in this country, but it was unfortunately very poorly managed by the controlling body – nowadays known as MotorSport South Africa. They can say what they want, but if you look at the state of our motor sport today compared to how other sports like football, rugby and cricket have grown in the professional era, it's pretty clear we've had the gear lever in reverse for the past three decades.

Whereas back in the day I used to earn R25 000 – a significant amount of money 25 years ago – for winning the Castrol Rally, today the prize money has all but disappeared. Given that motoring is a multibillion-rand industry in South Africa, that's fairly strange, wouldn't you agree? You even used to get money for travelling expenses if you were Gauteng-based and the rally was down in the Cape. Now we have a situation where not only are you receiving nothing from them, but you're having to pay MSA a fortune for a racing licence. It costs over R1 000 these days for the privilege of having a licence. On its own, that's not a lot of money, but it adds to what has become a prohibitively expensive exercise if you want to start racing.

Over the years I have seen a controlling body grow fatter and fatter on the fees of its members and the contributions of its sponsors without it reinvesting anything back into the sport. MSA has become a massive hierarchy that requires *all* the cash just to keep itself going. Its strategy seems to be: Create as many different formulas as we can because the more formulas there are, the more money we'll get. At the moment, nothing gets done in South African motor sport until the weight of the paperwork is equal to that of the car.

MSA certainly haven't done anything that I can see to help the drivers. Do you want to know why we've never had another Jody Scheckter in F1? It's not because we lack the talent, I'll tell you that much. We have some excellent racing drivers in this country, but they are just being managed so badly by MSA. For example, a few South Africans have won the Rotax Karting world champs over the past few years, and karting – as the likes of Ayrton Senna, Michael Schumacher and Sebastian Vettel prove – is a testing ground for emerging talent. But what have MSA done for our karting aces like Claudio Piazza Musso, Wesleigh Orr, Gavin Cronje and Caleb Williams? What have they done to help these guys get to the next level?

SuperVan can tell you far more colourfully than I can ...

'Sweet fuck all, that's what.'

Thank you.

Jody Scheckter got into Formula 1 because, in his day, there was an MSA 'Driver to Europe' programme. If you won the Formula Ford title locally, which he did, it secured you a drive in a competitive team abroad the following year. How's that for a great incentive? But that's all fallen by the wayside, because MSA need the money to pay their own salaries.

But it's not the only way they're curbing our talent. Guys like my old friend Dick Sorenson and his weight-handicap bullshit are still in operation, and while drivers are still being penalised for performing well, they have very little opportunity to shine.

It's genuinely very sad, because a lot of local talent has fallen through the cracks. Nowadays the only way for any South African driver to make it overseas is to have the surname 'Rupert' or 'Oppenheimer' stencilled on the side of his helmet.

A name like 'Sarel' on the side of a helmet also used to act as an incentive to the next generation of drivers. I had achieved things others could aspire to ... perhaps I was even a hero to some. By failing to develop and nurture our driver talent, the next gen-eration of up-and-coming drivers has no real heroes to worship and no role models to aspire to.

As I've mentioned, as a young boy I used to wander around the pits among the world's greatest drivers of the day. When I started competing, I had icons like rally stars Ewold van Bergen and Jan Hettema, as well as track heroes like Basil van Rooyen, Koos Swanepoel and John Love, to inspire me. These men made me want to be a professional racing driver. Having the opportunity to compete against someone like Jan Hettema improved my abilities tremendously. It gave me a head start on my peers, as I was so focused on beating the best, by the time I'd beaten them, anyone else was a walk in the park. Hettema was also a full-time professional – it's what he did for a living. He drove rally cars, which proved to me that, despite my father's views to the contrary, it was possible to pursue driving as a full-time career.

I just wish the current drivers would challenge MSA a little more and at least try to improve their lot. SuperVan stood up to them from day one, and, to his credit, so did Michael Briggs when he was dominant in Touring Cars during the mid-1990s. The problem these days is that the whole system – inadvertently or not – is designed to marginalise the driver. A combination of the huge budget you need to race in a top formula, along with all this handicap rubbish that doesn't allow a brilliant driver to stand out, has resulted in a dearth of motor-racing stars in this country.

Granted, motor-racing stars often come along with a large ego and a very manly moustache, but they also have the kind of power that can at least keep MSA vaguely honest.

The drivers are forever moaning and bitching about MSA, but I seem to be the only one who's ever really done anything about it. My opinions on the administration of motor sport were often quoted in the press, and for a while in the early 2000s I even had a column in *The Citizen* newspaper, where I would regularly tear strips off MSA.

Beulah Schoeman was MSA's managing director back then, and she made the mistake of writing a rebuttal to one of my columns in the newspaper. That, of course, opened the door for SuperVan to have a full go. As I recall, he launched a barrage of smart bombs that included wanting to know what their overly large staff complement were doing at their high-rent premises at Kyalami Business Park beyond sipping coffee and shooting the breeze. MSA could probably cut their staff by 75 per cent and operate out of a house somewhere. No one would notice the difference.

The drivers' cause isn't helped by the fact that the car manufacturers have representation on the various MSA committees. That should never happen – the manufacturers should have their own association where they sort out all their shit beforehand, then have a single representative who fights for their issues at MSA committee level. What you have now is a situation where individual manufacturers are fighting for their own benefits, instead of fighting for collective interests. The rugby guys have got it right – on the SA Rugby Board, the main sponsors each have a single representative, as do the players. Why is that not the case with MSA?

I feel sorry for the guys trying to make it in local motor sport today, I really do. There's no question that the years in which I competed were a time when South African motor sport was at its zenith, both financially and in terms of popularity. This was especially the case during the apartheid years, when our national rugby, cricket and football teams were banned from international competition. As a result, the focus shifted onto the local racing and rallying scenes, and our motor sport was featured on TV all the time. Drivers became well-known – even household – names.

At the time, I warned MSA that this wouldn't last. I repeatedly told them that at some stage, South African sport would return from the wilderness and that they'd better get their arses into gear if they wanted to compete for the fans' attention and sponsors' budgets. But they did nothing. Aside from the odd MotoGP or World SuperBike race, we've had no decent international motor races or rallies here since the 1993 South African Grand Prix.

Okay, there was the V8 Superstar Series that was run at Kyalami in 2009 and 2010, but that was little more than a joke and, in reality, an example of how corrupt motor sport can become. As there is always big money involved, motor sport inevitably attracts schemers and connivers. And there's no better example than the R600-million-plus that the Gauteng government forked out for 'motor-sport promotion' a few years back. No, that's not a typo ... more than *R600 million*.

Of that money, R150 million was spent over three years on the A1 Grand Prix, R444 million over seven years on the World SuperBike Championship, and R39 million over three years on an 'international' motor-racing series. Now let's take stock of that: well, the international A1 GP series was a total disaster, with the series eventually folding in 2009; SuperBikes were here in 2009 and 2010, and that was it; and the 'international' series turned out to be the Italian-based V8 Superstar Series, which is basically a bunch of has-been drivers – mostly Italian – driving V8 saloons slower than the local Wesbank cars.

And 'Superstars' is overstating the case slightly, as the only driver whom I'd heard of in the line-up was Gianni Morbidelli – a former F1 driver who had achieved precisely one podium and a total of 8.5 championship points in his seven-year F1 career. Superstar. No.

But that's not all. Thirty million rand in total was also spent on the Renault F1 roadshow, where a Renault F1 car did a few smoky doughnuts in Sandton; and then an unconfirmed sum of R65 million was forked out to slap a 'GO-GP.org' logo on the BMW-Sauber F1 team. How that was meant to promote motor sport in Gauteng, the Lord alone knows. The website was supposed to be a portal for Grand Prix fans, tourists and investors to flock to Gauteng in their droves, all excitedly spending millions of rands. Unfortunately, the droves stayed away – perhaps partly because the website never actually worked.

'The big winner' – and I'm quoting here from a statement issued by the Democratic Alliance's Jack Bloom in August 2009 – 'apart from the overseas motor-sport controlling bodies, is a mysterious local company called Nightsbridge Investments. They look set to score about R56 million in "management and consultancy services", taking 10 per cent commission for arranging the deals, and 12.5 per cent of income from events.'

It seems that, spotting a gap, Nightsbridge had persuaded individuals in the Gauteng government to push the deal through.

And has it benefited our motor sport in any way? Of course not. But it has benefited a few people's back pockets; back pockets that must be so stuffed that the beneficiaries can no longer sit down. No one knows where the R600-million-plus has actually gone. A parliamentary inquiry was launched, but it didn't appear to be conducted with too much enthusiasm and didn't seem to involve much forensic accounting.

The whole set-up is so crooked, it's a joke.

To be fair to MSA, the corruption obviously isn't their fault, but it is at least an indication that there is plenty of money out there, and if they played their cards right, the money could be utilised in such a way as to actually benefit South African motor sport.

Unfortunately, motor sport has also always been an effective way not only to launder money – as the Pauls had done back in the States, using their IMSA team to whitewash their drug business – but also to move money out of a country in contravention of foreign-exchange laws.

I know of a certain South African driver whose success in the US was kick-started by a sweet little forex deal. Let's call him Cliff, because if I told you who he really was, I'd get sued from here to California. Besides, in my experience, guys named 'Cliff' are always *skelms*. So Cliff hooks up with a South African businessman, whose name we shall similarly omit, and agrees to help him move millions of rands overseas. Because the authorities never really have any idea how much racing cars and their supporting equipment cost, Cliff was able to buy a banged-up racing car for, say, R100k, stick on a bunch of decals that gave the impression that it was a hugely exotic and therefore very expensive piece of automotive machinery, and then tell the government it was worth a million bucks. What did they, or anyone else, for that matter, know about the value of a racing car? And so a million rand slips out of the country. Cliff gets his cut once the car lands in the US. From those humble beginnings, Cliff has managed to build an impressive motor-sport business in the States.

So no, there is nothing MSA is doing to bring international motor sport back to this country. Everyone is doing their own little thing, and the dwindling crowds at the racetracks bear testimony to the fact. MSA cannot deny that only hard-core motor-sport fans come and watch these days.

Because what's the point? I mean, who would want to sit around watching a Group N Production race – our premier formula at the moment – where the winner of the previous meet is now carrying extra weight, and the grid gets swapped around for the day's second heat, with Heat 1's winner now starting in 10th place? It's all far too artificially constructed. I'd much rather watch a regional club race at Killarney. Because there are no MSA controls to screw it up, the racing is always more exciting, and these guys are doing it on a shoestring budget, too. And that brings me to another instance of how MSA continue to cock things up. Remember how everyone – quite rightly – complained that Touring Cars were killing South African motor sport with their huge budgets? Well, the same applies to Group N Production cars. This is supposed to be a relatively stock-standard formula, which, one would think, would keep costs relatively low.

Not exactly. It's going to cost you around R2.5 million to build one of those cars, not to mention what it will cost you to run it for a season. The reality is that they're far from being anything near a production car. You could probably run 20 genuine production cars for the kind of money it takes to run one of these Group N machines. And you wonder why there are only a handful of cars running in a Group N, Class A heat …

When it costs in excess of R10 million a season to run a team, sizeable sponsorships are required not only to pay your expenses, but so that you can make a little money to live off as well. Why must it be like this? You see, this is what really annoys me about MSA. Group N should never have become what it is. Fans don't care about lap times, only about close racing. Why do we have to have cars that appear to be stock standard but underneath allow hugely expensive mods? Who's benefiting from this? Run the bloody production cars as bloody production cars. You'll get many more entrants, you'll get closer racing, you'll get more fans at the races, and you'll therefore attract more sponsors' interest.

Another factor, of course, is that a huge budget makes you and your team very vulnerable. The moment there's any kind of economic downswing or any other reason that might cause the motor industry to tighten its seat belt, guess where the budget gets cut? That's right, motor sport. And to be honest, sometimes the teams do piss the money away. Remember that Wesbank team I bought from Opel at the end of 2001? Well, General Motors were spending R12 million a year on that little show. They had huge workshops, great, big race-day hospitality tents and staff that did everything from fixing the cars to spritzing the pot plants. And they didn't win anything.

In 2002, I ran the same team on R1 million. Whereas Opel had employed people to cook food for them, I sent out one of the mechanics to buy us pies. That's how you run a serious racing team. I kept on the top three Opel mechanics, but that was it – there was no budget for the rest. Instead of partying, we won the championship two years in a row. Motor sport has shot itself in the foot many a time getting caught up in a spending spree. I even see it in some of the Engen Polo Cup teams, where there are pretty big budgets involved. They need to be careful – a small change in circumstances and their sponsors could close their wallets and walk away. And then they're stuffed. The teams still haven't twigged that that's how it works.

If I were a sponsor, I wouldn't put money into SA motor sport in its current form. I was recently asked by someone with a large marketing budget if he should invest it in racing. 'Why the fuck would you want to go and do a stupid thing like that?' was my answer. At the moment the product is shit, and, as a sponsor, you're not going to get value for your money.

Whereas in the past we'd have live TV crossings to Kyalami on race days, that's all disappeared now. What you get these days is a few 30-minute highlights packages on SuperSport, with 10 minutes allocated to each formula. If you're sponsoring a car, what kind of pathetic exposure are you going to get out of 10 minutes of TV time? You'll be lucky if your car comes past once ... and only if the camera is zoomed in close enough for anyone to actually see your brand stickers. The truth is, it makes much more marketing sense to put your money into other sports. No, it's a very sad state of affairs. In fact, it's a total balls-up.

And I think I'll stop my complaining right here. There is, after all, not too much one can add to 'it's a total balls-up'.

As those annoying self-help business coaches like to say, 'Don't come to me with problems. Come to me with solutions.' Well, put me in charge and this is what I would do ...

To start with, I'd cut down on the number of formulas currently operating on our tracks. I don't even know how many there are any more, because every time I go to a race meet, there's another formula described as a 'South African Championship'. Instead of having our raw talent spread among all these little races, we should have our most talented drivers competing in a limited number of formulas. Not only will the increased competition improve their skills, but it will also focus sponsorship money and give the sport more exposure. MSA, of course, won't allow this. As I've said, the more formulas, the more licence fees and the higher the cut of the sponsorship fees that they get.

Our national series should consist of no more than a couple of single-seater formulas – Formula Ford, which teaches you proper single-seater car control, and maybe Formula VW, with their more sophisticated aerodynamics. There should also be a proper, low-cost Production Class series, and then a bigger, more expensive modified series, in which the manufacturers can participate. Add a couple of national motorcycle-series formulas and perhaps a regional historic car race to the programme, and you'll have a full day's racing for the crowds.

The next thing I'd do is franchise each formula, which is what they do in the US. NASCAR and Indy Racing League, for example, are both franchises that were purchased from the Automobile Competition Committee of the United States for a hefty licence fee. And because the franchisee is then running his franchise as a business, he tends to ensure that everything runs smoothly. If the franchise doesn't create a product the public likes, he can kiss his investment goodbye. For that reason, he will make sure that he has the best drivers and cars in the business.

The big advantage of the US model is that you can then fire 90 per cent of the MSA crowd. Because the franchisees are now running their own formulas, MSA would only need to ensure that the general competition rules – as dictated by the worldwide governing body, the FIA – are adhered to. If there are any disputes, MSA would then step in as the final authority.

I'm prepared to put my money where my mouth is, too.

My ex–Kreepy Krauly teammate and one-time Wesbank adversary, Ian Scheckter, and I are busy setting up a showroom stock championship. In other words, a proper Group N class with very few mods. Besides a roll cage inside the cabin and a bucket seat for the driver, that, my friend, is *it*. No special shocks, brakes, tyres – no nothing. The cars will have standard road tyres, although we will allow the teams to skim them – that is, remove some of the tread. This actually makes the tyres last longer, as with too much tread, they quickly build up heat around a track and wear out.

The classes will be based on a car's standard power output as set out in the dealership brochure, which makes it really easy to control. All you need is a dyno at each race, and anyone you suspect of cheating has to put their car on the dyno. If it's outside, say, a 2 per cent tolerance, which is standard, you tell him to take his car and piss off for the remainder of the season.

I reckon that to keep costs down, we'll limit the top class to about BMW M3-type horsepower – so somewhere in the region of a 340 kW max. That means you'll still have prestigious racing cars like the BMWs and the Merc C63 AMGs – and maybe even the Chev Luminas – battling it out.

We intend to run it as a two-tier competition, with inland championships at Kyalami, Zwartkops and Phakisa, and coastal championships at Killarney, Aldo Scribante and East London. And then we'll have a season finale for everyone, which will be a six-hour endurance race that counts three times the points.

I want it to be a stand-alone competition that doesn't run on the same day as MSA's national Wesbank Super Series. They can run all their formulas on their own on that day; we'll hook up with the club days at the various circuits and do our own thing. Having an event free of all that thunder means we can get our own naming sponsor and also generate our own TV show, which will afford the competing teams' sponsors more screen time.

The racing will be real cards-on-the-table stuff for the manufacturers, because there's no hiding your car's actual performance in this series. You can't do any under-the-skin stuff to boost poor performance. Your car will only get whipped by the other brands if it's genuinely slower. This is dead-honest racing, which petrolheads can appreciate. Because it involves relatively low running costs, we should generate big grids – hopefully up to 50 cars – and the fans will appreciate that, too. With all those cars of different abilities on the track, the fast ones will lap the slower ones near the end of the race, which will make for even more interesting racing. And if we can create that Holy Grail – interesting racing

– then the fans will flock in, closely followed by sponsors waving their wallets in the air.

Maybe, just like Scheckter and I did as youngsters, an up-and-coming driver will be able to drive his racing car to the track, enjoy the thrill of racing, and then drive it back home.

Who knows, he might even be the next SuperVan.

Hey, there's only one SuperVan.

Ag, piss off.

11

HOW TO (TRY TO) DRIVE LIKE SUPERVAN

Obviously it's impossible to drive like SuperVan, but here
are some tips anyway – including avoiding the number 4
at all costs

This is the chapter where, with my best Clint Eastwood stare, I
spit tobacco juice onto the dusty street and say, 'You'll never drive
like me, kid. Nobody can. But listen up and I'll give you a couple
of pointers.' Obviously you'll have to imagine Clint Eastwood
with an Afrikaans accent, but I'm as tall as he is and I used to
own a pair of cowboy boots when I raced in the States. As I
recall, they were made of snake skin.

1. LISTEN TO THE OLD FARTS
As a young gun new to the racing and rallying scene, I often
thought I knew it all. You could tell from my stage and lap times
that I had natural ability – and lots of it. And with a tendency
towards doing things my way, I could easily have made the mistake of not paying attention to what some of the older guys had
to say. Fortunately, I had my first team boss, Ewold van Bergen,
to guide me. As the manager of Datsun's rally team and a good
friend of my father's, out of respect I would listen to Van Bergen's
advice. That it happened to be very good advice was a real bonus.
Although he counselled me on rallying, a lot of what he said
stuck with me throughout my racing career.
    He would say things like, 'To finish first, first you've got to

finish,' and 'Try to win at the slowest possible speed.' While that might sound like ruminations from the Buddhist School of Motor Racing, it was actually very sound advice, which I would then give a more practical spin on the track.

Van Bergen taught me how to *think* my way to the chequered flag instead of just relying on my natural speed. If, for example, I had built up a comfortable lead, I learnt how to look after the car without sacrificing speed. I'd brake a bit earlier, use fewer revs and basically 'save' the car. That's not to say I'd drive any slower, or decrease my cornering speed, as that would inevitably have meant a loss of focus – which is when you fall off the track. I would just be a little softer on the brakes so as not to overheat them, and probably drop about 500rpm to go easy on the engine. It was a case of being easy on the equipment but not on the driver.

Aside from the philosophical stuff, Van Bergen also gave me the kind of practical advice you'd never get in a driving manual. He'd say, 'If you hit a rock during a rally stage and you're not sure how bad the damage is, drive to favour the other side of the car.' You were always clipping corners during a stage and you never knew what might be lurking in the grass verge. Sometimes there'd be an unexpected bump from, say, the right front wheel, and I'd make sure that I then absorbed any bumps in the road with the wheels on the left side of the car until I got to the next service point, where the crew could check it out.

Van Bergen was a canny manager as well. At the start of my rallying career, I was particularly *windgat* and, because I was trying to match the times posted by the guys in the faster works cars, I was often way over the limit. Because I didn't have the equipment, I was going as fast as I could all the time. Naturally, I crashed a lot in those days. But occasionally I would keep it together long enough to win my class in a rally and, while that was exciting initially, I was soon hankering after top honours. Winning your class was cool, but ask somebody three weeks later who had won the class and they'd have forgotten. But everybody knew who had been up on the podium celebrating overall victory. And that's what young SuperVan wanted. To accomplish such a victory, however, I needed to drive a modified works car.

I expected a works drive from my Datsun employers after driving my socks off to win the 1973 regional Pretoria News Rally in my own standard Datsun SSS. I had, after all, won a rally for my company in my private rally car. Van Bergen duly invited me to join the team … except that I wouldn't be driving a modified Datsun SSS, as I'd wanted, but one of the standard cars. Basically, exactly the same car I had been driving.

I was *not* happy. Not only did I *think* I was quicker than the rest, I knew it. Why should I not have the best car?

It took me a good few years to realise how clever Van Bergen had actually been. Back then I was still too raw a talent to be given a full-blown rally car. I might have been quick, but I was still crashing too regularly. I still needed to learn more control and finesse. If I'd been given the keys to a modified car then, God knows what I would've done to myself. Even when Van Bergen finally allowed me to drive one of his precious modified Datsun SSSs in 1975, it was the single-cam version. The twin-cam went to my more experienced, but slower, team leader, Jochi Kleint.

I was a lot more consistent by 1975, and Van Bergen's decision infuriated me. He wouldn't tell me why he'd given the twin-cam to Kleint either, which didn't help. He was the team boss and you went with what he said. I eventually figured out his reasoning, though. He knew that the twin-cam was quicker, but I think he also knew that I could still outdrive Jochi in the single-cam. The single-cam was a proven car, whereas the twin-cam still had some unreliability issues – we didn't know exactly what was going to break, and where. Van Bergen was being a smart team manager by putting the quick-but-still-hard-on-his-cars youngster in the reliable car, and the slower-but-easier-on-the-equipment guy in the more fragile one.

VW Golf aka The World's Kakkest Golf Why? Well, put it this way … in the two years I rallied this car – 1989 and 1990 – I posted 14 non-finishes. In my entire rallying career up till that point, I'd only registered 13 non-finishes

Audi Quattro Fresh from winning the American IMSA GTO championship, Audi SA brought these here for the Wesbank series. This is me testing the car for the first time. Within a few seconds, I knew it would be unbeatable

Ford Mustang The US-sourced ex IMSA GT Series car that I'd use to finally rip the Wesbank championship from the hands of Audi in 1994

Ford Mustang … and then again in 2000 and 2001 when I bought the re-bodied car back from Peter Lindenberg. I never really get emotional about cars, but I was quite sad when I sold this one at the end of 2001

Daewoo Cielo Driving what was basically an Opel Kadett in disguise, my old partner in crime Franz Boshoff and I would sensationally win the 1996 Castrol Rally on the car's debut

Opel Astra V8 Winning the final race of my career at Kyalami in 2002. I helped my young teammate Johan Fourie win the Wesbank championship in Heat 1 and then left them all in the dust in Heat 2. A fitting end to SuperVan's professional career of 35 years

Citi Golf Showing the youngsters that SuperVan's still got it. Here I'm swapping paint with Giniel de Villiers at the sharp end of the 2009 Golf Challenge race

Ford Galaxie 500 For the past few years I've been driving this 1963 7.0-litre monster in the SA Historic Saloons series. I'm not usually easy to pass, and in this big red block of flats it's an even trickier prospect

My navigator Chris Hawkins and I behaving like the cool hipsters we were. Second wife Tersia … Datsun T-shirts … so that must be 1973 and the end of the Total Rally in Lourenço Marques

My 'Leinad Lerás' racing licence … a scrambled version of my first and second names Sarel and Daniel. Having a secret identity allowed me to race for some privateer teams on the sly

Two great men … two great moustaches. It's that rivetingly exciting event, the Total Economy Run, and this time I was the co-driver navigating for none other than boxer Kallie Knoetze at the 1978 event. Not sure I know who the lady is, but Kallie clearly does. The third moustache lurking in the background also remains a mystery

The legendary manager of Ford SA's motor-sport endeavours, Bernie Marriner. Bernie was one of the best in the business at conjuring up sponsorship money and played as hard as he worked

Sarel chooses Jurgens for its towability and easy handling.

Making a buck outside of motor sport

During my first season in the US, SA driver Desiré Wilson would sometimes stand in for me if races clashed with my rallying commitments back home. Here she is talking to me and team owner and co-driver Giampiero Moretti at a 1983 IMSA race in Miami

The start of the 1984 24 Hours of Daytona. I'm on the left in the Kreepy Krauly March about to start a big dice with Mario Andretti on my left in the Porsche 962

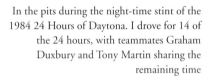

In the pits during the night-time stint of the 1984 24 Hours of Daytona. I drove for 14 of the 24 hours, with teammates Graham Duxbury and Tony Martin sharing the remaining time

Kreepy Krauly owner and founder Danny Chauvier celebrates as I cross the finish line to win the 1984 24 Hours of Daytona. That victory would put the Kreepy Krauly brand on the map in the US

Victory Lane at Daytona in 1984 and the win that launched my overseas career. Ever the businessman, Kreepy Krauly owner Danny Chauvier makes sure his product is in the shot

Our second March burns out in 1984. I was actually leading the IMSA Series race at Portland when a fuel leak caused the fire. When I pulled over to the marshal point, all the bloody marshals ran away. You can see how impressed I am with their efforts

Doing some promo work for the 1984 Castrol 1000 endurance race at Kyalami and providing some support for Miss Kreepy Krauly. As I recall, her heels were killing her

My first ever Le Mans in 1984 and my first ever drive in a Porsche 956. As part of Ken Fitzpatrick's Skoal-Bandit-sponsored outfit, we came third. Those scratches on my helmet are from scraping against the roof of the Porsche's cramped cockpit

My second favourite off-the-track pastime. I played a lot of golf in the 80s – particularly while racing in the US – I eventually got down to a 7 handicap. And yes, that's how you wore shorts back then

Le Mans 1987. My teammates David Hobbs and Chip Robinson and I looking suitably unimpressed after our Porsche 962 expired on the warm-up lap. We were out of the race before it had even started

Unlucky number four. Whenever I had this number on my car, things went horribly wrong. Without fail. I was forced to use the number in the 1992 Volkswagen Rally in PE, and not even using a Roman numeral helped. A rock rolled into the road and destroyed my Ford Lazer's suspension

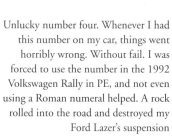

With my good friend and mentor
Ewold van Bergen at his 80th birthday
party in Paternoster, 2009

At Kyalami on the day I retired in 2002. The
grandstand along the main straight was renamed
in my honour

Me and Danielle

Morne van Zyl

I'm not quite ready to fade into the sunset yet!

I never realised it at the time, but Van Bergen was essentially putting me through rally school. I was 'payin' my dues'. Spit.

Of course, back then I thought it was all a load of crap, but now I can't thank Ewold van Bergen enough. The year I spent in the standard car taught me a lot about preservation tactics – how to keep everything alive and still go fast. And, thanks to that, throughout the rest of my multiple national-championship-winning rally career, I probably had the best finishing record of any driver.

I had learnt how to 'win at the slowest possible speed'.

2. LEARN SOME BASIC RACE CRAFT

There are some basic driving strategies you need to know if you're going to win races. These are the things that separate the smart drivers from the – no offence, Clint – cowboys, and with them you can even win in a car that's slower than those of your competitors. Sharpen your pencils and listen closely ...

Assist the car, don't fight it. Motor racing is all about the corners. Any monkey can plant his foot on the gas and nudge the needle as far right as it can go, but when the track bends left or right, then those knuckle-draggers get into trouble. That's where the real skill lies.

Contrary to popular belief, quick lap times are not about braking as late as possible when going into a corner. Yes, in a dice situation you do want to brake late and go in as deep as you can in order to get ahead of the guy you're racing, but that also slows both of you down. The moment you brake very hard, the weight of the car transfers to the front wheels, which affects the car's ability to turn in. For front-wheel-drive cars it's not too much of a problem, because the added weight can help with traction. However, on rear-wheel-drive cars – in other words, proper racing cars – that transfer of weight to the front creates understeer. The front tyres can't handle the power coming from the rear, and even though they're trying to turn in, they're basically getting pushed forwards, off the track. Needless to say, your tyres don't last very long when that happens.

No, what you want to do in order to set a fast qualifying lap or escape the field in a race situation is to brake slightly earlier, which will also allow you to step on the gas slightly earlier when you exit the corner. Fast lap times are about exiting corners quickly, and if you come out doing 4 or 5 km/h more than the rest, it will increase your speed down the next straight and you'll probably be going 8 or 9 km/h quicker. Basically, then, fast times are not about how fast you go into the corner, but how fast you can get out.

You can think of it this way, too: never fight the car – assist the car. A lot of drivers are intent on battling with their cars instead of the track. Some cars, like the Ford Galaxie that I occasionally raced in the historic saloon series, you have to manhandle a little. But even with the Galaxie, once you're into the corner, you've got to assist it out rather than fight it. The big Ford will always want to go straight, so you've got to coax it around a corner before once again unleashing that 7.5-litre V8 down the straights.

Defend that lead of yours, boet. What do you do when your tyres are wearing down and the guy behind you is catching up with you a couple of seconds a lap? Wave him through because you're such a jolly good sportsman? Fuck, no. You roll out your defensive strategy, because catching SuperVan is one thing, but passing him is another story, my good friend.

You know you can't go any quicker because your car is sliding around like a bastard, so you need to pre-empt your opponent's move. You need to start thinking. Your straight-line speeds might still be the same, but because his tyres are still okay, he's going to be quicker than you coming out of the corner. And he knows this.

What he's going to do, therefore, is hang back on entering the corner and then have a run at you coming out of it. It's the classic racing move. You can try to block him, but you can only block him so many times before you are either black-flagged or your competitor punts you off the track. No, in a situation like this, you should rather hang back with him, then make him brake and enter the corner at the same speed as you. That completely stuffs up his plan, and you'll still be in front when you both exit the corner.

Basically you're stuffing up the corner for other cars, but that's all you have to do at every corner. Because you're slowing number two down, an added bonus is that the guy in third place will also have joined your little dice. And, of course, that means the guy who has been hounding you now sees in his mirror someone trying to overtake *him*, which makes him less inclined to have a dart at you.

I often used this tactic in my Group N days in the late 1970s. My Ford Cortina was always heavier than the BMWs, Mazdas and Alfas, which meant it had a great appetite for tyres. For the first few laps of a race, my teammate Geoff Mortimer and I worked together and physically pushed each other to gap the rest of the field. It worked for a bit, but then Mortimer's tyres would drop off and the Alfas would eventually get to him. The Italian cars were the best on tyres and it was always just a matter of time before they appeared in my rear-view mirror. You had to have a plan ready.

Mine was to start sliding the Cortina all over the track. I'd still brake at the same point, but then drift the car sideways through the corner. As I was now blocking up the racing line, beyond hitting me, the Alfa behind me had to brake as well. As overheated tyres lack lateral grip but still offer the same traction in a straight line, I would have the same exit speed as I had on lap one ... and keep the lead.

Race one lap ahead. Racing from corner to corner is a complete waste of time. The only winner is the driver who crosses the finish line on the last lap. It's not the king of the late-braking crowd-pleasers who kamikaze'd his way past his nearest competitor at every other corner. He's only going to wear out his tyres and ruin the slim chance he might have had of winning the race.

No, to win the race, you have to plan ahead. If, for example, you're in third place, it's no use ducking and diving trying to pass the guy in second if there's still a long way to go in the race. It will only make him drive defensively, which will slow both of you down and allow the leader to escape. Rather drive clean lines, so that the car in front of you can also drive clean lines. Then you can catch up with the leader. And when everybody's together, the race leader is going to start worrying about the car behind him. And while those two are dicing and fucking up their tyres, who's sitting back in third with good rubber, waiting to pounce? That's right.

Make the others race each other and not you. If you are in the lead early on – and again we're talking about a situation where you're all doing similar lap times – get the guys in second and third to fight among themselves. This will allow you to bugger off and establish a bit of a cushion. I would slow everyone down going into a corner so that we would all be nose to tail, which then gives number three a sniff at number two. With them now involved in their own little scrap, which inevitably means they screw up their race lines and post slower lap times, you can now focus on some smooth, quick driving and gain half a second per lap.

Isolate your victim. If you do happen to be the guy in second, you obviously don't want to be involved in the scenario I've described above. You then have to isolate your victim in first place and pounce. Many a time I would physically push the guy ahead of me down the straights in order to get us away from the pack behind us. Because of the improved aerodynamics, two cars nose to tail are actually quicker than one. This is evident in NASCAR – two drivers will often work together, either to escape from the pack or to make up lost time.

Once we'd established a bit of a gap, I would then attack the car whenever I felt like it. I'd often use this tactic down the old Kyalami straight. I'd just drive right up his arse, floor it and push him for three or four laps until we'd built up a nice gap. Then I'd pounce. It's a bit like hunting.

Always leave it as late as possible. It's all well and good if you're in a superior car and you can just disappear into the distance, but if you're all doing similar lap times, then always leave your move for the lead as late as possible. If you go for it early, and everybody is doing the same times, then you're going to have to spend the whole race defending your lead. I wouldn't wait until the very last lap, either – that's a little *too* dicey, because if you do cock up one corner and lose the lead, there's probably little or no chance of getting it back. Rather make your move on the second-last lap, because then you've only got one lap to defend.

3. FOLLOW THE QUICK GUYS

During practice, get out there on the track and follow the fast guys around for a few laps. There are two reasons for doing this: 1. It'll provide you with a strategy to win the next day's race; and, 2. You'll learn things out there on the track that you can't learn anywhere else.

First bits first. During a practice, I'd make sure I was out on the track at the same time as my main competition. Not necessarily right on his bumper, but just somewhere around so I'd have an idea of what he was doing and why he was doing what he was doing. I'd then know where he was quick and where he wasn't. But I would never pass him – you don't want to show him your speed – I just wanted a good idea of what I would need to do during the race. You don't want any nasty surprises once the lights turn green.

Even if you're up against the same drivers week in and week out, which was often the case when I was racing in South Africa, it will still give you an idea of how their cars are behaving at different parts of the circuit. I'd know, for example, that Ben Morgenrood's Mazda always held its line through turn two so that I could take him on the outside of the corner without worrying that he might get off line and take me out. It also taught me never to take Terry Moss on the outside of any track in the country because he is a lunatic and would punt you into the gravel at the slightest opportunity.

As for the second reason, there have been a couple of drivers I've had the privilege of following. Both were Germans, and in both instances it was a real eye-opening experience for me. One guy showed me that there was a level of skill higher than my own, and the other taught me that there were limits I was just not prepared to explore. This last guy was a driver who'd soon lose his life – Stefan Bellof.

The first driver, however, was someone who'd soon be a seven-time F1 world champion. His name was Michael Schumacher, and following him would be something of a humbling experience for SuperVan, but you've got to acknowledge superior talent when you see it. During 1990, Schumacher was racing for the Sauber-Mercedes team in the World Sportscar Championship. I was racing a Kenwood-sponsored Porsche 962 for the Kremer team, and we were all at Belgium's legendary Spa-Francorchamps for one of the season's championship races.

From a driver's point of view, Spa is the best motor-racing circuit in the world. Even in dry weather, it's a very challenging track – the ultimate big-balls affair in motor racing. It's a high-speed circuit with no letting up anywhere. If you're on the right racing line, you can go flat out – which is what you have to do to win – but veer off that line by even a couple of inches and you'll be gone. And if you go off the track, you're going to go off in a big way. The circuit is not that dangerous – there are plenty of run-off areas – but you know there's one wild ride waiting for you if your car leaves the tarmac.

As it is a big track, it often has different weather conditions happening at different parts of the circuit. It can be dry on the lower parts, but rain at the top of the hill.

The first corner after the start is La Source, a hairpin right-hander. You come through La Source in second gear and by the time you hit the end of the pit straight, you're already in top gear. Then you still accelerate for another half a kilometre into the famous left-hand dip Eau Rouge, and up the hill into the Raidillon right-hander, before the long Kemmel straight and into the snappy left-right-left Les Combes complex.

Then it's through Bruxelles, another hairpin right-hander, through the fast double-apex Double Gauche, then another right-left-right sweep through Fagnes and Campus corners, and right into Paul Frère corner.

Next you have to steel yourself for the testicle-shrinking Blanchimont corner – a sweeping, high-speed, left-hand turn that's one of the scariest pieces of asphalt in motor sport. There's no option but to take it flat out if you want to post a decent lap time, but run wide on entry here – as some top drivers have done – and you're going to smack the tyre barrier very hard. The run-off area on this corner is smaller than most others at Spa, plus there's the small issue of an eight-metre drop on the other side of the barriers should they fail to stop you.

If you're still on the racetrack after Blanchimont, you've got to stand on the brakes for the Bus Stop chicane while still making sure that you have enough exit speed to nail the short start–finish straight before going into La Source once more.

Spa is all about maintaining your speed through the ballsy corners to make sure you're able to carry the momentum into the start of the long straights. You have to get Eau Rouge just right, otherwise you drop speed on the long Kemmel straight. Going into the Eau Rouge/Raidillon combo, you have to take a very early apex on the left-hander, then a late apex on the right-hander. Problem is, that final apex is a blind rise – it's like driving into a void. You know there's a long straight waiting for you, but you only catch sight of it at the very last minute.

After that, the downhill Les Combes complex presents a tough decision – of the three corners, you can take two flat out, but you have to back off in one of them. In your mind, you're always thinking that the ideal lap is to go flat out in all three – something today's Formula 1 cars probably do – but the sports prototypes back then didn't have enough downforce and you'd be off the track faster than you could say Michael Schumacher … and it's exactly here where the German overtook me.

And not just overtook me – he overtook me *in the rain*.

All three of the team's drivers had to qualify their silver C11 car, and the team's number-one driver, Mauro Baldi, had gone out and set a time of 55:1 on quali rubber. Jochen Mass went out next, and I think he was a couple of tenths slower … Then this young Schumacher kid got behind the wheel. On race tyres – and these were a second-and-a-half slower than quali tyres – he posted a 54:1 – a whole second better than the team's number-one driver, and on slower rubber too. He simply blew us all away.

We didn't qualify well, but it rained on race day and I was able to drive right through the field – I've always backed myself in the rain. Spa is a very fast track, but very technical, too, making it a sure-fire date with the Armco barrier if you veer even vaguely off line. I was going past Spa's famous Bus Stop chicane and above the noise of the rain hitting my car, I heard another sound. It couldn't be another car – no one in their right mind would attempt a pass down there. Especially in the rain. Anyway, there I was, thinking smugly what a rainmeister I was, belting down the hill, watching the cars in front of me squirming around … and the next minute this silver C11 Merc comes past me.

On the outside.

Down the hill.

I don't think SuperVan's eyebrows have ever lifted that high in his life.

I couldn't see who was driving, but I hung onto him for about three-quarters of a lap. But that was all I could manage. Whoever was in the car was clearly in a class above the likes of me. Not only was his braking unbelievably late considering the conditions, but he didn't care when the car started sliding – he would sort it all out on the way through the corner. Although the Merc slid all over the place, it never looked like he was going to crash. At first I thought the driver was Jochen Mass, but not even he could match this shit.

The Merc and I pitted at the same time and I made a point of trying to see who got out. I was so impressed that I had to know who the hell this driver was. Of course, it was Schumacher. After I got out of the car, I called Danielle over – she was at the race with me.

'See that guy over there? No, not him, he's a mechanic. That skinny German with the funny, skew smile. Yes, him. That guy is going to be a future world champion, trust me.'

And he was, but not even I had known then just how good this bubbly chap would become. He was having a wonderful time at Spa that day – I think he lapped the entire field. It was one of those moments I'll remember forever. Obviously, because of the heights he subsequently reached, the moment became even more memorable, but even then you could sense greatness in the guy. Rather than feel jealous or pissed off that he was faster than me, I just felt helluva privileged to have been able to follow him for part of a lap and to see what this youngster was capable of in a powerful car.

There was one other guy I followed around a couple of times who was just as quick as Schumacher, but for different reasons. Sadly, they were reasons that would kill him. In Stefan Bellof's

case, it was like following someone to the very edge of a preci-
pice. He was on the ragged limit all the time. It wasn't a case of
the rest of us not being able to do what he was doing … we just
weren't prepared to go that far.

When Bellof arrived on the scene in the early 80s, he was
immediately the quickest guy in world sports-prototype racing.
You get two kinds of fast: a very controlled and calculated fast,
like an Alain Prost; and the kind of fast that's often on the reckless
side. Ayrton Senna was like that, and so was Bellof.

I followed Bellof during practice sessions and he was forever
sliding the car. There was an exuberance to his driving that was a
joy to watch, but it also skirted danger far too often for my liking.
I could drive like he did for a balls-to-the-wall qualifying lap, but
not for the entire race. I wasn't comfortable doing it. Remember,
these were cars with big ground-effects set-ups, and getting them
to slide around took not only exceptional skill, but great bravery.
Do this all the time, though, and it moves beyond bravery to pure
foolhardiness.

Bellof was one of those rare talents that other drivers acknowledge as something special. You could see it in the way he handled
both the Porsche 956 and the Tyrrell 012, which he raced in F1.
His was a very positive and direct way of driving – a no-nonsense
approach that demanded the car do exactly what he wanted it to
do. Bellof won the World Sports Prototype Championship in
1984, and I think he still holds the famous Nordschleife track
lap-record at the old Nürburgring – a 6:11.13 he set while grab-
bing pole position in a factory Rothmans Porsche 956 at the 1983
ADAC 1 000 km Nürburgring.

We were all therefore very sad to witness his fatal crash at the
very circuit where Schumacher would later impress me so much.
At the 1985 1 000 km of Spa race at Spa-Francorchamps, his Brün
Motorsport Porsche touched Jacky Ickx's factory Porsche, sending
both into the barriers. Bellof's car went straight through the barriers and into a wall. The car burst into flames and he was killed.

Tragic, yes. I can't say that we were surprised, though.

The saddest part for us older guys was knowing that Bellof could've been one of the greats. He had the ability, but sadly he never made it beyond the crashing phase we all go through. If he'd survived another year and got into F1, I think we would probably have had another Schumacher on our hands.

4. DEVELOP YOUR BMT

Big match temperament. If you've got it, great. If you don't have it, go out and get it, because it doesn't matter how talented you are, without BMT you don't stand a chance in motor sport. Other drivers will soon pick up that you lack it.

I'll give you an example – Chip Robinson. Now here was one very talented Yank driver. He often partnered Al Holbert, driving a Porsche 962 in their IMSA team, and now and then he'd also compete in the World Sports Prototype Championship race in Europe.

In fact, Chip was my teammate for the 1987 Le Mans in the Jöest Porsche 962. He was very quick, but he just couldn't deal with pressure situations. Chip would invariably be among the fastest during practice, which meant he'd be the last guy to go out and do his qualifying lap. But we all knew that if one of us stepped up and put in a really good lap, Chip would fold and almost always mess up his quali lap at some point on the track.

As you can imagine, BMT was never an issue for SuperVan. In fact, the opposite was true. I relished this kind of situation, as it meant the spotlight was shining brightly on me, and what better light in which to display my driving ability? This confidence also gave me the platform to play a mind game or two with my opponents. They weren't of the subtle kind, either.

I remember one Sasol Rally – it must've been in 1992. Nic de Waal was leading the rally by something like 25 seconds in his four-wheel-drive Nissan Sentra. I was second, but driving a Ford Lazer – not the greatest rally car I've ever driven. There was only one stage to go, and no way on earth was I going to make up that time.

The situation called for a little wager.

'Hey, Nic!'

'Ja?'

'I bet you R150 … no … R200 that I'll take at least 30 seconds out of you in this stage.'

'Ag bullshit.'

Because he was leading the rally, De Waal was first on the road. I was second. Halfway through the stage, I came around the corner … to see Nissan parts scattered all over the road. De Waal had rolled his car in a big way. The rally was mine. Pieter de Waal – Nic's brother and team manager – went ballistic …

'How can you fall for shit like that!!!'

Man, it was bloody funny.

Throughout my rally career, I had no qualms about telling my competitors exactly how bad a hiding I planned to give them. I found this tactic to be a lot more effective than a subtle approach. It dovetailed perfectly with my driving strategy, too. During the Castrol Rally, for example, I would always make a point of letting my fellow drivers know that the Castrol was always won on the first night, and seeing that this was the first night, they were going to eat my dust. I would then get in the car and go berserk for three or four stages. I'd set scarily fast times that the rest of them could never achieve.

Obviously I'd never be able to sustain that pace for the rest of the rally, but it was enough to intimidate the hell out of the rest of the field. Mentally they'd all now be fighting for second place, allowing me take it easy and control the lead from the front.

From time to time, someone would call my bluff. One of the drivers might find himself on a roll and he and I would have a *moer* of a dice. It was fun, actually – it brought out the fighter in me. If the guy got in front, I'd make damn sure he knew that any mistake he made would lose him the lead. Whatever he did, he'd know I'd be right behind him, hounding the hell out of him.

I tried something similar with my former IMSA teammate, Englishman David Hobbs. He was my co-driver during my first IMSA season, driving the Chevrolet Corvette GTP in 1985, but for the 1986 season, he jumped ship to hook up with the new BMW-March team. Run by McLaren North America, these new cars ran a very powerful four-cylinder turbo motor, based on BMW's F1 engine. At the season opener at Daytona, I wanted to make damn sure Hobbs knew who had the better car.

'Hey, Hobbs. Today I'm going to show you exactly how fast I am. Today this guy from Africa is going to show you Poms how to drive a racing car.'

I went out and clocked a serious lap time – something like two-and-a-half seconds quicker than anyone else. I could see Hobbs in my rear-view mirror trying to keep up with me, but he didn't last, and the next thing all I could see was a new BMW-March spinning like a top. Although he didn't break the car, he cocked up his qualifying session completely.

Hobbs was one of the real characters of that series, and he and I got on very well, despite our rivalry on the track. He was also part of the Jöest Porsche team with Chip Robinson at the 1987 Le Mans. Hobbs was an outright clown and a wonderful mimic. I remember him teasing team owner Reinhold Jöest during the 1987 Le Mans. That was the year our car broke on the warm-up lap, which meant we had the whole of the Saturday to drink and cause a bit of kak. Hobbs kept on addressing Jöest as 'Herr Oberst' – and, talking in a funny German accent, kept on teasing him about German technology.

'You Chermans really like putting yourselves under ze pressure, ja? I mean, you haf developed ze V2 rocket 10 years before you haf actually used ze damn sing in World War II. It vos only ven ze war vos basically lost zat you take it out und aimed it at us. Vot is it vis you people?'

It was hilarious. Old Jöest's German crew nearly wet themselves.

As well as it worked for me, my in-your-face approach was not the only way to gain a psychological advantage. You could, for example, take the Björn Borg approach and isolate yourself in a bubble of concentration. You never knew what the guy was thinking – whether he was pissed off, nervous or happy. Just the same, focused expression all the time. It must've been very disconcerting for his opponents.

Prost adopted this kind of approach – very analytical – and it was tough to figure out what was going on under that curly mop of his.

Senna, on the other hand, was the in-your-face type – not so much with what he said, but with what he was prepared to do out there on the track. Senna wasn't an aggressive personality, but in the car he made it very clear to the rest of the drivers that he would do whatever it took to win, including crashing into them.

Which is exactly what he did to Prost at Suzuka in 1994. Senna was ahead of the Frenchman by 11 points going into the penultimate race of the season, in Japan, and he knew he'd win the championship if Prost scored no points in this race. Although Senna would later claim that he had wanted to make a point about the FIA's decision to change his pole position from the clean right-hand side to the dirty left-hand side, he famously drove Prost off the track at the first corner. Whether or not the FIA were conspiring to sabotage Senna's chances of winning the championship – as Senna suspected – his actions seemed to be a very direct, albeit a very cynical way of claiming his second world title. By attempting what was clearly an impossible overtaking manoeuvre at the first turn, Senna took Prost, and himself, out of the race. He won the championship, though.

I think Senna's actions intimidated the crap out of everyone – especially Prost. It seemed as if he was prepared to risk his life to win. That little French guy was an incredible driver and he really should've won more titles … and Senna fewer. But psychologically speaking, Senna had his number.

The Brazilian's approach was similar to mine, though clearly more extreme, and I have to say I do think it's the more effective approach. I just wish some of our local drivers would adopt it. I don't think any of them really want to dominate racing badly enough, which is why we don't have any motor-sport heroes … or any real sports heroes, to be honest. There are very few sports stars in South Africa that you can either love or hate, and, for me, that's a critical element in any sport. Everyone has just become so effing polite, it irritates the living shit out of me.

5. LEARN HOW TO DRIVE FOR A CHAMPIONSHIP

Winning races is only half the job done. To win titles, you need to be consistent. And that means choosing not to go for that high-risk, do-or-die banzai charge down the inside in a stupid bid for race-winning glory. If it's the last race of the season and you need the points, fine; but if it's earlier on, the smart thing to do is to settle for second and collect the points, thank you very much.

I learnt the wisdom of this early on. During the 1975 rally season, you'll remember that I left Datsun in a huff for Alfa halfway through the calendar. If I had stayed with Datsun and their great 160U, I would easily have won the championship. But because my real ambitions were focused on the racetrack and Alfa offered me that opportunity, I had to complete the rally season in the Alfetta, which, unlike Alfa's racing car, was a piece of shit.

I had built up quite a lead in the Datsun, but it immediately became clear that I hadn't a hope of winning any more rallies in the Alfetta that year. To win my first ever championship, I had to make sure that I accumulated points from then on in. Which I did, by placing in most races – because I had learnt my lesson the previous season.

After winning the 1974 Duckhams Rally, driving the standard Datsun SSS, I had become a little cocky, thinking that, because I'd beaten them once, I could beat them again. And because I was only in a standard car, I thought I had to be on the limit all the time. Bad idea. I crashed a lot. I reckon if I'd driven a little more conservatively and accumulated more points rather than go for overall wins, I could have finished second or third in the championship.

I was fortunate to have had that experience early on in my career and it was one of the major reasons I'd go on to win all those rally championships between 1977 and 1986. I wasn't too fazed if I didn't finish the first rally, or only came third in another. I knew that I'd win my fair share, and by steadily accumulating points in the rest, I'd be the one receiving the trophy at the season-ending awards dinner.

6. NEVER, EVER PICK THE NUMBER 4

It doesn't matter how good you are ... some things can't be explained. Like the number 4. Whenever I drove a car that was even vaguely associated with that number, shit would happen. And I mean bad, not good, shit.

The curse started early on in my career. After I won my first rally championship in 1975, I drove one rally with the number 4 on my car the following season. Back then, rather than always drive with number 1 as the current champ, there'd be a draw at the start of each rally to determine the starting order. And that would be your number. I got 4 ... and from then on, weird stuff would happen whenever I drew that number.

Often the shit would happen when I wasn't even near the car. It would be parked at a service point somewhere, and somebody else would reverse into it. Or the mechanics would be working on it, and suddenly it would move off the jack and the jack would go through the sump. It got so bad that I refused to drive with that number.

One particular instance really illustrates what I'm talking about: the 1992 Volkswagen Rally in PE. To my horror, I was drawn 4.

'No … screw that … I'm not driving with that number. I'm not even going to show up because it's just going to be kak.'

But the organisers wouldn't budge. Obviously I couldn't refuse to take part just because I didn't like my race number. All I could do was wait and see what 4 had in store for me this time …

I was very unhappy about the situation and even drove with roman numerals on my car in a vain attempt to avoid the inevitable. Because I lived in PE then, I knew the surrounding countryside very well, and by stage … wait for it … four, I was leading by over a minute. I came bombing past two guys standing on a bank watching the rally and, as I approached, the rock they were standing on broke loose, rolled down the bank, hit the front wheel of my Ford Lazer and broke the suspension. That was it. We were out of the rally.

Another time I was due to race a Porsche 962 for the Brün team at the Norisring. When I got there, I saw that the car had the dreaded number on its side. I warned the Brün people about what a bad omen this was and tried my best to persuade them to change the number *sofort*. They thought I was joking. They even made some comment about my superstition probably only being a southern hemisphere trait and that the German mindset was so strong, the curse would be rendered ineffective.

Okay then.

There were two one-hour heats that day, and I won the first one. Naturally, there were more German-accented sniggers in our pits. During the second heat, however, while heading for an overall win, I passed a slower car on the main straight on the very last lap. There's a hairpin right at the end of the straight for which you have to brake heavily, and as I turned in, I was T-boned by the guy I had just passed. His brakes had failed and he'd come sailing down the long straight, right into me.

When I joined the Chevrolet Corvette team in 1985, my car was initially allocated the number 40. I made them remove it.

I'm not even superstitious. But strange things happened whenever I had a race or rally car with the number 4 on it. Of all the races I've won – and over the years there have been many – not one of them ever featured a car with the number 4. In fact, I don't think I ever even finished any event with that number on the car.

7. AND THEN 'JUST DO IT'

Don't make stupid excuses. When they do badly, sports stars love placing the blame on everyone and everything but themselves. Don't blame bad luck, jet lag, an unfamiliar track … and don't ever let me hear that you're consulting a sports psychologist. Man up, you bunch of soft cocks. Especially you rugby okes and crick-eters. It annoys me when I listen to some player roll out the inevitable, 'No, we lost because it's been a draining tour and we were jet-lagged.'

Jet-lagged?

I remember finishing a Castrol Rally on the Sunday after-noon, catching a helicopter from Mbabane to Johannesburg, boarding a flight to the US, then the following day strapping myself into a 1 200bhp Chevrolet Corvette and stomping on the gas pedal. There was none of this 'Sorry, but I've got jet lag' bullshit. I had to get in and bloody drive, and drive fast or I'd be out of a job.

In fact, the more I drove, the better I got. I look back at 1984 to 1990 as the golden period of my career – it was a time when I was rallying and racing in South Africa, as well as driving the Porsches and Chevrolet Corvette overseas. Sure, the schedule was hectic, and all the flying was one of the main reasons I would eventually stop racing abroad, but driving those different cars certainly upped my game by several notches.

I didn't worry at all about different cars and different tracks, or the fact that I was going from left-hand-drive cars to right-hand-drive cars – I just wanted to drive. The variation was actually very beneficial. I developed a great feel for cars and it was one of the reasons why I was very good at setting a car up.

Back to making excuses – of course I realise rugby is a very physical game and you okes need your downtime, but don't give me that crap about how tired you poor Proteas are after playing cricket for eight months. Toughen up. You're getting paid a kak-load of money – and they tell me you don't even get taxed on it if you stay out of the country long enough with your girlfriend while exchanging messages on Twitter. Is that true? Can't be. Because after that piss-poor performance in the last Cricket World Cup, I'm already hacked off with you lot … and that might just push me too far.

And this rubbish about 'home-ground advantage'. I don't understand that either, especially when you're talking about a team sport. You're travelling with your buddies – don't give me this kak about how tough it is on the road. I was on my own out there travelling from track to track, country to country, just getting on with it. You race against the same guys, in the same cars, what's the bloody difference where you drive? Whether you're playing at Newlands or in Christchurch, it's the same-size field with the same-size opponents. Why must you be influenced by home ground? So what if one or two drivers knew the track better than me – I'd have at least two days to practise before the race, and if you didn't know the track by the end of it, you were never going to know it.

As for the 'partisan crowd support' argument: of course the crowd will be supporting the home team. So? That means you play worse? If a part of the crowd was cheering for my competitors, it would motivate me even more. To be honest, I loved competing in different parts of the world. Any free time I got, I'd be out there driving or walking around, taking in the local culture. No, I don't get this whole 'home-ground advantage' excuse.

Just like I don't understand the need for sports psychologists. As far as I'm concerned, if you're not tough enough to handle the pressure of professional sport, then you shouldn't be there. Go and do something else. I don't usually like speaking on SuperVan's behalf, but I can honestly say that he never sat around at a foreign racetrack thinking, 'I wish somebody could just give me a little pep talk.'

I was at that racetrack because I loved driving racing cars against other people and I loved to win. Now, shit, if that's not enough motivation for you, then you should step out of those fireproof overalls and take up yoga.

12

HOW TO CRASH LIKE SUPERVAN

You can't race cars and not crash. I certainly did – I had some big ones too. And I survived them all with hardly an injury. Luck? Maybe …

Crashes … yip, I've had my fair share. And, typically, they tended towards the spectacular. If you'll remember from the first chapter, I started quite young too, crashing my mother's Ford Fairlane when I was 12 and, of course, my father's precious Porsche Speedster a few years later. For me, cars and accidents were part of the package right from the beginning.

As an aspirant young racer I understood racing to be a dangerous pastime and a potentially fatal career. As I was growing up, one or two of my heroes would die each year – Formula 1 drivers Wolfgang von Trips, Lorenzo Bandini, Jim Clark, Piers Courage, Jochen Rindt and François Cevert were all big names who were killed when I was young. Somehow, though, their deaths seemed very far removed from my own experience. With a father involved in motor sport, I was deeply immersed in the South African racing scene from a young age, and even though I saw plenty of racing accidents, our drivers seemed to emerge relatively unscathed.

I suppose when you're young, you also have a sense of invincibility – in your mind, only old people die – and if you hit a tree or rolled the car, you always believed you were going to be all right. I'd crashed my parents' cars, and I'd even seen my dad crash the Speedster at the old Grand Central track near Pretoria. He wasn't wearing a seat belt and was thrown from the car, yet the only injuries he suffered were a couple of bad bruises.

I think that is why crashing, or getting injured in a crash, never bothered me much. Sure, some of my Formula 1 heroes had died, but life down here at the tip of Africa seemed very different. In my world, people walked away from accidents while brushing a little dirt off their shoulders. So, yes, I grew up around crashes and, frankly, they didn't seem that serious. The possibility of dying in a crash was simply something I never entertained.

When I first started rallying, I used to crash quite a lot. I was a youngster trying to establish himself on the scene, and I genuinely believed that I was better than the likes of Jan Hettema and the rest of the established guard. I wasn't just being *windgat*, either – my stage times in those early rallies certainly supported my self-belief. I might not have been the quickest, but given that I was in a standard car as opposed to the big guns in their modified machines, my times proved that I was the real deal.

Problem was, in order to beat or even equal those times, I had to be over the limit through most of the stages. *Way* over the limit. And you simply cannot drive on the edge for an entire rally. Unlike the smooth asphalt of a track, there are just too many unpredictable factors on a rally's road surfaces. You're going to have an accident. End of story.

I went off the road many times in those early days and destroyed a fair number of cars. But I always walked away from the wrecks. For me, crashing was not a disaster, though it might have been a financial disaster when I was funding myself. I maintained this attitude throughout my entire career and, despite some major prangs, it kept me injury-free for the duration.

Accidents didn't just happen on the track or in rallies. Even on the road, a crash seemed to be relatively harmless. I remember, for example, driving my Toyota Corolla to visit a girl in 1968 and being clipped by an idiot who'd skipped a red traffic light. My Toyota flipped onto its roof, then skidded for about a block. My head got a bit hot from the friction of the roof sliding over the tarmac, but other than that, I was fine.

Let me take you through some of my bigger shunts, where, despite the carnage, the worst injury I ever suffered in motor racing was two cracked ribs. This is how it happened ...

1992, FORD SAPPHIRE

On its own, motor racing is an unpredictable and dangerous environment in which to earn a living. Add Terry Moss to the mix and you up the ante significantly. Terry is a now-retired South African racing driver who won multiple saloon-car titles in both Wesbank and Group N. He's a nice enough bloke and he and I get on well these days, but put him in a racing car and he turns into – sorry, Terry – something of an idiot. I think it's a case of wanting to win so badly that common sense and caution get left back in the pits. It's not so much a case of the famous 'red mist' that descends as a 'red downpour'.

At the time of the accident I'm about to describe, there was also a fair amount of needle between Ford and Audi, the two manufacturers for whom we respectively drove. Having become somewhat bored driving their all-conquering Quattro Wesbank car, SuperVan had issued instructions that he and I should leave Audi for Ford in order to show the world just how good a driver he was. I therefore swapped teams in 1991. My fireproofs now sported a blue oval rather than the interlinked four rings. Or to put it another way, I no longer *vorsprunged durch technik*, but kicked ass with pure US of A muscle.

Moss was my replacement at Audi and was obviously dead keen to ensure that the Wesbank title not only stayed with the Audi team, but became his. Given that Moss's *normal* state of mind is 'fired up', one can only imagine what happens when he's actually fired up.

Despite beating the Audi in the 1991 season-opener race, which gave me immense satisfaction – I mentioned it in Chapter 7 – the Sapphire wasn't good enough to win consistently and Moss claimed the championship. At the start of 1992, Moss – being

Moss – was once again all fired up to make sure that he retained the championship. And of course, SuperVan being SuperVan, I was equally determined not to let this unholy event happen again.

One of the early races of the season was at the Welkom track – now, of course, known as the Phakisa Freeway – and I was following Moss down the straight, lining up a pass into a big 180-degree corner. I'd been slipstreaming Moss and, using the slingshot effect of the slipstream, moved out from behind his Audi and passed him at about 300 km/h.

But as I went by, he clipped the back of my Ford, which turned it sideways in front of him and sent the car, with me inside, off the road and into the gravel. This, remember, is all happening at 300 km/h. Did Moss do it deliberately? I think he did. But even giving him the benefit of the doubt and saying it was an unintentional clip, it was still one monumentally stupid piece of driving.

The moment the Ford hit the sand, the wheels dug in and the car went arse-over-petrol. It started rolling sideways for what felt like a helluva long time and then executed a couple of backwards, end-over-end rolls just for good measure before eventually coming to a halt.

All in all I rolled sideways nine times and end-over-end three times. Those end-over-end rolls might look spectacular, but they're actually easier on your body than sideways rolls – they happen a lot slower and therefore generate far less G-force.

It was a big shunt ... the biggest of my career. I didn't realise it at first, but only once I'd undone my safety belt, switched off everything so there'd be no fire and climbed out ... and then had a look at what remained of my car, did I realise it. I walked away, but when I tried to climb through the safety fence, I began to feel the pain. Although my whole body ached, the sharpest pain was on my left side. I was carted off to hospital for a check-up, where it was discovered that, incredibly, the only injury I had received were two cracked ribs.

Normally in an accident such as this, you just kind of hang on to the steering wheel for dear life, but during those initial sideways rolls, my left hand had come off the wheel and I'd smacked myself in the ribs with my own elbow. That was basically it. All they could do was put some light strapping around my chest. To this day, I've never been in a cast for any motor-sport-related injury.

That was basically it for the Sapphire too. Simply put, the car was fucked. It wasn't just a case of the body panels being graunched – at that speed, the roll had totalled the body, the chassis and the engine. Everything was stuffed. We needed a new car ... which is when we bought the Cougar.

Naturally, I was not a happy individual. After I'd been to hospital and they'd strapped me up, I went out for dinner with Danielle. All the drivers were staying at the Holiday Inn, and who was at the bar but my good friend, Mr Moss. He hadn't once inquired about my well-being and here he was, having a drink.

We exchanged words.

Mine were obviously peppered with every expletive I've ever known – I recall the words 'poes' and 'you' being two that came up quite often. His were unrepentant. He wouldn't admit any fault.

Neither did MotorSport South Africa, which, frankly, was no surprise. In the court case that followed, the accident was deemed a 'racing incident'. I knew Moss was fully responsible, though ... and so did my fellow drivers. Full credit to them, as a number of the guys took Moss on about his reckless driving. I remember Michael Briggs in particular telling Moss exactly what he thought of his on-track behaviour.

But I had walked away relatively unscathed, for which I was grateful. It was not the first time I'd had a big shunt and had escaped unharmed.

1982, FORD ESCORT BDA

It was dusk, Day 2 of the 1982 Castrol Rally, and I was chasing down Tony Pond. Even though the British driver and his potent

2.4-litre Nissan Stanza were ahead of me on the time sheets, I was at the wheel of that wonderful 2.0-litre BDA Ford Escort and therefore confident of catching him.

Although I was first on the road, with Pond starting behind me, the Englishman had initially been quicker than me. It was a fairly long stage, and at some point I had received word that he was now a couple of seconds ahead. There would be a bit of a rest at the end of the stage and a regroup before we'd start the night stages. I definitely needed to be in the lead by that time – it would allow me to be first on the road, which was always a good thing at night, especially when it was as dusty as it was on that Castrol.

To win back those few seconds, I had to take some risks, and my navigator, Franz Boshoff, and I were prepared for some over-the-limit driving. It was game faces on, helmets strapped extra tight. This was going to be a serious stage.

It being dusk, visibility wasn't great, but with the stage starting on a slight downhill, I could see about a kilometre into the distance. There was what appeared to be a dip, then a little rise, and beyond that a gap in the tree line (remember, we had no pace notes back then). It looked as if the road was pretty much straight all the way, which would allow for flat-out acceleration through all the gears. Franz and I looked at each other, nodded, and off we went.

Only the road wasn't straight.

Turns out that it turned sharply right at the top of the rise in front of a deep donga, after which it carried on straight through the tree line. We couldn't see the right-hand turn until we got there, by which time, of course, it was *way* too late. I couldn't possibly brake in time. I had two options: I could either stand on the middle pedal and try to scrub off as much speed as possible before we rolled into the donga, or SuperVan could accelerate and try to jump over the donga.

SuperVan usually gets his way in these situations. And I must admit, his logic made sense ... we were going to crash anyway, so we might as well try to gap it. So I put foot in a somewhat optimistic attempt to fly across a six- or seven-metre donga without anything resembling a ramp ... or any kind of landing area on the other side, should we miraculously get across. Only bush and small rocks would be there to greet us.

I'm not sure what was going through Franz's mind – it's not as if I had the time to ask him. I had to make a split-second decision and ...

... ja ... no. We didn't make it.

For a tiny moment I'd thought we might, but the Escort ploughed nose first into the opposite bank, about a metre short of the lip. Not a bad effort, I thought.

Then the car just rolled and rolled and rolled and rolled and rolled ... out of sight of any other competitors coming past. No one knew we had gone off the road. Because I had accelerated in my attempt to clear the donga, there weren't even any telltale skid marks on the road to indicate an accident. Thanks to the Escort's strong roll cage and our safety belts, we appeared to have survived. The car, though, was a total write-off. The bodywork had concertinaed around the roll cage, but at least we were okay.

Initially, though, Franz thought he was bleeding to death ...

When the car finally came to rest on its wheels, the first thing I asked – after I'd done my own mental check and had wiggled all the body parts one wiggles when one finds oneself in such circumstances – was, 'Are you okay?'

'No!' said Franz in a panic. 'I'm bleeding!'

'Shit!' I thought, he must be bleeding internally because I can't see any blood. 'Where?'

He pointed to his legs and feet. But there was nothing ... no blood. I said, 'Where?!' and he said, 'There!' I go, 'But *where*?!' and he shouts, 'There, there!' And so on.

Then I realised that the windscreen-washer bottle inside the car had come loose and, because it was next to the engine compartment, the water was sort of lukewarm, which was why Franz was feeling all this warmish, wet stuff.

'There's no fucking blood, it's water! Now get out of the fucking car before it catches alight!'

One's language does tend to get fairly colourful in that sort of situation.

It took us 10 minutes to get out of the car and back up to the road. I know this because car number five passed us just as we got back up, and the cars leave at two-minute intervals. It was a big accident and our rally was obviously over, but Franz and I suffered nothing worse than some painful bruises and stiff muscles, and, of course, one soggy racing overall.

1980, MODIFIED FORD ESCORT

I suppose there haven't been too many instances in the history of motor sport where one shunt shuts down an entire formula. It happened here, though.

It was the final race of the 1980 Manufacturer's Challenge Saloon Car championship – a series that had really whipped up public interest. Started in 1979, it was basically a silhouette series – in other words, the cars had to 'kind of' look like the donor saloons they were based on and they had to have an engine from the same stable. You could, for example, shoehorn a Ferrari engine into a Fiat ... both brands were in the same stable. To say the rules offered a broad interpretation is something of an understatement.

With the promise of some very exciting and fairly exotic machinery on our local tracks, the series attracted the big car manufacturers, the big-name drivers in local racing, and the crowds. It all produced some very, shall we say, 'spirited' driving from those behind the wheel. And SuperVan does love a bit of spirited racing.

By the series' second year, I had a decent car – a Ford Escort with a European-spec Group 5 Ford Capri 3.4-litre Cosworth V6.

Sharing the track with me were the likes of Geoff Mortimer and his V8 Chevair, Dave Charlton in a twin-turbo, rotary-engined Mazda 323 screamer, Basil van Rooyen in his Ferrari-powered Fiat 131 with its turbo-charged V6 straight out of the Lancia Stratos rally car ... and Ian Scheckter in a BMW.

BMW started Scheckter off in Eddie Keizan's old BMW 530 chassis, onto which they had grafted all sorts of wings and flared wheel arches, and stuck in their legendary straight-six engine from their CSL racing car.

By now the stakes were high and the teams had pretty hefty budgets. There was a little needle, too – the English press, led largely by a journalist called Harvey Thomas of *The Star*, were always writing up Scheckter, while the Afrikaans press were behind me. The fact that we were probably the biggest names in local motor sport back then – he was a multiple SA Drivers Champion and I was the SA Rally Champion – obviously added to the drama as well.

That year, the races were usually contested between the two of us. Our cars were pretty evenly matched and Ian and I would always qualify in the front row of the grid and generally swap door-handles all the way through. As far as motor-sport fans and my peers were concerned, I think that series really confirmed me as a serious racing driver. Before that, I was seen more as a rally driver who would appear on the racetrack and slide cars around rally style. I was often referred to as 'Sideways Sarel'.

Scheckter, on the other hand, came into the series with a big reputation. He had blown everybody into the weeds in our big single-seater formulas – the SA Formula 1 series and also Formula Atlantic. Even though there were a lot of door-to-door dices, I had his number. I remember one specific instance where I even out-braked him with two wheels on the dirt. Scheckter thought I was going to lose it and take us both out, so he backed off. I don't think he'd ever seen a move like that before. Obviously, I kept everything under control and took the lead.

This incident set the scene for what has gone down in South African motor-sport lore as 'The Prang of all Prangs' …

We were racing at Kyalami, and after another opening-lap dice, I'd managed to open up a lead on Scheckter … only then to be held up by some backmarkers. Scheckter closed up again and was right up my arse all the way through Barbecue Corner and into the old Jukskei Sweep. Jukskei was never the best place to overtake – it was a very quick, slightly off-camber corner that only had one racing line through it.

Cue some serious Scheckter brain fade …

With both of us nudging 250 km/h, he dived up my inside, I stuck to the racing line (the only line) and he hit the side of my car. Predictably, off we went. How we didn't roll I still don't know, but there was a shower of dust, grass, fences and expensive bits of Escort and BMW all over the show. We were okay, but the cars were completely buggered.

I was livid and, with our cars coming to rest a few metres apart, I climbed out of the wreckage with the intent to seriously *moer* him. What I saw when I got out, though, made me laugh out loud. Scheckter had taken shelter under the embankment, because the incensed crowd – clearly pissed off that he'd messed up a very entertaining race – were pelting him with beer bottles.

I saw Scheckter again in the pub at the post-race prize giving. Normally these are very pleasant affairs where we all get together to have a party and talk shit, but that night I was feeling very aggrieved. Our team manager, Bernie Marriner, made sure Scheckter was kept out of my sight, and I suspect that the BMW guys were on the same page. Scheckter is not a very confrontational guy, but I think everyone knew I was just waiting for an excuse to *klap* him. Actually, I reckon if anyone had said something wrong that night, I would have decked them.

The debate carried on in the press in the weeks that followed, and eventually MotorSport South Africa convened a hearing. For once MSA took my side and found Scheckter guilty of dangerous driving. But it didn't amount to too much. He was given a small fine, which was nothing more than a slap on the wrist.

Scheckter's BMW was a total write-off, so they had to build a new car. At least my Escort was repairable, and while BMW were busy building the new car, I won a couple of races in Scheckter's absence. When Scheckter did return, it was with a completely tricked-out racing car. This BMW bent the already sketchy silhouette rules to breaking point, and their fancy new monocoque chassis was immediately two seconds a lap faster than any other car. By now, none of the other manufacturers was prepared to spend the kind of money needed to take on BMW, and the series fizzled out … basically thanks to that accident.

My relationship with Ian Scheckter remained somewhat strained for a few years afterwards, but it improved when I drafted him into our Kreepy Krauly–sponsored IMSA-series March in 1984. From then on we became good pals, and these days Scheckter stays with me when he comes to Cape Town, and I stay with him when I'm in East London.

Whenever we attend the same public function, *that* accident always comes up for discussion. We always get asked to explain what really happened … at which point I hand the mike over to Scheckter and say, 'I think the perpetrator is the best person to answer your question.'

Scheckter usually tries to palm off the crash as 'just a racing accident', saying that we were all much more aggressive back then and he *had* to try to get past me. That's my cue to tell everyone that he's talking shit.

MAYBE IT'S JUST LUCK?

I know people find it a little strange when I tell them I've never really worried about dying in a racing car. Surely, they think, somewhere at the back of his mind there must be this little kernel of fear.

No. Seriously. Nothing.

Aside from the fact that having fear as your co-driver will never make you a race winner, my life experience has shown me that there are many other ways of kicking the bucket. I didn't need to look any further than my own family. My mother and father both died of cancer in their 50s – and within two-and-a-half years of each other. That's some serious shit to deal with. In the back of my mind, I probably figured that I wouldn't make it past 50 with my family history, so what the hell, I might as well enjoy life while I can.

I also quickly realised that you don't have any time to think about the possibility of your impending death during a racing accident. You're way too busy trying to sort out your predicament. Remember that incident in the Kreepy Krauly March at Road Atlanta when it burnt out during testing in 1984?

A quick refresher: There must have been a fuel leak near the March's turbo, which then ignited, causing the rear suspension's highly flammable magnesium strut to burn through. The car suddenly spun as if it had hit an oil patch, and through the rotations I saw the flames from the rear shoot past me. When the car eventually stopped, a marshal ran up with a fire extinguisher.

No need to panic then.

Then the fuel tank exploded.

As I was trying to unclip the four-point harness seat belts, I felt a big *whump*! as the bloody fuel tank beneath me ignited, buckling the floor pan and pinning me in the belts. The marshal aimed the nozzle of the fire extinguisher at my rapidly burning March, hit the button and ... nothing happened. As his eyes grew very big, he turned tail and ran, which is when I realised I was now in some fairly deep shit.

Now *this* would be a good time to panic.

The explosion had blown a hole right through the floor pan and flames were now coming into the cockpit, engulfing the whole left-hand side. And guess which side the car's only door was on ...

I remember feeling surprisingly calm, and I somehow managed to get my belts undone in order to climb through the flames
and open the door to roll out of the car ... which then proceeded
to burn to a grey, melted pile of metal right in front of me. With
the flames starting to broil my arse through my fireproofs, I'd
simply had no time to worry about dying – I had too much to do.
And that, I think, is one of the major reasons why I'm not scared
of dying in a racing accident. I know I'd be so busy trying to
prevent the prang or getting myself out of the car that the fatal
moment would come without me even realising it.

In a crisis situation, I seem to have the ability to keep my
thought processes under control and think my way out of things.
I do admit, though, that a certain amount of luck has had something to do with it. Then again, they do say that you create your
own luck – don't make me quote Gary Player on this one – and
perhaps that is true on some metaphysical level, where one supposedly creates one's own reality.

Or maybe it's just fate. When it's your time, it's your time.

I say that because one guy can have a *moer* of a crash – like
me – and simply walk away, feeling a little stiff the next day. And
another guy can have a fairly innocuous-looking prang – like
NASCAR legend Dale Earnhardt had in 2001 – and be dead.

Have a look at the YouTube footage of his fatal accident at
the 2001 Daytona 500. It's hard to believe he would've had much
more than some serious bruising. Earnhardt's flanked by two
cars coming into Turn 3; he seems to get a nudge from one car,
which sends him left to the bottom apron, but he overcorrects,
sending his No. 3 Chevrolet up the track, where it clips another
car before hitting the wall nose first.

Because he connects with the concrete wall at a 55-degree
angle, the impact doesn't seem that severe. It's not as if the car hits
the wall straight on and comes to a sudden halt. At the angle he
hit the wall, it appears to be more of a glance, and the car slides
sideways for a long time before coming to a halt. You expect the

guy to climb out and slam his helmet on the ground in disgust at being taken out on the very last lap of NASCAR's most famous race.

But no. The driver whose car Earnhardt had clipped comes to a halt right next to him – he gets out of his car, walks over to Earnhardt, looks inside, and suddenly starts waving his arms frantically for the medics. Dale Earnhardt was already dead … his neck had snapped when he hit the wall.

It was dumb luck. The angle of the impact and the estimated 256 km/h speed at which it had occurred had brought a whole lot of forces into play that conspired to snap his neck. As you now know, I was in the NASCAR business and I know what a monumental pile-up the cars can cause. Those NASCAR accidents are crazy – the whole race is a bit surreal, actually. You're sitting in a pack of 40 or 50 cars, nose to tail and travelling at over 300 km/h. Inevitably, somebody touches somebody else, and then it's just mayhem.

Guys spin, hit the wall, hit other cars, and slide along the grass. You sit there in your car – fortunately built to withstand a nuclear bomb – spinning like a top, getting smacked by what seems to be every car in the field, and there's nothing you can do about it but stand on the clutch to keep the motor going in case you're somehow in good enough shape to continue the race once it's all over.

Eventually the spinning starts to slow down – by this time you've probably slid for a kilometre – and you climb out feeling a little knocked about, but not much more. In the one crash I was involved in, I even took a massive side impact, which bruised me quite badly. Actually, it did more than that – a couple of months later, when I was back home, I started getting out of breath whenever I did anything physical. Like jogging. It got so bad that I eventually saw a specialist, who gave me an ECG, but he couldn't pick anything up.

I was so convinced that something was wrong, I got him to

have another look, and it was only after he'd stuck a little scope into my artery that he discovered one of them was pinched closed. For it to have happened to that artery, reckoned the doc, my body must have taken a huge impact that was strong enough to basically fold my heart. It was obviously the NASCAR shunt.

My point is this … I'd taken all these big knocks in NASCAR and survived in good shape. And even the one time it could've been serious, because of the pinched artery, I still came through without any serious repercussions. Yet Earnhardt has this little smack against a wall with hardly another car involved and, because of a load of forces vectored in a certain way, he is dead. Had the impact angle been one degree different or the speed at impact 2 km/h faster or slower, he would probably have survived. That's how small the margin can be between life and death in this sport.

So what's it about? Luck?

Here's another example – and probably one closer to the Earnhardt incident …

During a 1995 Touring Car race at Kyalami, I T-boned Shaun van der Linde at high speed. He had spun in the esses ahead of me and I was on the outside of a gaggle of cars, entering the corners. As we entered the esses, the guy ahead of me swerved out of the way, and suddenly my field of vision was filled with a BMW parked in the middle of the road. It couldn't have been more than five or six metres away …

There was no time to take evasive action, so I hit Van der Linde square on at exactly 147 km/h. I know this from the car's telemetry. The same telemetry also indicated that I had decelerated from 147 to 0 km/h in 0.7 seconds. I had my hands on the steering wheel and the deceleration was so rapid that the negative G-force generated through my arms and hands actually bent the steering wheel.

The marshals thought I was badly hurt, because once I had unstrapped the seat belts and climbed out, I collapsed on the ground. They were all looking at my head, thinking I probably had a serious head injury ... but the pain was coming from a little further south. In the impact, the seat belts had squashed my one testicle so badly, I couldn't even speak. The next day I had a ghoen the size of a tennis ball.

Other than that, I seemed to be all right – we still had a big piss-up that night at the track's bar. The next morning was a different story. Apart from one very unhappy ball, it felt as if I had pulled every single muscle in my body. I was so sore that instead of going back home by plane, I arranged for a car to drive me back to PE so that I could at least lie back. I was seriously buggered.

As I got older and more experienced, the crashes got fewer, but as we all know, even the best drivers in the world – from Sébastien Loeb to Sebastian Vettel – sometimes get it wrong. At the top level of any motor sport, you're going to be up against a bunch of guys with very similar abilities and to cross the line first, you often have to push the limits a little. And when you push the limits, it's just a matter of time.

I had my last big one in 2001. The owner of a 1971 Ford Escort BDA Mk I, a guy called David Sutton, asked me to drive the car in an international classic-car rally that was held here in South Africa. The rally ran across the entire country and finished in Durban, and included some stages in the Western Cape that were the very same gravel roads used in the annual Cape Rally – a national rally championship event.

As a part of the national championships, the Cape Rally featured all the local big shots like Serge Damseaux, Jannie Habig and Enzo Kuun in their state-of-the-art 4×4 rally machines. Our classic rally wasn't just using the same special stage routes as these pros, but we drove them the day after the Cape Rally guys had been through.

The classic rally wasn't merely a parade of old cars piloted by drivers making sure their valuable possessions were kept nice and safe. Most of them were rich European guys out to have fun in the southern African sun, and they were giving it stick. What a pleasure! I could therefore show them what a car like a Ford Escort BDA Mk1 could *really* do. Even though I'd competed in the BDA Mk II, I felt at home the moment I hit the accelerator on this older version. And I was quick. Very quick. What did you expect – in a BDA, on the same stages as the current pros? How could SuperVan not make an appearance?

After we compared my times through the stages to those of the Cape Rally, it turned out I was only two seconds behind the time set by Cape Rally leader Serge Damseaux. And I was ahead of Kuun, Habig and the rest of the national championship field. Or, to put it another way – a 56-year-old driver in a 30-year-old car would've been lying second in a current national championship rally. That's me in an old rear-wheel-drive tjorrie beating youngsters in their fancy new rally cars.

Naturally, SuperVan made sure he pointed this out to them. I went along to one of the Cape Rally service points ...

'What? Did you guys all have problems?'

'No, why?'

'Well then, how do you explain how an old car and an even older driver can come here and fuck you all up?'

Yip. They were quite sheepish. I will admit that that day gave me immense pleasure, especially as there were quite a lot of wet sections where the 4×4 cars should've nailed me.

Unfortunately, as this is the chapter on big crashes, you've probably guessed that this story does not end on a high note. The classic rally moved on to the Eastern Cape, where I wrote off the BDA, rolling it while bombing it up the Otto Du Plessis Pass between the towns of Ida and Clifford. I slid a little wide in a corner, but as I didn't think it was anything serious, I kept my right foot planted as we went over a patch of grass.

Except it wasn't just a patch of grass.

It was a patch of grass covering a ditch. There was no way I could have known, and the car dug in and flipped. I rolled that nice little Escort into a ball of bent metal. Needless to say, old Dave was very unhappy with me, but that's rallying. It's a very unpredictable type of motor sport and there was no way I could have known that that was a ditch and not just another grassy patch. As they say, thems the risks. Dave was very, very pissed off, and I never saw him or his crew again after that day.

And that was the last one … I haven't had anything close to a major shunt in over 10 years. I still compete in the odd race here and there, but it's mostly in the Historic Saloons series, where everyone is fairly careful not to get into any major scraps. Besides the occasional incident where someone like Mini Cooper Guy needs to be put in his place, it's very clean and we give each other a lot of space.

Looks like my 'luck' has held so far …

13

PEDAL TO THE METAL – STILL

Some reflection, some plans … and some fun and games
with the Japs

The final chapter. It's the one where you're supposed to reflect on
your life and maybe throw in a few wise, philosophical state-
ments and sound advice that years of experience can bring. And
I think you're supposed to bask in the glow of past glories, too.

Well, I'm not much of a philosopher – unless 'to finish first,
first you have to finish' counts. Nor, for that matter, am I much
of a basker. That implies sitting on one's arse, probably wearing
a pair of sunglasses, as the bright light of glittering memories
washes over you.

I'm not ready for that part yet. I still want to do stuff. I still
want to drive a racing car at every opportunity I get. Racing is
still in my blood. It was my career for 35 years, and even though
I may have retired from competitive racing, it doesn't mean the
fire has dimmed. Practically every day for over three decades I
used to go out and scare myself shitless. Take that away and life
can get a little boring.

I mean, there was a time back in the late 80s when I was
driving some of the finest cars on the planet every weekend. I'd
get out of my Audi Quattro rally car, board a plane, and then
climb into a Porsche 962 in Europe, or a Chevrolet Corvette
GTP in the States. Yes, all the flying was kak, but apart from that
it was great to go from one car to another. There was always
something to look forward to. Even if I had a shit result in one
race, I knew I could have another go the next weekend. At one

point I was racing 44 weekends of every year. And what are there ... 52 weekends in a year?

Going from rally cars to sports cars week in and week out might be an adjustment for some drivers, but I was so used to it by then that it was easy making the switch. I could, for example, mentally delete what had happened in the Corvette the week before in order to focus all my attention on the rally I needed to win in the Quattro.

Remember, too, that I was constantly shifting from right- to left-hand drive and back again. Having to deal with such great variation helped develop my ability to set up cars, which is always a great asset for any racing driver. It wouldn't even take a lap or three to rewire my brain for different cars – it happened immediately. I was on top of my game. In fact, our test sessions at the tracks always took less time than those of the other teams. I would simply get straight in, head out, get the tyres warm, do a hot lap, then come back in and say, 'Okay, change this', and do another lap. Whereas the other guys were going 30 or 40 laps, I would be doing maybe 15.

Your memory bank expands with experience – I knew a Porsche should do this and a Corvette won't do that or this is a rally car and it doesn't do any of it. When you're driving competitively on a weekly basis, you just get completely dialled in. One of the reasons Michael Schumacher was so dominant during his time at Ferrari was that they had their own private test track at Maranello and the guy was just driving and testing all the time. These days, with the ban on testing in F1, he's looked like a different driver in his relatively unsuccessful comeback with Mercedes-Benz. The simple truth of the matter is that a guy who's driving an F1 car just about every day is going to be sharper than the one squeezing into the driver's seat every two weeks.

In between all this, in 1988 I even found the time to break the outright South African land-speed record ... in an Audi, of all cars. Until then, the South African flying-kilometre speed record was held by Mike d'Udy. D'Udy, driving a 6.0-litre Loa T70 sports prototype on a closed-off section of road along the Cape's West Coast in 1968, had set an average of 308 km/h for the two required runs. With a modified 500 turbo saloon, Audi had recently set an endurance speed record at the banked Nardo test track in Italy, and the South African chaps thought it would drum up some nice publicity to bring the car over here and have a crack at the record.

The attempt was set for late November 1988 on a flat piece of public road between Bothaville and Welkom. We first took the car to the Welkom racetrack, where the engineers worked on the engine mapping, and then headed for this piece of road that had the required less-than-1 per cent gradient. The test driver got in and posted 320 km/h on both runs, then I got in and set 356 km/h one way and 362 km/h on the return for a new record average of 358.92 km/h. I remember that the Audi's gearing was very long – obviously installed for its Nardo record attempt – and I never even got it past fourth gear. With proper ratios, I reckon we could've gone even faster.

The whole event was pretty uneventful, to be honest. A low-flying helicopter was filming the attempt and, aside from the turbulence it caused, which momentarily upset the car's balance, the actual event was all fairly straightforward. Of course Audi made a big song and dance about it, but I was doing those speeds at Le Mans every lap, so from a personal point of view, its excitement level was up there with scratching my arse. In 2002, Grant van Schalkwyk upped the record to 388 km/h in his low-drag, 9.5-litre Spirit of Dunlop special, but I believe I still hold the record for our class.

Apart from the thrill of international competition, I also miss the fun and games I had back then. And this time I'm not talking about the parties. I miss the subterfuge. I miss the sneaking into countries that would normally ban South African sportsmen and women from competing within their borders. Life as a racing driver was pretty exciting. But life as a South African racing driver travelling abroad was even more so. We weren't that welcome overseas back in those dark days of apartheid, and, while you could enter a country on a tourist visa, competing was not allowed.

This didn't stop me, and I became fairly skilled at slipping into countries without raising any border-control alarm bells. I don't mean slipping across the border in the back of a car boot in the dead of night, but flying or driving into a country via towns or cities with less intense security. If, for example, I had a race at Monza, I wouldn't fly into Rome, but rather land in Venice – where they were far less *paraat* – and make my way to the racetrack from there.

I did get caught out once, though. The Japanese eventually nabbed me. *Hai!*

As I've mentioned, I raced there a few times in the mid-80s with George Fouché. Even though I was granted a six-month visa, I was only given it because I had signed an affidavit stating that I wasn't there to participate in a race, but merely 'to buy parts for a racing car'. Right. Fortunately they cocked up the spelling of my name every time I entered the country – I was Van Merwe, Van Ban Sarl and many other mangled variations of my *suiwer* Afrikaans surname.

Not that I minded. Their systems couldn't match up the Mr van der Merwe who was in Japan on a part-buying mission with the Mr Ban Sarl who was driving a Porsche 962 remarkably quickly round their Fuji racetrack. Unfortunately, though, the little fuckers eventually put two and two together. Landing in Tokyo for my third visit to 'buy parts' ended in my arrest. The immigration officer studied my passport for longer than usual, and I began to suspect that the game was up. Next thing, another official-looking Japanese chap arrives with a guard in tow.

There wasn't any confrontation – the guy just repeated, 'You no come here … you no come here.' They put me on the next flight out. Despite telling the Japs how much I was beginning to like sushi and that Japanese people did not all look alike, they escorted me onto the plane … and I said *sayonara* to Japan.

I was escorted aboard a British Airways flight bound for London, and the poor crew had no idea who I was or what I had done – only that I was some type of criminal the Japanese did not want. I could've been a murderer or a terrorist for all they knew. But my deportation worked out well for me – the crew stuck me in the deserted first-class cabin, which made the journey from Tokyo to London as comfortable as a long plane journey can be.

The next morning, once we'd landed at Heathrow, the whole commotion started up again. I think I was interrogated by every flipping cop in Scotland Yard, who wanted to know who I was and what I was up to. I was there the whole day, with someone keeping an eye on me at all times. They wouldn't let me out of their sight in case I blew up Big Ben or some other English icon we wicked Afrikaans South Africans were just itching to dynamite.

Eventually I'd had enough.

'For fucksakes, get 10 of your armed men and march me over to the South African Airways counter. They will know who I am and vouch that I'm very good at racing cars, but very bad at being a terrorist. Besides, I really like Big Ben.'

The SAA crowd were great – they confirmed I was who I said I was and gave me a ticket home on board a flight that evening.

The Belgians didn't like me much either. Which was fine with me, because I'm not that wild about them. Weird bunch of people, the Belgians. I was stopped at Brussels airport and told to go back to the UK from where I'd come. Which I did. And then I simply hired a car and came across on the ferry. This time they let me in. Idiots.

I once made the Canadians very nervous as well. I was on a flight from London that was scheduled to land in Detroit, but because of major storm activity we were re-routed to Quebec … of all places. Turns out the French-speaking Canadians aren't quite as *laissez-faire* as their brethren back in *la belle* France.

We landed fairly late in the evening – around 8 p.m. – so we were forced to spend the night there. The airline arranged accommodation at a local hotel for all the passengers ... all the passengers except me. As a South African *sans* a Canadian visa, they wouldn't allow me out of the airport. Words were exchanged – I argued that I was far keener to get the hell out of Canada than they were to see the back of me, and that I was therefore unlikely to make a run for it. My argument did the trick. Eventually, at 2 a.m., I was given a hotel room. With an armed guard posted outside the door.

Strangely, some of the countries who officially boycotted South African sportsmen and women didn't actually give too much of a shit when one made an appearance. The Germans, for example, didn't really worry much. And, true to form, the French didn't give a damn. As usual, they always seemed more than happy to do the exact opposite of what other countries wanted them to do.

Even the Aussies didn't seem that fussed. Their main concern was that I wasn't in their country as part of a South African sports team. Individual sportsmen were apparently okay, but South African teams were not welcome. I just had to convince them that I was part of a German privateer Porsche team and all was great. Mate.

The Yanks were the least concerned about my comings and goings. They gave me a 10-year visa and left me to my own devices. Having an apartment and, therefore, an address in Indianapolis, helped. But anything south of the border was a no-go zone. As a South African, I couldn't, for example, travel to Mexico. This became a problem when a whole bunch of us got drunk in San Diego one night and decided that a little jaunt to Acapulco was a helluva good idea.

I was in the Hendrick Motorsport Chevy Corvette team, and the Yanks in the team thought a trip to Mexico was just what was required. You only needed a US driver's licence to cross the US/Mexican border, so we all piled into a van, handed over a bunch of licences at the border post, and we were in. I was really nervous about going into Mexico, because, if we were caught, as a South African I would've been thrown in jail. I don't know about you, but being in a Mexican jail is possibly even less appealing than being in a South African one. Luckily, we had a designated driver to deal with the border officials and made it safely in and out. The rest of us were so drunk that we could barely remember which country we were born in.

I miss the characters I used to race with back then. Funny guys like David Hobbs and Hans-Joachim Stuck, the witty ones like Derek Bell and Klaus Ludwig, and the ones that defy any categorisation ... like Willie T Ribbs.

Willie was an American driver. And black. Not a common sight in US racing, I can tell you that much. He was a real character, though – funny as hell – and we got on like a house on fire. Some Yank TV network would be busy interviewing me and next thing Willie would stick his head in the frame and, with a huge grin on his face, say, 'Hey, Van Der Meer ... kill any of my brothers lately?'

And the TV crew would go, 'Cut!'

It was an unlikely friendship – the white guy from apartheid South Africa and the African American – but he and I had some fun times. Willie was a pretty good driver as well, being the first African American to drive in the Indy 500, as well as NASCAR's Winston Cup. He wasn't too successful there, though. Declaring on live television that it was time somebody showed NASCAR's good ole boys how to drive was not the smartest career move. I think Willie started 24 NASCAR races ... and those good ole boys put him in the wall 24 times.

Yup, I miss those days a lot. I really do. I'm still doing the odd race – and the classic saloon stuff is a helluva lot of fun – but I miss the high-powered cars. Sliding the big Ford Galaxie around Zwartkops or Killarney is great, but it's not the same as driving the Chevrolet Corvette at Daytona or the Porsche 962 at Spa.

But one does have to be realistic. You do – to quote Kenny

Rogers – have to know when to fold 'em, and I retired at the right time. At 55, I was older than most drivers when I called time on my career, but I'd also started very late, only going to the US when I was 37. Most importantly for me, though, I was still competitive when I retired and not some drooling old fart functioning as little more than a mobile chicane out there on the track.

These days, when I do race, I know I've lost the outright pace I had back then, but experience makes up for a lot. I can force other guys to do things they really don't want to do, and that helps. Most drivers still race from corner to corner and a lot of the time I can persuade them to continue with this short-sighted strategy. Once their tyres start to go, I can pick them off. I may be 65 now, but believe me, I can still do it.

Of course, I have to occupy my time in between these races, and most of my spare time is taken up by my Spirit of Africa business. It's basically an off-road competition for teams of two people who have the opportunity to test their 4×4 abilities in some really tough African conditions. My partners are Volkswagen, and their Amarok bakkie is the official competition vehicle for the event. VW supply us with 23 cars to use. We have elimination rounds before the big finals are held at a challenging location. In 2011, this was in Mozambique.

It's pretty intense work for Danielle and me. Each of the two elimination rounds takes place over three months and we host 15 new teams every week. We run everything from a camp site, and Danielle works like a demon to make sure that everyone's comfortable and well fed. You can visit www.amarok.co.za for more details on the next event.

It's been a very successful venture so far, and something I kind of lucked into. It began in 2000, when I was a partner in the Eco-Challenge – also an off-road event, but one with more of an eco-conscious angle. In 2004 my partners and I had an argument about the direction the business should take. I wanted something more driver-focused, and they wanted it to be more environmentally focused. Nothing wrong with that at all, but I knew my skill lay in teaching people how to drive.

I broke away then and started the Spirit, which has now developed a life of its own and has turned into a very good business that's basically killed off all the competition. That wasn't my intention; it's just turned out this way. I think the format of the Spirit is right; I happened to come up with the right idea at the right time.

So far, it's been great, I have to say. Apart from the good times I've had with the contestants who have taken part over the years, it also solved an issue that had been of some concern to me when I was still racing. I had earned money from motor sport for so long that it was difficult to think what the hell I was going to do afterwards. I could buy a business, but I've never been someone to sit behind a desk all day. Me and SuperVan in an office? All day? It just wouldn't work.

But setting up a business once I'd retired from racing hovered in my mind all the time. I still needed an income once I stopped racing, but because I retired from racing about 15 years after most of the other guys my age, it was pretty late in the day for me to get a new venture going. I looked at someone like Chris Aberdein, my ex-teammate at Audi, who'd retired from motor racing in his early 30s and had gone on to be a hugely successful businessman who owned his own helicopter company, as well as doing very well in alternative-energy ventures.

Now that the Spirit has really taken off, I can focus on some new ventures – not least of which will be that showroom stock formula I told you about in Chapter 10.

FOR THE FINAL WORD, OVER TO …

Am I satisfied with my achievements? Am I leaving behind a legacy I'm proud of? I think it's best to leave the final word to SuperVan …

Yes. It's a good idea to give me the final say – it's worked well enough for us over the past 45 years – and yes, I am satisfied with what I've achieved. More than satisfied, actually. A South African has yet to match my feats either as a rally or a racing driver, never mind the combined achievements. And that's not being *windgat*. It's a fact.

Of course I have some regrets, mainly that I only got to race overseas in my late 30s. That's practically retirement age for a racing driver. The fact that I was still able to be successful was a testament to my ability. If I'd got there a decade earlier, I would without a doubt have won some of the world's biggest sports-car races. I was that good.

Not winning Le Mans is another regret – especially after coming so close in my first-ever race there in 1984. I reckon I was unlucky not to have won the greatest of all endurance races at least once. If I'd taken up the offer to drive for Mercedes, I probably would have won it.

In 1987, I was approached to drive one of the Sauber-Mercedes team cars, but got offered another Porsche drive for more money. It was at a time when, thanks to our dear government's apartheid policies, it looked as if not even I could slip in and out of foreign countries any more. Figuring a total ban was imminent, I decided to accept the Porsche deal and the cash, thinking I might as well get what I could while I could. The Sauber-Mercedes team went on to win Le Mans in 1989 and dominated the World Sports Car Championship in 1989 and 1990. That could've been me.

I should also have raced in the States for a little longer instead of stopping at the end of 1989. Granted, my schedule was way too hectic, but I probably should have quit the World Sports Car racing in Europe and continued to race the IMSA series in the States. Time zones were the big issue, but apart from that, America was really easy for me. Everyone spoke English, I had an apartment there and I'd made a bunch of friends.

Another reason why I decided to quit the States was the political situation back home. After PW Botha's infamous 'Rubicon' speech, it seemed that any hope for a peaceful political reconciliation in the country had been lost. As tricky as it had been for me to travel overseas to race, it looked as if it would now be practically impossible.

After PW had waved his finger, licked his lips and shouted his short-sighted, defiant nonsense to the rest of the world, I suddenly found myself stranded in the States after all SAA flights in and out of the US were cancelled. My air ticket was useless. Fortunately, though, I could pay in a bit extra and catch one of the BA flights. But it seemed as if travelling to and from the US was going to be one big hassle from then on.

At one stage, I even entertained thoughts about getting another passport. What was the point of being South African? We had an idiotic government whose apartheid policies were ripping apart the country and involving us in the war in Namibia, which was costing billions. It all seemed so bloody pointless. So ja, I was pretty pissed off with and sad about the general situation.

But even when the chips were down, I knew in my heart I'd never leave. Africa was where I wanted to live, no matter what happened. After a long stint in the US and Europe, even landing in Nairobi would give me a sense of coming home. I love Africa, not just South Africa.

Aside from it being so crowded, the weather makes the northern hemisphere a shit place to live. And I could never live in Australia. I don't like Australians. They live in a bloody police state. Every single time I went to Australia, I'd get a speeding fine. Their speed limits are even worse than America's. Even in the damn Outback, there's some bloke sitting behind a bush with a radar gun trying to clock you breaking the 100 km/h speed limit. They have so many cops trying to enforce their freedom that it's impossible to live there.

Talking of speed limits, I must admit to a propensity for ... shall we say ... 'forgetting' about them from time to time. My forgetfulness has resulted in more than a few run-ins with the gentlemen from the traffic department. I was once caught doing 211 km/h. Not the fastest I'd ever driven on a public road – not by a long shot – but certainly the fastest at which I've been trapped.

It happened some time around 1990, when I was flying along the West Coast road in the Western Cape. Despite writing to the traffic authorities and promising to pay whatever fine they wanted, I was nonetheless requested to appear in the Hopefield magistrate's court. With my racing schedule, it was a big inconvenience, but what could I do?

I arrived at the court, only to find that there was no parking to be found anywhere. Word had clearly got out that I'd be appearing in court, and what seemed like the whole town had turned out to see what would happen. Expecting to be nailed, I'd brought along R5 000 in cash to get me out of my latest speed-related indiscretion, and I stood meekly before the judge.

But it turned out that the judge was a SuperVan fan, and he declared that I was probably a safer driver at 200 km/h than most of the people in his court who drove at 60 km/h. He gave me a R600 fine, prompting a round of applause from the spectators.

I doubt whether a similar scenario would happen in this country today. As with Australia and the States, we, too, are fast becoming a police state. Rules and regulations seem to be issued from Pretoria on a weekly basis. I reckon Namibia is the place to go to – it must be a great country to live in. You'd have to live in Windhoek, where you can easily get in and out. Although I own property in Swakopmund, it's difficult to travel from there, whereas a Joburg–Windhoek flight takes about the same time as Joburg–Cape Town. Also, Windhoek is not densely populated and their government is effective and corruption-free.

But don't get me started on that. Let's finish something instead … the story of me. And Sarel.

I've lived. I've raced. I've rallied. I've had a lot of sex. It's cost me a lot of money. And I've also made some good friends in my life – many of them ex-competitors of mine. I guess you could even call them my previous enemies. The fact that we get on so well these days means a lot to me. Ian Scheckter, Serge Damseaux, Jan Hettema and even old Terry Moss – these are guys I scrapped with on and off the racetrack during my competitive years, but we're all mates now.

In a way, I seem to be the catalyst that brings them all together. And it makes me feel really good. I think in any sportsman's life – or in any walk of life, for that matter – recognition from your peers affords you the greatest satisfaction. Sure, some of that initial recognition might have been on the negative side – okay, a *lot* on the negative side – but the fact that after all these years we can sit down, talk shit and get pissed together, is great. I thank them for that. I know I was a bit of an abrasive bastard when I was racing, but I was never nasty or vindictive, and I do value their friendship now.

So, yes, I have some regrets, but I am happy with the cards life has dealt me and I am satisfied with the way I've played them. I've got a wonderful wife in Danielle, and I'm lucky in and thankful for the way in which she has supported me for the past 23 years. And I have three great kids.

I consider myself a lucky man.

I also consider myself a man who has not taken himself too seriously. Stroppy alter egos aside, I know who I am. And that's someone who can drive just about any car faster than almost anyone else. Apart from that particular skill, I'm fairly normal. Unlike a lot of other so-called 'celebrities' I've had the misfortune to encounter, I do not feel that I'm qualified to espouse great wisdom on topics like politics and space travel. Make no mistake, it's helluva entertaining to watch these celebs talk the considerable amount of crap that they do, but what makes them think that they're experts in areas beyond kicking a rugby ball or acting (really badly) in a local soapie is beyond me. I can only shake my head and smile at these youngsters. So you wore a national jersey for a couple of years … that somehow makes you and your opinion more important than everyone else's? No, boet.

I know I'm sounding like an old codger, but this is the rather sad reality of modern celebrity culture. That's not to say that there aren't some decent guys around. Young Schalk Burger – now there's a real what-you-see-is-what-you-get youngster. Just like his old man, there's no bullshit about Schalk. He never pretends to be someone he isn't.

It also isn't true to say that there weren't any pretentious types around in my day. There was the one chap – sort of shortish and often seen marching up the fairway dressed in black – who would come across as so well-mannered, polite and squeaky clean that he'd make Gandhi look like The Bandit King of Kolkata.

I've always admired the guys who weren't prepared to hide behind their public persona. They would always call a four-iron a four-iron. I'm talking about golfers like Denis Hutchinson, Simon Hobday and Dale Hayes, tennis stars like John McEnroe and Jimmy Connors, Springbok players Frik du Preez and Piet Uys … and Kallie Knoetze. Now there's a guy I always thought handled himself the right way. Kallie was Kallie. He's as rough and ready as they come, but he doesn't pretend to be anything else. If he didn't like something, he'd say so. He's got one helluva sense of humour and he's not afraid to take the mickey out of himself. Kallie never took himself too seriously, and that's why 'Die Bek van Boomstraat' has become such a South African legend.

I first met Kallie on one of the early Total Economy Runs. As you can imagine, this event and I were never going to be friends – frugal driving in a crappy little fuel-sipper was not my idea of fun. Fortunately, in 1977 I was paired up with Kallie as a 'celeb' team, which happily transformed the whole event from a potential ball-ache into one big party.

I can't remember what car we were driving – one of the Sigma

Corporation's entirely forgettable vehicles – but Kallie turned out to be the perfect driving partner, funny as hell and up for anything. I installed myself in the passenger seat, lit a cigarette and told him all he had to do was listen to me and we'd be fine. Needless to say, economical driving was a foreign concept I reckoned was best left to the experts, and within no time at all I had old Kallie four-wheel drifting around corners like he'd grown up in Helsinki. Kållje Knøetzë.

In those days, Kallie was in the police force, and a couple of weeks later I got a call from Chris Heunis, Kallie's partner on patrol and himself a Springbok rugby player. He and Kallie were driving around in their Valiant when they got a call to hightail it to the scene of a crime. Instead of the usual route, Kallie took them along some dirt roads he reckoned were a 'short cut'. Much to Chris's surprise, his partner was exuberantly sliding the car all over the show.

'What the hell has gotten into you, man?'

'I've been rallying,' was the reply from a very pleased-with-himself driver.

Actually, Kallie and I hadn't only been rallying…

As I recall, one or two women were involved as well. In fact, I seem to remember one of the women being the wife of a fellow contestant. The poor guy came looking for her and Kallie had to drop over the balcony of our hotel room. We were only on the first floor. (I think.)

But that's Kallie for you. He gets it. Kallie knows his role is to entertain the public (and, yes, sometimes the public's wives). No more, no less.

Same goes for me. I never felt that my success as a driver made me any better than anyone else. My abilities behind the wheel, however, allowed me to entertain South African motor-sport fans for more than three decades.

And of that, I am very proud…

INDEX

INDEX

Do you have any comments, suggestions or
feedback about this book or any other Zebra Press titles?
Contact us at **talkback@zebrapress.co.za**